COPING IN POLITICS WITH INDETERMINATE NORMS

SUNY series in Political Theory: Contemporary Issues
edited by Philip Green

SUNY series in Radical Social and Political Theory
edited by Roger S. Gottlieb

Coping in Politics
with Indeterminate Norms

A Theory of Enlightened Localism

Benjamin Gregg

STATE UNIVERSITY OF NEW YORK PRESS

Cover art: Bill Wiman
Night Lights, 1998
watercolor, 54 x 40 inches

Published by

STATE UNIVERSITY OF NEW YORK PRESS, ALBANY

© 2003 State University of New York

All rights reserved

Printed in the United States of America

No part of this book may be used or reproduced in any manner whatsoever without written permission. No part of this book may be stored in a retrieval system or transmitted in any form or by any means including electrostatic, magnetic tape, mechanical, photocopying, recording, or otherwise without the prior permission in writing of the publisher.

For information, address
State University of New York Press,
90 State Street, Suite 700, Albany, NY 12207

Production, Laurie Searl
Marketing, Anne M. Valentine

Library of Congress Cataloging-in-Publication Data

Gregg, Benjamin Greenwood, 1954–
   Coping in politics with indeterminate norms : a theory of enlightened localism / Benjamin Gregg.
     p. cm.—(SUNY series in political theory. Contemporary issues) (SUNY series in radical social and political theory)
   Includes bibliographical references and index.
   ISBN 0-7914-5781-8 (alk. paper)—ISBN 0-7914-5782-6 (pbk. : alk. paper)
   1. Social justice. 2. Social norms. 3. Social policy—Moral and ethical aspects. 4. Justice and politics. I. Title. II. Series. III. Series: SUNY Series in radical social and political theory

HM671.G74 2003
303.3'72—dc21

2002192959

10 9 8 7 6 5 4 3 2 1

For Nicholas and Saskia

Contents

Acknowledgments ix

Introduction 1

I
THE PROBLEM: INDETERMINATE NORMS

1 Indeterminacy in Social and Political Norms 19

II
THE SOLUTION: BASIC COMPONENTS

2 Coping with Indeterminacy through Proceduralism 39

3 Coping with Indeterminacy through Pragmatism 61

III
THE SOLUTION: LOCALISM WITHOUT PAROCHIALISM

4 Enlightened Localism in Social Critique 93

5 Enlightened Localism in Public Policy 117

6	Enlightened Localism in Law and Morality	141
	Coda: Social Cooperation in the Absence of Political Unity	161
	Notes	171
	Bibliography	189
	Index	197

Acknowledgments

For careful and engaged readings, generous and thoughtful criticism, and a collegial devotion to scholarship in the specific sense of pushing me again and again to make my arguments the best they can be, I am deeply grateful above all to David Braybrooke, who with unflagging energy and cogent insight, suggested any number of ways I might better reach for what I grasped for in this book. For thoughtful readings and useful responses I am also indebted to Joseph Carens, Fred Dallmayr, J. Donald Moon, Alan Ryan, and Michael Walzer, and to Richard Posner and Dick Howard, reviewers for State University of New York Press.

Chapter 3 draws on, but substantially revises, work that appeared as "Jurisprudence in an Indeterminate World: Pragmatist not Postmodern," *Ratio Juris* 11, no. 4, 382–398, copyright © 1998 by Blackwell Publishing. Adapted with kind permission of Blackwell Publishing.

Chapter 4 draws on, but substantially revises, work that appeared as "Possibility of Social Critique in an Indeterminate World," *Theory and Society* 23, no. 3, 327–366, copyright © 1994 by Kluwer Academic Publishers. Adapted with kind permission of Kluwer Academic Publishers.

Introduction

THE PROBLEM OF NORMATIVE INDETERMINACY

This work in social theory concerns the possibility of justice in a world of what I shall analyze and describe as "normative indeterminacy." Indeterminacy refers to the lack of clear, distinct, and rationally persuasive knowledge. It refers specifically to knowledge of what a normative rule means, and how groups and individuals should apply it. I shall oppose it to two kinds of determinacy: epistemic and normative. *Epistemic* determinacy is a matter of knowledge. It refers to definite knowledge of the meaning of texts such as legal statutes, or statements of public policy, or claims of political philosophy. But it equally refers to cultural practices such as the ways in which racial, sex-based, or class-bound identities are constructed in a given society. *Normative* determinacy is a matter of action. It refers to definite knowledge about norms as themselves direct guides to behavior, or as cues to the interpretation of texts that regulate behavior, or as directives to the interpretation of cultural practices that also regulate behavior. In short, this book is about the intersection of epistemology and politics. It analyzes that intersection in multiple ways.

In its strongest form (stronger than forms actually held by almost anyone today) the thesis of indeterminacy asserts that, where norms are indeterminate, no theory, rule, or principle constrains us (whether citizen, judge, social critic, or policy maker) to interpret or apply the norm in a particular way. Consequently a normative question or problem could have many different answers or solutions—yet all of them valid. But if different answers are equally valid, then discursive validity can no longer serve (it might seem) as a criterion to guide public policy (if it ever could so serve). In that case communities would forfeit at least one form of rationality in public life, in the formulation of politics, and in other attempts to construct a better society.

Many, perhaps most, spheres of daily life cope quite well with the inability of social rules—of some rules, some of the time—to yield determinate outcomes. But in some contexts indeterminacy is far more than merely theoretical. This is especially so in some political, legal, moral, and cultural contexts of social integration. Consider the legal sphere. A legal system forms one among a number of vitally important, because consequential, sets of social and political norms. Although few scholars or judges or legislators today view law itself as something static, the notion that judges make rather than find law implies to many observers consequences such as unequal or arbitrary treatment of individuals. Where law can be determinate, however, it might well have an exclusively "correct" meaning and "proper" application. In short, it might have that most valuable of intellectual or moral commodities: one "right" answer. If justice through law is predicated on such qualities as consistency and (more ambitiously still) objectivity, then normative determinacy (in whatever form) might seem a prerequisite for justice.

This book demonstrates that such determinacy is not necessary for justice, in a legal sense or more broadly in a political and social sense. It addresses the problem of indeterminacy by asking two basic questions: First, how, in a complex modern society, in a liberal political order, is nonauthoritarian politics possible under conditions of normative and epistemic indeterminacy? This is a descriptive question: How is social equity, how is legal justice, possible where aspects of the social, political, and legal order appear to be arbitrary, inconsistent, and subjective? I argue in chapter 2 that a theory of pragmatism can explain why indeterminacy in social norms is not always a problem in the day-to-day functioning, or even legitimation, of modern polities.

Then, in a narrower context, with respect to the social uses of rules, I argue that the meaning and application of norms often need not (indeed, often cannot) be consistent over time or between cases. In practice, the validity of any given interpretation or any given application of norms can only be relative to the particular community of interpreters. I argue that this sort of relativism need not lead to epistemic or moral nihilism, so much so that I analyze such relativism as a form of "weak objectivism." Something can be "objective" if it can sustain tests of "reflective scrutiny." That which has been so scrutinized then contrasts with the unreflected convictions of so much of everyday social and political life. Yet a weakly objective standpoint is still distinct from the strong objectivism of putatively universally valid or transhistorical standards. Weak objectivism refers to less-than-absolute objectivity. Under weak objectivity, decisions can be given objective grounds for the most part—but not grounds that will be valid *semper, ubique, et omnibus*. Weakly objective grounds are locally rather than universally valid. But locally valid though they may be, they are objective in an important sense.

The thesis of indeterminacy raises a second question, one that forms the prescriptive pendant to the previous descriptive question. It asks, How should a society deal with indeterminacy? I respond to this question, as I do to the first, with a theory of "enlightened localism." My theory first responds to these questions methodologically, with a consideration of the basic components of coping with indeterminacy: through proceduralism (chapter 2) and pragmatism (chapter 3). The theory of enlightened localism then answers these two questions—How do modern, liberal societies cope with indeterminacy? and How should they cope with it?—in three central spheres of normative behavior: in social critique (chapter 4), in public policy (chapter 5), and in law and morality (chapter 6).

NORMATIVITY, INDETERMINACY, AND LOCALISM

Thus three concepts operate at the core of the theory I develop in this book: 'normativity,' 'indeterminacy,' and 'localism.' Here I provide an introductory treatment of the three concepts in terms of an extended empirical example especially (and poignantly) significant in societies of diversity. But to begin with more general considerations: Societies are not structured in normatively neutral ways; they do not often distribute social goods equally; they do not often impose social burdens equally among the populace. But even as they persist in being normatively problematic in such ways, human societies are also much more than merely random collections of people. They are more than this or that solidarity among members of this or that community who, for whatever reason, share certain characteristics and certain understandings. Human societies, like the individuals who compose them, do not stand free of context; they are multiply embedded. They are embedded historically, in the common heritage and experience of some of their members. Although always open to interpretation and revision, that heritage and experience cannot be freely chosen, no more that it can be freely discarded. Nor can the historically embedded society entirely choose its future; any given past, any particular history, constrains the parameters of its future. Societies are also embedded culturally, reproducing in their citizens traits customary and habitual, linguistic and aesthetic, culinary, cognitive and spiritual—but also normative, the trait of central concern in this book. Human societies organize individual persons in transindividual ways; they pattern individual subjects in intersubjective ways; they integrate individual agents with each other in complex interactions. These multiple connections—transindividual, intersubjective, and interactive—are often inflected with power. The reference to power means that, through these connections, some groups may dominate others; that some may reproduce their privileged status generation after generation, while others endure systematic discrimination generation after generation (though some communities, once subordinated, are later assimilated to the society and culture that once marginalized them).

To recapitulate my claims thus far: societies are embedded culturally; many of the ways in which people are culturally integrated are normative; some of these normative relationships are matters of power politics, as in the sorts of distinctions I've been drawing, between dominant and dominated persons, between subordinated and assimilated communities, between privileged and victimized groups. These distinctions are in fact various articulations of political, social, and legal power. In other words they are never "value-free" but always, and deeply, normative, as inherently evaluative of conduct "good" and "bad," or of belief "right" and "wrong." This book analyzes articulations of power as reflected in the politics of norms. It analyzes political power epistemologically, in the ways in which this or that group renders this or that indeterminate norm determinate, and thereby establishes the corresponding societal standard for behavior and belief, for knowledge and practice.

And this book emphasizes the politics of normative indeterminacy. At the level of epistemology, its analysis is abstract; at the level of politics, concrete. Abstract, for example, are the presuppositions—some conscious and some unconscious—that reinforce or challenge the social constructions of race that daily play out as hierarchies and subordinations. Very concrete is the practice of racism; very concrete are the social institutions that perpetuate racism. In its elements both abstract and concrete, the politics of race involves normative indeterminacy. Distinctions between racist and nonracist behavior or belief are deeply normative. The terms *racist* and *nonracist* are indeterminate whenever a society cannot agree on their meaning. Indeterminate are distinctions between racism and its alternatives whenever a society cannot agree on the appropriate response to racism (as is almost always the case). Various groups at various times struggle over alternative ways to render these distinctions determinate. Hence in epistemology this struggle is always political. This abstract dimension of racial politics finds concrete expression in the design of public education. Some designs perpetuate racist practices; others seek to avoid racist practices; still others would overcome the enduring consequences of past racist practices.

What about racism in public education? American society has long provided many African Americans with a public education strikingly inferior to that provided many European Americans. Although in the United States today there may be agreement on this point, there is no agreement on how racial subordination continues, and certainly no agreement on how best to remedy what is by now a commonly perceived problem. On the one hand, the Civil Rights movement, as well as political liberals more generally, have long sought racial integration of public schools as a solution. And the relevant major court cases decided after *Brown v. Board of Education*[1] in 1955 urge "balancing the student and teacher populations by race in each school, eliminating single-race schools, redrawing school attendance lines, and transporting students to achieve racial balance" (Bell 1995a:25). On the other hand, years earlier W. E. B. Du Bois argued (as others argue today) that the

> Negro needs neither segregated schools nor mixed schools. What he needs is Education. What he must remember is that there is no magic, either in mixed schools or in segregated schools. A mixed school with poor and unsympathetic teachers, with hostile public opinion, and no teaching of truth concerning black folks, is bad. A segregated school with ignorant placeholders, inadequate equipment, poor salaries, and wretched housing, is equally bad. Other things being equal, the mixed school is the broader, more natural basis for the education of all youth. If gives wider contacts; it inspires greater self-confidence; and suppresses

the inferiority complex. But other things seldom are equal, and in that sense, Sympathy, Knowledge, and the Truth, outweigh all that the mixed school can offer. (1935:335)

Du Bois does not oppose racial balance. He argues that racial balance in public schools does not necessarily entail improved educational opportunities for the now integrated black students,[2] and that racially integrated schools are no sine qua non of improving educational opportunities for black pupils. For his part, Derrick Bell argues that "providing unequal and inadequate school resources and excluding black parents from meaningful participation in school policymaking are at least as damaging to black children as enforced separation" (1995b:10). Instead, American schools should focus on "improvement of presently desegregated schools as well as the creation or preservation of model black schools" (Bell 1995a:26).

I observe, then, two mutually incompatible normative standpoints backing integration. One sees racial integration as socialization into a-racialism, into color blindness, into chromatic neutrality. On this view, public school can be the site of rationalism, objectivity, professionalism, and impersonal neutrality. It can provide educational opportunity to children without distinction of race. A competing standpoint argues that racial integrationism is not a question of black children joining white children for a better education, but only of black pupils mixing with white pupils in the hope that the blacks might enjoy better facilities and perform at higher levels. On this view, society simply needs to place underprivileged black youth in "white" schools, to deliver them into white, middle-class culture. Stokely Carmichael attacks both standpoints: "You can integrate communities, but you assimilate individuals. Even if such a program were possible, its result would be, not to develop the black community as a functional and honorable segment of the total society, with its own cultural identity, life patterns, and institutions, but to abolish it. . . . The racial and cultural personality of the black community must be preserved and the community must win its freedom while preserving its cultural integrity" (1971:39).

One norm—that of the Civil Rights movement, the National Association for the Advancement of Colored People, and many political liberals—champions the racial integration of public schools. A different norm, equally well-intentioned, criticizes racial integration for the

> complete acceptance of the fact that . . . to have a decent house or education, black people must move into a white neighborhood, or send their children to a white school. This reinforces, among both black and white, the idea that "white" is automatically superior and "black" is by definition inferior. For this reason, "integration" is a subterfuge for the maintenance of white supremacy. . . . Such situations will not change

until... integration ceases to be a one-way street. Then integration does not mean draining skills and energies from the black ghetto into white neighborhoods. To sprinkle black children among the white public in outlying schools is at best a stop-gap measure. The goal is not to take black children out of the black community and expose them to white middle-class values; the goal is to build and strengthen the black community. (Carmichael and Hamilton 1967:54–55)

Racial equality here means the preservation of a racial identity and heritage: "The racial and cultural personality of the black community must be preserved and that community must win its freedom while preserving its cultural integrity. Integrity includes a pride—in the sense of self-acceptance, not chauvinism—in being black, in the historical attainments and contributions of black people. No person can be healthy, complete and mature if he must deny a part of himself; this is what 'integration' has required thus far" (ibid.:55).

The indeterminate norm of racial equality—to which I return in chapters 1 and 2, and then again in chapter 6—has allowed me to introduce two of the concepts at the heart of this text: 'normativity' and 'indeterminacy.' It introduces the third key concept of this book as well: 'localism.' The meaning and application of *racial equality* is indeterminate because it allows for two or more mutually exclusive alternatives. One alternative regards integrationism as a "progressive rejection of local bias and parochialism in favor of the impersonality of centralized authority" (Peller 1995:135). Another asserts that antiracism must seek local control, in the sense that a "school system in an all-white neighborhood is not a segregated school system. The only time it's segregated is when it is in a community that is other than white, but at the same time is controlled by whites" (Malcolm X 1970:16). This question of localism, of local culture and preferences, of local practices and beliefs, forms the third element of the theory I develop here. The theory distinguishes between two forms of localism: a parochial form and a form I call "enlightened." This book is an extended brief on behalf of the latter.

TWO FORMS OF LOCALISM: PAROCHIAL AND ENLIGHTENED

On a spectrum of positions in political theory in which the defining issue is the extent to which complex modern societies can establish and sustain agreement on normative bases, I locate myself near authors skeptical that consensual agreements can be reached, and who reject objective foundations for whatever agreements might take shape. But I also reject a pure and simple relativism and deploy elements of pragmatism and proceduralism to show the possibility of normative agreement under circumstances that discourage it. Of course a theory of enlightened localism cannot assume that its own principles (pragmatism, relativism, and proceduralism) are part of any given society's shared understandings. Rather these principles serve as tools by which the theory can uncover and develop possibilities of shared understandings that already exist in many of the communities that make up a society.

I argue more generally that politics needs to span the tension between the more limited conditions of a local standpoint and the less limited conditions of a perspective beyond that standpoint. As I shall emphasize, particularly in chapter 4, rule-governed social behavior guided by enlightened localism can begin with cognitive and normative standards immanent to a society's cultures, understandings, and practices, but it must exceed them as well. In exceeding them, normative behavior neither ceases being situated nor starts being universal. It does not cease being situated: It cannot escape the conditions of collective life, including those (like parochialism) that discourage rational perception. It does not get very far toward universality for the same reason. Less than universal, validity lies across disputes or among communities within society. Enlightened localism can span this tension without breaking on it if it resists appeals to universal criteria which, because of the multiplication of normative standpoints in our "disenchanted" modern world, are not (and likely never were) available or plausible to so many of us in contemporary societies.

Disenchantment implies social fragmentation. Even though normativity equally informs diverse spheres of society—from politics to religious faith, from law to social critique—the multiplication of competing worldviews, together with the rise of empirical science, has fragmented shared worldviews. These phenomena also discourage the creation of shared worldviews where none has existed before. Complex modern societies are characterized increasingly by a heterogeneity of normative convictions, commitments, and intuitions. Norms of various worldviews appeal to sources of justification not equally available or plausible to all or even many of the heterogeneous groups that make up contemporary liberal societies. Under these conditions no single worldview can possibly resonate with all groups or every individual.

A normatively fragmented society compels us to distinguish critically among competing spheres of normative value. It also compels us to distinguish critically among competing spheres of cognitive validity. In a society tolerant of competing belief systems, coping with differences in worldview is possible only across heterogeneous groups, and only across normative commitments. It is not possible to cope by reducing one worldview to another. It is possible only by giving full weight to the participants' perspectives as well as to perspectives beyond those of the local participants. It is possible only by speaking to the particular self-understandings of the affected groups and relevant worldviews—as well as to the supraindividual understanding generated by what I shall develop as the weakly objectivating approach of enlightened localism.

If, in making normative choices, members of a legal community cannot appeal to a single worldview of universal validity, then they can appeal only to the reality in which they are already situated, to the way of life in which they already find themselves. Social critique offers an example of finding criteria of critical judgment this side of universal validity, as I show in chapter 4. Critique, like its normative foundation, can be mounted only in actual social, historical, and cultural contexts. The norms of critique are always *our* norms, *our* creations, and *our* understandings; the norms are always relative to us, the critics, indeed *these* particular critics rather than *those*. For adjudicating among competing worldviews, precisely a local basis offers itself in the absence of a universal one.

A self-reflexive, enlightened relationship of a society to itself is a relationship characterized by relativism, yet a relationship nonetheless robustly critical, in the following sense. If the local and extra-local dimensions of knowing are sundered, neither is possible; if local understanding and nonlocal knowledge cannot be bridged, then nonparochial knowledge is impossible. Were all knowledge and discourse merely an ethnocentric projection, then no knowledge or discourse could be a tool of rationally persuasive social science; there could be no legal justice among very different kinds of people; there could be no democratic politics in societies of diversity. Epistemologically there would be no possibility of developing, across diverse communities or within a cosmopolitan society, anything like a freely consensual standpoint toward contentious issues of public policy. Among disparate communities or within the entire society, self-indulgent and grossly partisan viewpoints would be the only viewpoints possible. Knowledge and action would be possible only as manipulation. For these reasons viable public policy, socially responsible jurisprudence, and progressive public philosophy must each be able to entertain criteria of truth distinct from its own. To entertain alternative criteria of truth is to reject reductionism, to employ a form of relativism.

On the one hand, an account of translating between or among competing viewpoints must invoke claims to validity that can be vindicated in ways plural, hence local, rather than ways monological or universal (or ways that otherwise reduce one standpoint to another). On the other hand, the validity of a conviction, even though necessarily situated and embedded and thus oriented on local standards, must also transcend any particular community if it is to be more than parochially local. If it is to be local in an enlightened sense, it must be the localism of a local consensus that nonetheless escapes parochialism by overshooting any particular worldview without positing some universal one. To overshoot is to escape the "gravitational pull" of any particular local commitment or perspective.

MAKING NORMATIVE JUDGMENTS

To describe my position as "enlightened" need not privilege it rhetorically over its many competitors. The notion of enlightened self-interest indicates an awareness that some forms of self-interest are problematic. Enlightened self-interest, then, claims to be a less problematic alternative (even if not unproblematic). Similarly my concept of 'enlightened localism' implies that, while localism is problematic, my version avoids or overcomes at least some of its problems, and copes well with others. Whereas terms such as *pro-choice* and *pro-life* represent rhetorical swordplay by imputing to the respective opponent a view that the opponent probably rejects (many pro-lifers do not regard themselves as "anti-choice" and many pro-choicers reject the label "anti-life"), the term *enlightened localism* does not impute to parochial localism characteristics that parochial localism would reject as a fair description of itself. Parochial localists (some of whose work I analyze) view parochialism as morally and intellectually viable, indeed as the only viable position today. They reject many of the values and ideals of the European Enlightenment—modernist all of them—for a variety of alternatives I shall examine in the course of this book. Parochial localists would reject my position as utopian. I draw less pessimistic conclusions than do parochial localists about contemporary possibilities for rational communication and human flourishing.

'Enlightened localism' is not a slogan but a normative and explanatory concept. It might be described as a sociology of moral knowledge because it begins with the given norms of actual communities. It begins descriptively with the mundane perspective of the participant and then seeks prescriptively to enhance the mundane perspective of groups and individuals. That perspective must cope with the often indeterminate normativity of communities in complex modern societies.

The theory in all of its parts is concerned with practical implications: how people in fact cope with normative indeterminacy—and how they might better cope if guided by a theory of enlightened localism. "Practical implications" are practical in two senses: They concern *consequences* of human behavior, and they concern peculiarly *normative* consequences. In both senses human societies as a whole, groups and individuals within them, and the worldviews they hold, regularly judge or prioritize normative standards that may include criteria such as explanatory comprehensiveness, logical coherence, or conceptual economy; practical efficacy or moral acceptability; empirical adequacy and empirical predictability; even aesthetic appeal.

In contexts from politics to law, from public policy to culture, groups and individuals judge some normative standards nonconsensually. Revisions and qualifications are part of the normal activity of judging such standards. In cosmopolitan societies few comprehensive normative judgments are conclusive, uncontested, or satisfactory to everyone concerned. But they can still be constitutive of political community; they can still be meaningful and useful to enough people over long enough periods to sustain both the belief, and the desire to believe, in the possibility of correctly judging by epistemic standards. Within any modern liberal society, the apparent impossibility of ever achieving that kind of correctness (which may not exist) does not entirely vitiate the strength or coherence of the belief in the possibility of correct judgment. In fact, such belief may have a regulative function without which people could not discharge the everyday, practical necessity of making normative judgments about social institutions, cultural practices, and political beliefs.

ENLIGHTENED LOCALISM WITHIN THE TRADITION OF SOCIAL AND POLITICAL THEORY

A theory of enlightened localism offers no blueprint for the just society; rather, it offers an extended argument for the plausibility and potential of communities within society reaching some degree of social and political agreement under conditions that discourage agreement. Enlightened localism concludes from the frequent phenomenon of normative indeterminacy that we cannot develop a theory of the just society unless we pay attention to particular social contexts and actual, shared norms. From such conclusions other analysts, on the political and cultural left as well as the political and cultural right, might draw inferences as debilitating for scholarship as for politics. My conclusions are debilitating in neither way, as the self-consciously positive term *enlightened localism* suggests. It is a spatial metaphor, in three senses simultaneously. It is an argument about "position," about a golden mean. It marks a middle ground between, on the one hand, purported moral and epistemic certainties; and, on the other hand, the perspectivalist conviction that humans cannot generate nonarbitrary or nonidiosyncratic meanings. Second, it is spatial in a geographic sense: Societies need agreement on norms in a particular locality, hence a localism whose norms are not generalizable to all of society. And third, it is a spatial metaphor in the sense of calibrating the political consequences of group size: Societies need to consider the preferences of groups within the general population that, because they are relatively small in size, might be ignored by larger and therefore often more powerful groups.

A theory of enlightened localism locates itself within the broad expanse of Western political theory. Through the millennia, coping with normative indeterminacy has been a major concern of political theory, preconceptions otherwise notwithstanding. That concern situates this book among any number of figures. By way of example, briefly consider 2,200 years punctuated by three influential figures of disparate interests, yet equally preoccupied with social stability and political integration under conditions of indeterminacy. Plato (c. 430-347 B.C.E.) provides a static solution to the problem of indeterminacy; Machiavelli (1469-1527), a dynamic one; and Adam Smith (1723-1790) conceives of society in a way that renders indeterminacy not particularly problematic as long as people simply share certain common moral sentiments.

In the *Statesman*, Plato associates social solidarity with shared values and purposes. The interweaving of members of the polity, their linking together, "can never be lasting and permanent if vicious men are joined with other vicious men or good men with vicious. . . . But in those of noble nature from their earliest days whose nurture too, had been all it should be, the laws can foster the growth of this common bond of conviction, and only in these" (1952:233). Shared social values and purposes are, by virtue of being shared, determinate. Determinacy in this sense can be created.

> There is no difficulty in forging these human bonds if the divine bond has been forged first. That bond is a conviction about values and standards shared by both types of character. There is one absorbing preoccupation for the kingly weaver as he makes the web of state. He must never permit the gentle characters to be separated from the brave ones; to avoid this he must make the fabric close and firm by working common convictions in the hearts of each type of citizen. (ibid.:233)

Plato is urging the greatest possible normative determinacy by extending shared values and purposes to all parts of society, so much so that he predicates social unity—which he understands as normative determinacy—on substantial uniformity within society.

Determinacy on the Platonic conception is a matter of shared norms; indeterminacy so sorely taxes a society's energies and resources that social instability follows from it. Stability is socially more economic than instability; politically, it is more fruitful: statecraft for Plato is possible only in those areas of social life at least temporarily free of instability. Determinacy allows politics to go beyond a merely defensive mode (one way to respond to indeterminacy) to politics that can deal with social differences based on some underlying sharedness. Politically, points of normative determinacy imply or entail or implicitly raise questions about the points of normative indeterminacy that a polity needs to address for its own survival. Epistemologically, to place any part of a field into question requires that at least one part not be placed into question; a question can be posed only from some standpoint not itself in question (at that moment, at least). Disagreements can be discussed only within the context of at least some agreements; indeterminacy can be dealt with only from within determinacy; controversy can only be resolved when, on other issues, there is agreement and determinacy. If a majority of Americans accepts the authority of the Supreme Court because the majority agrees with its holdings in many cases, the majority likely will not withdraw that trust even when it disagrees with this or that particular holding. An area of normative agreement within society is precisely that space within which disagreement can be engaged: where it accommodates the challenges of dissenting opinions and dissenting groups; where it reaches out to dissenters without breaking on the tension between them and the mainstream; where the community relates flexibly to groups and beliefs that reject a great deal of communal opinion and practice.

In *The History of Florence*, Machiavelli analyzes normative indeterminacy as the complexity of competing social interests between the nobility and the people: The "only party feeling which seemed occasionally to glow, was that which naturally exists in all cities between the higher classes and the people; for the latter wishing to live in conformity with the laws, and the former to be themselves the rulers of the people, it was not possible for them to abide in perfect amity together" (1878:60). He studies normative indeterminacy within the nobility (between the new and the old nobility): "Violent animosities amongst the nobility enabled the companies of the Arts to establish this law with facility; and the former no sooner saw the provision which had been made against them than they felt the acrimonious spirit with which it was enforced" (ibid.:61). Machiavelli examines normative indeterminacy within the people (between the higher and the lower classes): the "hatred of the lower orders towards the rich citizens and the principals of the Arts, because they did not think themselves remunerated for their labor in a manner equal to their merits" (ibid.:127). And he investigates it between artisans and merchants and their respective guilds: "The nobles of the people and the major trades were discontented at the share the minor trades and lowest of the people possessed in the government; whilst the minor trades were desirous of increasing their influence, and the lowest people were apprehensive of losing the companies of their trades and the authority which these conferred" (ibid.:144).

He distinguishes between normative disagreement he takes to be natural, hence inevitable, and normative disagreement born of competition among competing interests, coalitions, and efforts to obtain preferential treatment. Whereas Plato seeks to turn indeterminacy into determinacy, Machiavelli views a "cabined" or "delimited" indeterminacy as politically beneficial. Indeterminacy can be controlled in this sense through the joining of interests into factions and then through the contest of factions. Factions are like islands of local normative agreement in a sea of general normative disagreement. The frictions entailed by competing factions need not destabilize society; normative indeterminacy and the frictions it entails offer distinct potential for social improvement: "In every republic there are two different dispositions, that of the populace and that of the upper class and . . . all legislation favorable to liberty is brought about by the clash between them" (Machiavelli 1975:218).

Machiavelli counsels against reducing normative indeterminacy unto complete determinacy; against grinding competition down to uniform agreement; against eliminating political factionalism in the polity. He urges its containment, as a kind of spontaneity within order rather than order without spontaneity; he advises regulating factionalism and then harvesting its potential for positive influences on the polity. Whereas Plato enjoins normative determinacy, unity through conformity, Machiavelli urges "contained indeterminacy," interest-propelled clashes of indeterminacy within a larger, determinate order. Whereas Plato sees political society as order through unity, and stability through normative determinacy, Machiavelli in *The Discourses on the First Decad of Titus Livy* sees political progress through the satisfaction of competing interests, and the perpetuation of a degree of political indeterminacy: The "blending of these estates made a perfect commonwealth; and . . . it was friction between the plebs and the senate that brought this perfection about" (ibid.:216).

Adam Smith does not seek to eliminate indeterminacy, as Plato does; nor does he seek to limit and then to harvest it, as Machiavelli does. He regards normative determinacy as necessary to modern capitalist society only to a very limited degree. This kind of society connects members of the polity to each other only indirectly, and very loosely at that, often not even consciously. The normative determinacy that does associate them with each other is a general affective correspondence among individuals at the level of feelings: What observers of a man's problems or sorrows feel will

> always be in some respects different from what he feels, and compassion can never be exactly the same with original sorrow; because the secret consciousness that the change of situations, from which the sympathetic sentiment arises, is but imaginary, not only lowers it in degree, but in some measure varies it in kind, and gives it a quite different modification. These two sentiments, however, may, it is evident, have such a correspondence with one another, as is sufficient for the harmony of society. Though they will never be unisons, they may be concords, and this is all that is wanted or required. (Smith 2000:23)

On this view, social integration is not threatened by indeterminacy as long as members of society experience certain shared (and in that sense determinate) moral sentiments. Determinacy at this minimal level is sufficient to allow persons to enter into the minds and hearts of others, which is the extent necessary to achieve integration amid difference.

> To produce this concord, as nature teaches the spectators to assume the circumstances of the person principally concerned, so she teaches this last in some measure to assume those of the spectators. As they are continually placing themselves in his situation, and thence conceiving emotions similar to what he feels; so he is as constantly placing himself in theirs, and thence conceiving some degree of that coolness about his own fortune, with which he is sensible that they will view it. . . . As their sympathy makes them look at it in some measure with his eyes, so his sympathy makes him look at it, in some measure, with theirs. (ibid.:23-24)

What Plato and Machiavelli construct as political and social authority (normative determinacy) here dissolves to community understood as a sphere of widespread normative indeterminacy.

As an argument about "position," about a golden mean, enlightened localism also invokes Aristotle (384-322 B.C.E.), among others. Its task, while related to work from Aristotle to Adam Smith and beyond, is also different, in its concern with contemporary landscapes in politics and society. Perhaps any historical era is ripe for golden means. Certainly ours would seem to be, when intellectual life in the West at the dawn of the twenty-first century offers elements of a cultural right pronouncing moral and epistemological verities implausible to many groups and individuals, and elements of a cultural left resigned to, perhaps even celebrating, potentially nihilistic perspectives such as some forms of postmodernism (which I discuss in chapter 3). A theory of enlightened localism locates a middle ground between right-wing foundationalism and left-wing anti-foundationalism, between universalism and radical particularism.

OVERVIEW

This book has three parts, each with its distinct function within an ensemble. The first part, in which the first chapter alone figures, lays out the problems for belief and behavior of social and political norms that are uncertain because they are indeterminate. Chapter 1 analyzes central aspects of indeterminacy in normative rules. It shows that arguments against the indeterminacy thesis, whatever their merits, cannot refute, preclude, or otherwise dispose of the thesis, or vitiate its repercussions, for normative rules in particular or normative judgments generally.

The second part, made up of the second and third chapters, identifies and develops the two basic components of my solution to the problem: proceduralism and pragmatism. Societies are possible only by coordinating behavior among countless individuals and across diverse groups. Although ever-greater differences in political and moral values often preclude agreement on many issues of public policy, they need not prevent agreement on procedures for adjudicating differences.

Chapter 2 works out a new version of political proceduralism. Unlike older versions of proceduralism, the proposal does not operate on the logic of complete neutrality; rather, it is sensitive to certain factors of "local" import. Using the example of procedures for electing representatives to congress, chapter 2 shows that an "enlightened localist" proceduralism would deal with the problem that usual forms of proceduralism cannot address: vote dilution of racial minorities. Race-conscious districting, far from violating the logic of neutrality sought by proceduralism, can in fact better realize proceduralism under conditions of racial inequality and residential segregation. Under such conditions, "neutrality" is best sought where race consciousness (rather than color blindness) serves as a short-term proxy for a suite of distinct political interests of an otherwise "voiceless" subcommunity.

Chapter 3 develops pragmatism as a means of coping with indeterminacy, using jurisprudence as an example. Within contemporary jurisprudence only pragmatism and postmodernism regard law as deeply indeterminate with respect to meaning and application. Both assert the absence of ultimate foundations for knowledge and morals and the necessity of drawing on local standards to render law determinate. Still, a pragmatist jurisprudence is not postmodern, as often asserted. Pragmatism allows for nonparochial forms of localism; legal critique that is more than idiosyncratic, arbitrary, and subjective; a viable notion of autonomy of the group and individual vis-à-vis legal institutions; law without mass delusion; and a notion of justice as singular not plural, yet more than simply authority.

The third part of this book explores several possible applications of my proposed solution to indeterminate social and political norms, a solution I have defined as enlightened localism. Chapter 4 applies enlightened localism to social critique. It first addresses indeterminacy in critique, then critique from a "decentered" standpoint, and finally critique among competing belief systems. The concern here is more with the general problem of making social policy under conditions of epistemic indeterminacy, than the problems (analyzed in chapter 3) of interpreting texts under conditions of indeterminacy. The issue is not whether borderline cases exist, but whether instances of normative indeterminacy running deep within the life of contemporary communities can be resolved, and resolved in different ways.

Chapter 5 applies enlightened localism to public policy, asking, Which particular subcommunity's interests should prevail over the different interests of the community as a whole? Might different normative communities bridge their differences in productive discussion? I explore these questions through two topical issues: Should parents have legal rights with regard to the compulsory education of their minor children? (Here we have ambiguity in the role of the state within a community.) And should immigration be available to almost anyone who desires it? (Here we have ambiguity in the relationship of insiders to outsiders, residents to nonresidents, citizens to noncitizens: relationship concerning any one country's decision to admit or not admit noncitizens.) I show how a public policy of enlightened localism might deliberate on these issues by analyzing three areas of policy critical to both issues: boundaries, citizenship, and rights. First, in a public policy of enlightened localism, the relationship between local and nonlocal boundaries of authority might take the form of contract instead of regulation. A contract may realize a horizontal relationship between local and nonlocal levels of authority, as an alternative to a vertical or hierarchical relationship. Second, citizenship in complex modern states is a combination of agreement and disagreement between the citizen and other members of the polity. Not all forms of disagreement are socially deleterious. A public policy of enlightened localism embraces forms of nonconsensus because it recognizes the potential advantages of diversity, disagreement, and challenges to values and perspectives held by the majority (or otherwise defining for the status quo). Third, public policy implies one or the other notion of citizenship, and notions of citizenship imply certain rights, including rights both individual and collective: the right of collectivities to regulate entrance, the right of individuals to exit collectivities, and the right of some outsiders to enter and the right of some entrants to become citizens.

Chapter 6 shows that, in coping with indeterminacy, normative choices between the individual citizen's social identity constructed in terms of one set of collective identities, or in terms of another set, can be made only in the language of law and morality. For law and morality provide a medium by which social structure, where it confines or oppresses individuals (for example, racial identity that functions in terms of a hierarchy of chromatic and moral value), can be transformed into structure that enables and empowers individuals (for example, racial identity that serves to construct solidarities both to create positive self-images and to advocate for legitimate group interests). This constant "translation" is necessary because color consciousness and color blindness each carries more than one political and moral valence simultaneously. Similarly, social structure and individual agency each carries more than one valence simultaneously (thus the individual experiences both noncontingency, in his or her social environment, as well as contingency, in his or her competent behavior in that environment). A self-determining legal community can make normative choices among these kinds of options by drawing on the transformative power of law and morality to decide in what instances to prefer structure over agency (to prefer for example the principle of constitutionalism over the principle of democratic theory), or, with respect to public policy, when to prefer color consciousness over color blindness (when, for example, messages from a racially oppressed group would fall on deaf legislative ears if phrased only in color-blind terms). It can do so without undermining the mutual moral identification among individual human beings as equals, as individuals equally worthy of respect and dignity. And it can do so because of the complementarity between law and morality: Some legal norms need morality for ultimate grounding, whereas law enforces some norm-conformative behavior where moral cognition is not sufficiently anchored in citizens' hearts and minds.

In the coda I argue against claims that the fragmented conditions of normative and epistemic indeterminacy preclude progressive politics. I reject calls for somehow transforming locally valid norms into universally valid ones, calls for a political unity with universalistic features. But the fact that the only political universalism possible today is a spurious, imagined one, is not the end of the story. Progressive politics in a secularized age can be had in the radically democratic sense of a politically enlightened localism. Such localism allows a cosmopolitan population to achieve solidarity by rooting political life in the participation of all affected and concerned persons—citizens who relate themselves to each other communicatively, despite all differences, all fragmentations, and all plural normative commitments. It allows for social harmony in which the parts are not seamlessly integrated but nonetheless hold together in their differences. And it allows for rational social critique, through which social equity, political fairness, and legal justice may be sought without some special form of political responsibility owed to society as a whole.

PART I

THE PROBLEM: INDETERMINATE NORMS

CHAPTER 1

Indeterminacy in Social and Political Norms

In all of its parts this book is concerned with rules and with norm-governed behavior. In particular it is concerned with the far-reaching social and political significance of normative indeterminacy.[1] The thesis of indeterminacy asserts that norms whose meaning and proper application are unknown or unclear cannot be used without the intervention of interpreters. Indeterminate norms cannot be used without the direct and vital intervention of human agency in social structures, such as society's political and legal regime or cultural understandings. Only the interpreters, never the indeterminate norms themselves, can decide which meanings and which applications are politically or morally acceptable, and which are not. A norm that cannot be understood or applied without first being interpreted is indeterminate. The need for an interpreter signals indeterminacy; merely to experience difficulty in applying norms, where the difficulty can be resolved without an interpreter, does not. Thus the mundane traffic norm—automobiles and pedestrians shall stop on the red light—is clear in meaning and application, whereas the constitutional norm that all citizens are legally equal is quite useless until the meaning of *equality* is specified with respect to the relevant concrete social context. Specification can only be cultural and political, that is, contingent and valid only intersubjectively; it can never be valid absolutely and objectively.

Indeterminacy in the meaning and application of norms is not peculiar to any one kind of norm or any specific set of social, political, or legal issues. It characterizes many kinds of norms, though hardly all aspects of all norms in all instances. Indeterminacy is a problem only for some norms, and only some of the time. But those norms for which indeterminacy is a problem tend to be ones among the most significant for a country's social and political organization.

In the introduction I discussed several examples of normative indeterminacy without benefit of an explicit definition. I offer one now. *Normative* I define in a special and perhaps unusual way. I refer to a subclass of rules or standards that are embedded in, and expressive of, commitments to a way of life, or worldview, or political vision, or to other systems of profound cultural values. Normative rules (what I shall simply call *norms*) are rules or standards that are everything other than indifferent or disinterested; they are everything other than "neutral" or "objective" or "valid as such." By contrast, nonnormative rules or standards are either technical (as in instructions for operating a machine) or conventional (like the rule that traffic keeps to the right).

Technical or conventional concerns imply nothing about right conduct in a moral or political sense. They involve right conduct solely in the instrumental sense of achieving a pre-given and morally unquestioned goal. (In many cases, but not all, the goal here admits to no moral consideration, as for example in questions of mathematics or the solution to problems of mechanical engineering.) This is precisely the point: Questioning a goal, especially with respect to its moral desirability, is a normative issue and never technical or conventional. In this book the word *norm* either implies, or entails, or presupposes, this or that normative worldview. Even though a conventional or technical worldview is not a logical impossibility, it is empirically unlikely because no individual life can be lived, and no human society is possible, without confronting and coping with normative questions, day in and day out. Norms are forms of moral commitment, whether conscious or not. They are forms of commitment within some overarching perspective, one having to do with what people should believe and how they should behave (according to the norm in question), with how they should think or act in some sense moral or political. In this way I associate norms and norm-governed behavior with human agency, particularly in association with a person's free will. I affiliate norms with behavior, which the individual can thematize, reflect upon, cognitively challenge or defend, rationally reject or embrace, consciously preserve or modify. I focus on the individual's normative behavior given his or her interests in constructing or furthering *this* kind of society rather than *that*.

This book examines a variety of norms, each—as I shall show—a system of profound cultural values: social and political norms in general (this chapter), procedural norms (chapter 2), pragmatist norms upheld by people conscious of the norms' own relative validity (chapter 3), norms of social critique (chapter 4), norms that might guide public policy (chapter 5), and the sometimes competing, sometimes complementary norms of law and morality (chapter 6). In this broad span of ordinary human behavior, indeterminacy is not often a problem of politically paralyzing proportions. But I treat precisely those circumstances in which it is, and I propose ways to cope with problems of this magnitude.

The present chapter examines central aspects of normative indeterminacy by understanding how it occurs in different kinds of social, political, or legal rules. Humans employ norms because norms do valuable work for them. They do valuable work in people's daily confrontation of the unceasing demands of social life. To accomplish the tasks demanded of them, norms need to be determinate. In each particular instance, norm users need to know what the norm in question means and how to apply it. Many legal and political norms are as determinate as most technical norms; but some are deeply indeterminate, and they tend to be norms of unusual social significance. Norms significant to the lives of millions of human beings in profound ways tend to be the broadest, the most philosophical, and for that reason the most culturally contingent, the least technical, and the least "objective." By contrast, the constitutional rule that the president of the United States shall be at least thirty-five years of age is highly determinate; a claim for example that "years" in this sense be understood in terms of "dog years" (whereby one year in the life of a human being somehow corresponds to seven in a dog's life) has no purchase in American political culture. The meaning of this particular constitutional provision is not hard to elicit: It is a hypothesis about calibrating the kind of maturity in experience, thought, and vision that would seem appropriate to the highest office in the land, and even if one might disagree with the precise number of years specified, no one will argue about the intention of the rule's authors, and none will disagree with their goal.

Consider the socially profound norm of that part of the Fourteenth Amendment to the U.S. Constitution specifying that no state shall "deprive any person of life, liberty, or property, without due process of law; nor deny to any person within its jurisdiction the equal protection of the laws." In 1896 the Supreme Court interpreted the Amendment's norm of legal equality to mean that equality allowed separate but "equal" public facilities for Americans of different races.[2] In 1954 the Court rejected this interpretation entirely on the claim that such separation is inherently and necessarily unequal.[3] The constitutional words in question in 1896 were precisely those again in question in 1954. Their indeterminate meaning allowed for mutually exclusive plausible interpretations.

The norm of racial equality is indeterminate in the following question: Would the racial segregation of public schools facilitate equal citizenship or undermine it?" Making determinate that which is initially indeterminate is a cultural and political act. Any answer presupposes norms or values not contained in the question itself. The norm user is like the person who creates private property on John Locke's (1632–1704) theory—namely, by "mixing" his labor with the natural environment: The norm user brings about determinacy by introducing into the given norm something of him- or herself. Different norm users likely introduce different considerations (or values, goals, or needs), at least sometimes, and likely come up with different answers. Under these circumstances normative questions will not find answers valid in the eyes of all affected parties, relevant persons, and concerned citizens. Validity, then, cannot be absolute but only dependent, resting on the various contingencies of specific cases. Coping with contingency is a matter of political judgment, such that "doing norms" is deeply political business: With what authority does any given interpreter interpret? On what grounds should one interpreter's construction trump a competing construction? What renders one interpretation valid (even in the normatively minimal sense of "legally enforceable") and another not valid?

These are vital social questions. To secure its existence over time, every society must find at least temporarily satisfactory answers to at least some of them. But how can a society reconcile one answer with a different answer to the same question it may reach at a later time? How can a society reconcile a current answer with one to the same question reached earlier, perhaps by a previous generation—or perhaps more recently but under different circumstances, in terms of a different cultural and political *Zeitgeist*? In most cases any one answer to an indeterminate question will not forever solve the problem of indeterminacy for that particular question. For example, legally binding interpretations of legal equality and inequality in the United States have, over long periods of time, changed dramatically, and of course we have no reason to expect that currently obtaining interpretations will obtain in the future. Elsewhere I have argued that successive majorities on the Supreme Court over time have tended to expand the definitional inclusiveness of legal equality.[4] We have no reason to assume this trend is waning, let alone exhausted.

Again, indeterminacy is not always a problem, nor is it often a problem in many aspects of the daily social life of many citizens. But when indeterminacy is a problem, likely one or the other of the following seven theses applies: norms are not self-interpreting, the meaning and application of norms are contingent, norms are inherently incomplete, indeterminate norms can be interpreted only in ad hoc ways, the purely formal application of indeterminate norms is impossible, systems of norms contain inconsistent premises, and any one normative choice is subsumable under competing norms.[5]

NORMS ARE NOT SELF-INTERPRETING

To apply a norm is to interpret it; to interpret it is to reconstruct its meaning and therefore the criteria of its validity. The very identity of a norm first emerges with its interpretation. Because it is interpretive, identity is variable or changeable, never settled. Meaning is created time and again. The creation of meaning is contingent on all sorts of factors such as the interpreter's choice of method, or various kinds of presuppositions, or the speaker's political beliefs. Canons of interpretation cannot eliminate these interpretive uncertainties. A canon is a set of interpretations formally or informally recognized by an authoritative interpreter, such as a court of law. Canons are themselves general norms for the use of language. They employ general terms that themselves require interpretation and that cannot, any more than other norms, provide for their own interpretation (Hart 1961:123).

Norms by themselves are insufficient either as explanations of, or directives to, action. Particular situations do not await human actors, already marked off from each other, labeled as instances of a general norm whose application is in question. Nor can any norm itself step forward to capture its own instances (ibid.).

These epistemological claims illuminate concrete political phenomena. In this chapter I return to the norm of racial equality I considered in the introduction. That norm is not self-interpreting, which creates a dilemma for public schools trying to understand and practice it. Does it mandate race consciousness or color-blind neutrality? Could the experience of colored pupils in a colorblind school ever transcend the larger society's racial culture? Or does color blindness suppress all cultures but the socially dominant one, assimilating black pupils to the norms of white, middle-class pupils? Does color blindness pursue racial integration as the emancipation of black students from second-rate citizenship (itself entailed by second-rate education)? Does integration pursue emancipation into racial neutrality—or emancipation into the specific practices of white Europeans and white North Americans whose "traditional categories of liberal and enlightenment thought do not constitute an a-racial or culturally neutral standard that measures social progress in overcoming partiality, parochialism, and bias" (Peller 1995:142)? Parochially local are assertions to superiority by one race over another. Universalist are assertions that "all men are equal" and that race is therefore irrelevant politically, legally, and morally. But if the universalist assertions in fact fail to challenge the parochially local ones, they (unintentionally or not) merely perpetuate aspects of the subordination of one race by another. (In the coda I shall revisit the question of universalism.) An enlightened localism, by contrast, does not offer a negative understanding of race (either as the idea of superior and inferior races, or the idea that all race consciousness is racist); it offers a positive one, as a racial group's positive self-image. The norm of racial equality might then be interpreted (in public schools, for example) as mandating a positive form of race consciousness, not chromatic agnosticism.

Enlightened localism, then, offers a critical perspective on the supposed universalism of racial neutrality. The beliefs of the businessperson, the teacher, the nun, or the journalist are unlikely to be politically or morally neutral. Their normative beliefs are likely to be highly relevant to what they believe and how they act; their beliefs are likely to guide what they advocate in the public sphere, or would advocate given the chance. But in North America or Western Europe the social paradigm of the businessperson, the teacher, or the journalist may be one of normative neutrality—their racial identity supposedly irrelevant to their position. But in societies dominated by members of the white race, "professionally correct" businesspeople or journalists perhaps are expected to be "culturally white" and "culturally middle class" (which after all is what "neutrality" often means). Even as the white, middle-class mainstream understands itself as ethnically and racially neutral, for people of color to be middle class, and to be members of the professions, may then mean to deny their racial or ethnic identity. A culture of neutrality may equally subsume ethnic difference and identity among whites. The goal of authentic, group-specific identity (a self-conscious form of localism) reveals another, unconscious form of localism: the localism of racial whiteness. It reveals the fact that whiteness is not some racially neutral category, an unmarked marker of others' race. To have forebears from Ireland or Sweden, from Poland or Italy, is to be something other than simply and neutrally "white";

it is to be, no less than every nonwhite race, situated in a racial localism. But this realization hardly condemns us to racism; not all localism is parochial. *Enlightened* localism, as I shall show, is a means to race consciousness that, unlike race blindness, can facilitate racial equality and resist racial subordination (hidden or otherwise, conscious or unconscious).

Whereas universalism stresses similarity and blends out difference, enlightened localism highlights plurality and recognizes difference. In the context of racial politics, it highlights the plurality of ways in which race offers itself for definition. In part it does so by recognizing the different work that each definition might do. On one definition, race in a racist society is a metaphor for the subjugation of some groups and the privileging of others, for the stigmatization of some communities to the benefit of others. On another definition, race is understood as a mode of political resistance, exposing the problems of defining racism as only the overt, frontal rejection or exclusion of people of color. Racism understood only as formal exclusion is blind to (and thereby facilitates) more subtle forms of racism that manifest themselves in devastating statistical disproportionalities: unemployment, rates of crime and incarceration, single-parent households, teenage pregnancies, lack of health care, lack of health insurance, reduced life expectancies—but also relative absence in a variety of social spheres, from scholarship at universities and research institutes to leadership positions at the various levels of politics. If formal exclusion were the whole of racism, then such jarring disproportionalities and conspicuous absences from sites of social power and prestige could not be ascribed to racism.

Yet a third definition of race is cultural, race as self-identified by its own members rather than by a definition imposed by nonmembers. Thus the "literal biological truth that blacks (or members of any other racial or ethnic groups) are not born with genetic inclination for 'things black' . . . obscure[s] the fact that 'black' (like most racial or ethnic classification) also defines a culture" in the sense of a "shared heritage of language patterns, habits, history, and experience" (Williams 1995:192). Race understood as a self-identifying culture does not entail race as some essential or monolithic or genetic culture—as if all members shared all the same beliefs, or all members behaved the same way, or approached the world exclusively in terms of their local culture. Nor does race defined as a self-identifying culture (a fourth way to understand race) entail blindness to the overlapping of an individual's multiple identities. In other words, a self-identifying racial group can still identify ways in which members' identities are composite and are differently composite: A black woman is no less female than African American; Supreme Court Justice Clarence Thomas is no less black than a committed political conservative.

A fifth definition combines aspects of previous definitions: It combines race as a self-identifying culture with race as a mode of resistance. The categorization of a group in terms of race need not be unilateral where the categorized and thereby subordinated group reappropriates the category for itself and even unites around it, subverting race as a means of subordinating people of color into race as a means of empowering them. In this sense Kimberlé Crenshaw distinguishes

> between the claim "I am black" and the claim "I am a person who happens to be black." "I am black" takes the socially imposed identity and empowers it as an anchor of subjectivity. . . . "I am a person who happens to be black" . . . achieves self-identification by straining for a certain universality (in effect, "I am first a person") and for a concomitant dismissal of the imposed category ("black") as contingent, circumstantial, not determinant. (1995a:375)

Black people seeking to make determinate the norm of racial equality might deploy one claim in one social location, and another claim in a different social location. Instead of withdrawing from a marginalized social location, they would deploy it as a strategy of identity politics, toward wringing positive or progressive political and economic consequences from racial categorizations.

MEANING AND APPLICATION OF NORMS ARE CONTINGENT

We have no evidence that any norm refers back to something beyond the reach of time and change, to something based on some essential human nature or human purpose that might be disclosed once and for all by the right theory, if only we could uncover, discover, or recover it. Rather the creation, interpretation, and application of norms are themselves contingent, some given by historical chance, some embedded in culture and institutions that change only over generations.[6] Other definitions and interpretations of norms are constructed in individual situations rather than carried over from the past. For example, in the twentieth century the apartheid Republic of South Africa classified visiting Japanese businessmen as "honorary whites." The racial norm of white could not be self-interpreting or entirely stable even in a regime constructed around rigid understandings of race and the massive privileging of the white race in particular. Because norms are not self-interpreting, the meaning of a norm is not stable but rather contextual. Some normative decisions are made as the occasions require, and groups and individuals often can entertain conflicting sets of norms (such as the apartheid state's "white Japanese"), inasmuch as the conditions of correct choice are ambiguously defined.[7] Norms, then, can operate "well" or "properly" even as they operate inconsistently. In this example: Japanese are not "white" as apartheid intended "white."

History and experience provide ample evidence that the meaning and application of some very important norms are contingent on the context of use. Thus a particular race, or the female sex or a disfavored religion or the language of an ethnic minority, has often been treated as a deviation from the norm of socially dominant groups. Of course none of these identities or descriptors is neutral or a-normative, including those of the dominant groups, even if the latter may appear neutral in the peculiar sense that provides the standard by which others are classified or judged or placed within some kind of hierarchy. In precisely this sense great civilizations through the ages have defined themselves as superior to their neighbors (the Chinese word for "China," *zhōng gǔo*, is literally "country at the center," at the center presumably of the entire world). In this sense the culture of the white race for the past several centuries has defined itself as superior to races of color.[8] In this sense, across all cultures and all times, most males have defined themselves as superior to females; and today many heterosexuals define homosexuals as deviant from the norm—namely (and conveniently), themselves. In these cases *white*, *male*, and *heterosexual* function as norms by which *black*, *female*, and *homosexual* are defined as inferior, and therefore often as the subjugatable other.

In North America and Europe for hundreds of years now the unmarked marker of race is the racial category of "white." In a culture of whiteness only nonwhite "appears," that is, becomes the object of a great deal of social, political, and cultural categorization in which the question of race appears. In these contexts the racial category white is often invisible—or rather "negatively" present as the "not other" in terms of which all other races (all "others") are identified. The majority culture identifies the minority cultures without being defined itself—and certainly not being defined by the minority cultures it identifies. In this way the dominant culture reifies a racial norm (or a norm of sex, or of sexual orientation, or some other norm), positing the "natural" superiority of what in fact is a thoroughly social construction: the supposed superiority of one race over another. In this way the meaning and application of some norms are contingent on the context of their use.

NORMS ARE INHERENTLY INCOMPLETE

Any specific application of a norm, chosen from a range of possible applications, is context-dependent, and is so for a variety of reasons. First, norms never define an activity's character or possible range of conduct completely or exhaustively. Nor can all the conditions be specified under which an account holds up; sometimes an account formulated to interpret one situation will not offer an equally valid interpretation of another, even though the account employs the same terms. The norm of merit, as a criterion for the distribution of social goods—such as entrance to universities or professional schools or the granting of governmental contracts or the distribution of broadcasting licenses—is indeterminate in some respects. Race in a racist society has a different political value and social status than in a nonracist one. In a nonracist society the meritocratic norm might well function in a color-blind fashion. In a racist society, however, color-blind meritocracy may subvert plausible goals of meritocracy if in fact it perpetuates a system of entrenched privileges for one race and systematically deprivileges others, such that members of the disfavored race or races never really have a chance to compete with others on the basis simply of merit (an argument from the uneven playing field).

Second, the gap between norms and their context of application limits the capacity of norms to affect individual and group behavior. No possible meaning of a norm can be exclusively valid; no norm can imply one and only one kind of behavior. The meaning of a norm may change as the norm is applied under different circumstances, or to different concrete situations. In circumstances or situations in which racism prevails, a meritocratic norm cannot be racially neutral in the sense of operating "outside the economy of social power—with its significant currency of race, class, and gender " (Peller 1995:132). The meaning and proper application of the norm of meritocracy differs according to whether it is applied in a society where race, class, or sex are predicates of inequality.

Third, the very invocation of a norm alters the situation to which it is applied. It does so because actors, norms, and situations ceaselessly inform and mutually elaborate one another. Like actors and situations, norms do not appear except in a weave of practical circumstances. The actor, norms, and the present definition of the situation are intertwined and together constitute that situation; no one of these elements can be abstracted out and treated as either cause or effect. Norms are useful only if they are usable within such practical, contingent circumstances. Because of actors' ever-shifting body of social knowledge and practical interests, actors never judge a situation once and for all. Every judgment is only situationally "absolute," based on the realization that some later determinations may well change the certainty of the here and now. Judgments about legal equality, equal opportunity, and racial equality cannot be made independently of the social context of their application, for we (the persons affected, the participants, the concerned) can know *only situationally* what "equality" is. For example, standardized tests designed to generate scores to guide the allocation of college admissions and scholarships might be thought to be meritocratic but in fact, perhaps because socially privileged groups likely design them, may reflect unnoticed preferences that have a racial or economic bias. The word *yacht*, to be associated with the related word *ship* on a multiple choice question on the Scholastic Aptitude Test, is less likely to enter the experience and vocabulary of a young, inner-city student from an impoverished background than that of a solidly middle-class student. Not knowing this word indicates nothing about scholastic aptitude even though the missed question would be scored as scholastic inaptitude. In this case the criterion of selection is not merit, and the distribution of resources and opportunities merely reflects existing, nonmerit-based privileges. And even if the invocation here of the meritocratic norm may alter the situation (it might have the unintended consequence of drawing attention to important inequalities among the norm's addressees), the meaning of meritocracy cannot be independent of its context of application.

Because of their abstract character, norms are incapable of specifying what to do in every contingency and must be defined in terms of the occasions of their application; this is their core ambiguity. Any competent norm user must construct what a norm means with reference to a larger organizational context (Rhoads 1991:194). Just as typifications gloss the particulars they typify, so norms cover an indefinite range of contingent, concrete possibilities. Because norms must be applied to specific configurations of circumstances that may never be identical with each other, norms are applied again and again for the "first time." Thus the meaning of the norm of racial equality in the United States changes as the racial status of whites (and not just blacks) change. In this sense, when Derrick Bell (1995a:22) claims that racial equality is not possible for blacks in America wherever equality "threatens the superior societal status of middle- and upper-class whites," he is claiming that racial equality can only be achieved when it is a goal not solely of the victims of racism but also of nonvictims, indeed only when the respective interests of black and white Americans converge.

INDETERMINATE NORMS CAN BE INTERPRETED ONLY IN AD HOC WAYS

The meaning of a norm is "found" or "discovered" within the situation in which the norm is applied. In the end, every instance of an indeterminate norm's application can be accounted for only separately, by reference to specific, local, and contingent determinants. The meaning of a norm is elaborated in ad hoc ways to cover the idiosyncrasies of a situation within which it is applied. The norm may be "stretched" if need be to fit the particular situation. Alternatively, the relevant events of a situation are reconstructed to fit the criteria of the norm.[9] Where "black" functions as a norm of positive political identity, the racial marker may function only if it is neither monolithic nor essentialist. It may function only where it does not posit a unitary definition of that group or community; it may function only where it does not misrepresent the ad hoc features of the group.

In the case of African Americans it may function only where it does not portray or assume the group to be cohesive simply because all members have colored skin (in fact not all African Americans have colored skin); where it does not assume a singular, unified "black point of view"; where it does not infer from membership in a racial group that all members share the same set of cultural or ethical beliefs or practices; where it does not presuppose that members of a racial group who do share some kind of group consciousness do so because they work and reside in the same geographic area. Where "black" functions as a norm of positive political identity, there it can be interpreted solely in ad hoc ways. At the level of the individual this means, for example, that a black person "must *learn* to be 'black' in this society, precisely because 'blackness' is a socially produced category" (Gates 1992:101). Accordingly, as the category "blackness" changes over time, what one learns when one learns to be black changes, too. At the level of the group this means that no one segment of black America can represent all of black America, because members of a racial group may experience their race differently in different parts of the country (in this context one thinks of the multiple differences between the Deep South, the San Francisco Bay Area, and Idaho). No one segment of black America can represent all black America because different members of the same race may not share precisely the same identity (consider, for example, the ways in which differences in economic and social status may produce subjective differences in racial identity). And no one segment can represent the entire group because not all members of the same race share all the same race-related interests.

If the norm is one of positive political identity, then it fails in a political sense where it is interpreted in under-inclusive ways, privileging some members of the identity group by subsuming other members under the ones it privileges. In this sense feminism fails where it essentializes the category "woman," as if all women were essentially the same (in other words: as if white, middle-class women could be proxies for all other women). The struggle against racism fails politically where it essentializes color (as though, for example, black men could be proxies for black women *tout court*). Toward realizing the norm of positive political identity, groups can reinterpret the situation to fit the norm, rather than interpreting the norm to fit the situation; in such a case, the norm is treated as determinate, and the social or political meaning of the situation as indeterminate. In this sense the corrective to essentializing identity is the recognition that each individual is an intersection of multiple identities. Membership (chosen or, more often, ascribed by others) in any given group captures only some of the individual's multiple identities. Any group identity excludes most of the identities of each of the members and privileges some intersecting identities (for example, black and male) to the exclusion of others (black and female). The corrective to essentializing identity is politics at the intersections of multiple identities. This is the politics of coalition building, the politics of coalitions of various intersections of some identities and across others. Crenshaw sees in such coalitions the "basis for reconceptualizing race as a coalition between men and women of color," such that "in the area of rape, intersectionality . . . explain[s] why women of color must abandon the general argument that the interests of the community require the suppression of any confrontation around intraracial rape" (1995a:377). Coalitions among any number of marginalized identities would seem possible. For example, "race can also be a coalition of straight and gay people of color, and thus serve as a basis for critique of churches and other cultural institutions that reproduce heterosexism" (ibid.). Bell points to possible coalitions across racial difference on the basis of class identity: "[M]any poorer whites oppose social reform as 'welfare programs for blacks' although, ironically, they have employment, education, and social service needs that differ from those of poor blacks by a margin that, without a racial scorecard, is difficult to measure" (1995a:23).

PURELY FORMAL APPLICATION OF INDETERMINATE NORMS IS IMPOSSIBLE

Formalism describes a process in which the arbiter derives and applies norms whose content is completely independent of the process of their application. The arbiter applies or enforces a norm without contributing to or modifying its content.[10] But in cases in which the relevant norm cannot itself provide guides for its "proper" application, the arbiters necessarily go beyond formalism in their interpretation of that norm, thereby exceeding any purely formal application. In this sense litigation "tests" relevant indeterminate legal norms against their possible applications. Because none of the alternatives that arbiters have at their disposal is necessary, the preference for one alternative over another is likely to be guided by influences quite beyond the norm itself. To apply an indeterminate norm, the arbiter must make a substantive judgment, quite beyond all formalism.

The formal application of a norm of racial equality might be thought to exclude any consideration of race in governmental or legal classifications of persons for distributing social benefits or social burdens. *Brown v. Board* holds the classification of citizens in terms of their race to be unconstitutional because it is violative of the Fourteenth Amendment's guarantee of equal protection—unless a particular racial classification serves a "compelling governmental interest" and is narrowly tailored to accomplish that goal (in the sense of being neither over-inclusive nor under-inclusive). The Civil Rights movement (in which *Brown* played a significant role) urged Americans to focus not on racial differences among themselves but on characteristics shared by them, "universal" characteristics of the unencumbered subject of political liberalism, for whom race is a merely personal characteristic of no particular valence. On this view, race consciousness can only be racism, the only alternative to color blindness. On this view, legal norms can function as racially neutral instruments for identifying and eradicating racial bias, discrimination, and inequality in the organization and reproduction of social life, and in the integration of individuals into mainstream society. This is the view of the majority opinion in *Metro Broadcasting, Inc. v. F.C.C.*,[11] which found that "any set-aside designed to increase the voices of minorities on the airwaves was itself based on a racist assumption that skin color is in some way connected to the likely content of one's broadcast" (Crenshaw 1995a:375).

The purely formal explication of a norm of racial equality misses its own goal of racial neutrality or color blindness. In a society marked by racism, an appeal to color-blind law, or an appeal to constitutionalism free of race consciousness, can itself be racist in the sense of sustaining the position of the dominant race and the subordination of disfavored races, in this way preserving racial hierarchies. Neil Gotanda (1995) shows how legal norms that mandate color blindness in the interpretation and application of the laws are inevitably race conscious. He shows how constitutional interpretation that would be color blind in fact employs one or the other of as many as four distinct notions of race. (1) Race as a traditional marker of social status, although now largely discredited, "remains important as the racial model for efforts aimed at eradicating intentional forms of racial subordination, with their implication of racial inferiority" (257). (2) Race is formal as a politically neutral descriptor of skin pigmentation or ancestry, in ways entirely "unrelated to ability, disadvantage, or moral culpability . . . [and quite] unconnected to social attributes such as culture, education, wealth, or language" (ibid.). (3) Race marks experience when it refers to "past and continuing racial subordination" (ibid.) and entails the likely unconstitutionality of any racial classification by the state. (4) Race marks culture ("broadly shared beliefs and social practices"), community (in the "physical and spiritual senses of the term"), and a group's self-understanding (ibid.:258).

Another notion of the purely formal application of norms is the idea of law as something entirely independent of politics. The idea here is that legal institutions can mediate competing interests, and apply and interpret the laws, in apolitical or politically neutral ways, in ways free of power politics. But the very categories with which law picks out certain aspects of social and political life and ignores others—the categories that construct the law's view of the world, the categories that represent social and political life in a legally relevant way—are hardly apolitical. Technical categories such as jurisdiction or standing—or, for that matter, procedure, the topic of chapter 2—allow for a great deal of discretion in their interpretation and application. Here norm usage is neither automatic nor consistent because following a norm is not necessarily, or always, or perhaps often, a process of logical deduction, yielding unambiguous conclusions. Relevant norms do not merely emerge once a social situation is determined. No purely formal invocation of norms and the deduction of conclusions from them can be sufficient for every authoritative legal choice; jurisprudence must be supplemented by norms external to itself. Equality, for example, makes noncircular commands and imposes nonempty constraints only in the presence of concrete ideals (Tribe 1988).

Positing such ideals is a choice of values, not an explication of meaning by allegedly neutral professional standards of craft (such as allegedly neutral "reasoned elaboration"). The norm of racial equality cannot itself determine whether a color-blind or a color-conscious approach best realizes, or approximates, or embodies that norm. (In the coda I shall entertain yet a third option: that these two approaches might be complementary and might both be used, but differently, according to circumstances.) The norm of racial equality can tell us that race should not be a marker of social status. But it cannot tell us if race should never be used by the state to classify (thus it cannot tell us if race-based affirmative action realizes or contradicts the norm of racial equality). It cannot tell us if communities might be formed on the basis of race, or if any such community necessarily violates the norm of racial equality (hence it cannot tell us if the creation of all-black electoral districts realizes or contradicts the norm of racial equality). The answer to these various questions can only be given by concrete ideals beyond the norm itself. In other words, the meaning and proper application of indeterminate norms depends on factors external to those norms. Meaning and application are then likely to be ad hoc, shifting as the external factors shift (in a racist society, race-based affirmative action might be consistent with the norm of racial equality, but could become inconsistent as society overcomes its racism).

SYSTEMS OF NORMS CONTAIN INCONSISTENT PREMISES

An open set of unstated conditions of the norm's application always remains. Not only do the rules of a game not cover all possible contingencies (does the norm of racial equality change somehow if society becomes less racist?), the explicit rules fail to cover the full range of contingencies of their own application (does the norm of racial equality entail color-blind or color-conscious means to the goal of that equality?). Differences among situations falling under the jurisdiction of norms reduce the fit between norms and their contexts of application; exceptions arise that limit their generality. Carried to an extreme, this process leads to a complete denial of the existence of norms, which then dissolve into the complete uniqueness of any given situation. Consequently, for many norms and resulting conclusions, one could probably identify a counter-norm justifying a contrary conclusion.[12] On the other hand, some highly formalized sets of norms may apply consistently to mutually inconsistent descriptions of behavior, events, or circumstances.

The norm of racial equality illustrates both aspects of this thesis in concrete ways. For it admits the premise of equal treatment according to neutral norms as well as the contrary premise that, in a racist society, color blindness only perpetuates existing racial inequalities. It admits the premise that race should be irrelevant in relations among citizens; that any form of race consciousness is likely racist; that discrimination on the basis of race is irrational in its choice of criterion by which to distinguish people; and irrational when measured against the basically color-blind spirit of the Constitution and the political system in general; and that participation in the public sphere can be race blind. This premise supports the claim that racial segregation in America has harmed black citizens deeply and enduringly, and that racial integration is the antidote and only plausible alternative. The norm of racial equality equally admits the contrary claim that liberal integrationism actually (but unintentionally) sustains a racial hierarchy by presupposing that civil rights for black Americans above all means the right of blacks to associate with whites (that, in the words of Malcolm X, "what the integrationists . . . are saying, when they say that whites and blacks must go to school together, is that the whites are so much superior that just their presence in a black classroom balances it out" [1970:17]).[13] In fact probably few integrationists are saying this, although they nonetheless may be blind to certain aspects of the situation. For it remains that, here, racial justice is not racial neutrality; that here, race consciousness need not be racist in the way that white or black supremacist consciousness can only be racist.

Again, the norm of racial equality admits the premise that "blacks must gain access to white schools because 'equal educational opportunity' means integrated schools, and because only school integration will make certain that black children will receive the same education as white children" (Bell 1995b:7).[14] And it equally admits the contrary premise that a

> segregated school system, or a segregated community, or a segregated school, is a school that's controlled by people other than those who go there. But in an all-white neighborhood, where you have an all-white school, that's not a segregated school. Usually they have a high-caliber education. . . . So the schools in Harlem are not controlled by the people in Harlem, they're controlled by the man downtown. . . . On the other hand, if we can get an all-black school, that we can control, staff it ourselves with the type of teachers that have our good at heart, with the type of books that have in them many of the missing ingredients that have produced this inferiority complex in our people, then we don't feel that an all-black school is necessarily a segregated school. It's only segregated when it's controlled by someone from outside. (Malcolm X 1970:16-17)

ANY ONE NORMATIVE CHOICE IS SUBSUMABLE UNDER COMPETING NORMS

One normative decision may be subsumable under more than one competing norm. To make a normative decision is to choose among competing norms, all of which may fit many past decisions yet each of which might urge different action in the instant case. A norm does not compel (or preclude) a particular action in which particular action or result can be incorporated into that norm, once reinterpreted.

Hence, in any given case, precedent or stare decisis neither leads to nor requires any particular result. Available to choice are a wide range of precedents, and a still wider variety of past interpretive decisions. Choice may be guided, consciously or not, by factors external to law, such as social and political judgments about the case's substance, parties, or context. Further, not precedent itself but how one chooses to read any particular precedent controls. Choice is guided not by strict logic but by interpretive goals and interests of persons or institutions with the authority to interpret. These are influenced by contingent factors such as which categories currently obtain, or by what types of argument are currently considered (by whoever decides) appropriate to the kind of case at hand. With respect to law in particular, even if stare decisis were an ideal basis for decision, it applies only after a precedential ruling; the precedent establishing a norm is itself outside that norm. Stare decisis cannot justify the manner in which it interprets law in that all-important first decision or holding or opinion on a particular matter, and to which it refers from the other end of a chain of decisions.

That first decision (about a norm's "proper" meaning or application) is unavoidably ad hoc. This example is instructive for areas of norm usage quite beyond the legal sphere. At least two interpretive problems faced by the first interpreter are similar to those faced by the latest interpreter, and precisely these problems hold equally for all areas of norm usage. First, no categorical distinction can be drawn between matters of definition and matters of fact. Even allegedly "analytical" truths are simply those for which no one has yet offered any alternatives that might lead us to question them. "Facts" and texts are unavailable apart from interpretation: Observation is theory-laden and theory is value-laden. Interpretive strategies are not put into execution only after reading; these strategies themselves give texts their shape, making them rather than passively arising from them (and sometimes remaking them subsequently, for example, upon an interpreter's reexamination his or her theories). Linguistic meaning to some extent is conferred by the reader or readers; it is not wholly given a priori or objectively.

Second, the constitutive responses of the text's reader(s) are variable. Further, the intentions of the author(s) may well be unavailable to other individuals, especially to succeeding generations. Hence even if the authors' intent is an appropriate guide to interpreting a rule, a piece of legislation, or a constitution—and proponents of this view have yet to convincingly tell us why this should be the case—only the authors can have known exactly what that intent was, and the authors may be long dead or otherwise unavailable, and/or may have had conflicting intentions submerged in compromise such that intentions are unclear (as often happens in jointly authored legal and political texts). The meaning and application of norms can only be contingent upon the authoritative readers at any given time. Individual readers may offer different readings at different times, and over time the authoritative readership will change.

Consider the norm of localism, of local control, of local control of schools. This norm can in turn be subsumed by the idea, expressed for example in cases such as *Milliken v. Bradley*[15] and *Dayton Board of Education v. Brinkman*,[16] that "local autonomy" is a "vital national tradition."[17] "No single tradition in public education is more deeply rooted than local control over the operation of schools; local autonomy has long been thought essential both to the maintenance of community concern and support for public schools and to quality of the educational process."[18] But the norm of localism can also be subsumed under a contrary norm, on the claim that local control, as understood in the previous sentence, "may result in the maintenance of a status quo that will preserve superior educational opportunities and facilities for whites at the expense of blacks" (Bell 1995a:24). The counter-norm might advocate localism in the form of "model" all-black schools, or all-black magnet schools, or at least predominantly black schools. In that case, "judicial rejection of the 'separate but equal' talisman seems to have been accompanied by a potentially troublesome lack of sympathy for racial separateness as a possible expression of group solidarity" (Tribe 1988:1479), as well as a possible resource in cultural strength, "especially given the importance racial solidarity and exclusivity can have for associations organized to promote the interests of oppressed minorities" (ibid.:1480).[19]

This chapter, having analyzed central aspects of indeterminacy in normative rules, sets the stage for the entire book. It completes the book's first part, identifying the basic problem of indeterminate norms. The second part examines two ways of coping with indeterminacy. The first is proceduralism. I shall argue for a form of proceduralism sensitive to significant contingencies at the local level. The enlightened localist accommodation of local factors saves proceduralism from the unintended but unavoidable perpetuation of inequalities that would in fact violate its own logic of neutrality.

PART II

THE SOLUTION:
BASIC COMPONENTS

CHAPTER 2
Coping with Indeterminacy through Proceduralism

The preceding chapter illustrated the phenomenon of normative indeterminacy with respect to the legal norm of racial equality. It articulated one possible enlightened localist response to the question of local control of public schools. "Control" here would never bar any racial group from attending any public school. But in the case of majority-black districts, the idea of local control would urge interested communities to pursue more or less all-black magnet schools (or other forms of mostly black "model" schools). In the specific context of public schools, enlightened localism responds to the indeterminacy of "racial equality" with an alternative to the standard liberal policy of racial integration of all relevant institutions under all circumstances. The alternative recommends itself where the relevant neighborhoods are isolated racially, such that integration of the relevant schools is possible only by busing large numbers of students over long distances. It recommends itself wherever racially balanced integration is pedagogically ineffective, even detrimental. In such circumstances enlightened localism urges racial separateness or self-segregation with the aim of promoting the interests of a beleaguered group, long an object of systematic racial discrimination; with the aim of promoting the internal solidarity of the group; with the aim of drawing on the group's own cultural strengths in its battle against political marginalization and a multiply discriminatory environment.

This chapter and the next will show how, on the theory of enlightened localism, this conclusion is neither arbitrary nor ad hoc. Chapter 1 traced out the basic contours of normative indeterminacy as a pressing political problem. This chapter and the next pursue a different goal but one intimately related in the book's overarching argument. They provide the basic components for coping with the profound social and political problem of indeterminacy: They take a stand, first, on proceduralism; and second, on pragmatism. To cope with indeterminacy is to settle on working norms, norms that work under conditions normatively heterogeneous. In this chapter I contend that proceduralism (and in the next chapter, pragmatism) helps create shared understandings even in the face of the deep normative differences characteristic of modern liberal democracies (perhaps not only these, but I will focus on these alone). Shared understandings are not the sole means for coping with indeterminacy, but politically they are the most promising means of achieving sustained social cooperation of most citizens on an everyday basis. A shared understanding can become a shared motivation. Social integration seeks the sustained cooperation of the integrated in part by seeking shared understandings and shared motivations.

Among those shared understandings are norms. As we have seen, norms here are neither permanent nor static; they are products of history, of culture, of political choice, and of myriad other contingencies. They sometimes change dramatically in light of social upheaval; or as unanticipated consequences of technological development; or following political choices by a community (sometimes even by an entire society). Shared understandings cannot be complete and exhaustive solutions to the problem of normative indeterminacy. But they can cope successfully with indeterminacy and diversity. Successful coping means partial solutions, fallibilistic answers, and interim strategies, within an open-ended process of repeated attempts to "get it right." Coping does not preclude reasoned and thoughtful public policy; it does not foreclose rational and persuasive social critique; it does not defeat legal and social justice. Nor does it rule out heightened forms of sociality even under conditions that discourage society-wide agreement, such as diverse normative commitments within a single populace. This chapter and the next examine the nature of the "sharedness" possible through enlightened localism.

Let us being with proceduralism. Sharedness through proceduralism exhibits two features. First, it is medial in nature: It is neither determinist nor relativist. Second, the sharedness of understandings so generated is always less than total; social cooperation and public integration never require complete agreement. Here, in this interstitial space, enlightened localism goes to work, seizing on the politically promising space between irreconcilable disagreement and consensual agreement.

As a means of dealing with normative indeterminacy, proceduralism recommends itself precisely where governmental bureaucrats, judges, and legislators have the task of serving a citizenry of diverse normative commitments. Carrying forward the topical example developed in the introduction and chapter 1 (and to which I will return once more in chapter 6), this chapter considers legal equality with respect to black citizens of the United States today. In particular it looks at questions of legislative representation and voting procedures. Proceduralism offers itself as a means indispensable to efforts to secure legal equality and democratic polities.[1] In politically useful ways it can "capture" the complex intersections of law, politics, and race. Capturing those intersections cannot be undertaken from some normatively neutral position above or beyond the social dynamics of race and power. From the standpoint of enlightened localism, proceduralist means to dealing with racial inequality are themselves normative, are themselves politically committed one way or another. Any enlightened localist position is committed normatively. It therefore stands in a relationship of some tension to the notion of normative or political neutrality that characterizes the conventional formalist conception of proceduralism.

On that conception, a system of political representation through popular voting is procedurally fair only insofar as it is neutral vis-à-vis each participant. Proceduralism on the enlightened localist alternative is neutral only to the extent it provides each participant the capacity to equally influence outcomes (as a voter, for example). I shall develop this argument in terms of race, arguing that, in the proceduralism of voting arrangements, race as well as "racialized geography" (a term that will become clear in later pages) can serve as political proxies for representing local preferences in the national legislature.

Proceduralism on this understanding contributes to a political system more capable than conventional proceduralism, conceived formalistically as strict neutrality, of representing issue-based groups. A political system more capable of representing issue-based groups is more capable of winning legitimacy in the eyes of heretofore disenfranchised and currently underrepresented groups. With respect to race, proceduralism understood as strict neutrality entails color blindness, which is to say: strict indifference to the racial identities of those persons affected by the procedure's outcome. Against proceduralism so conceived I shall argue that, in a racist society, only a color-conscious proceduralism provides fair representation in the public sphere.

PROBLEMS IN APPROACHING RACE IN TERMS OF NEUTRALITY

Neutrality, as a basis for approaching race toward the goal of racial equality, fails in the face of five reasons.

1. Impartiality can mean open-mindedness even as the open-minded person remains situated and therefore of somewhat partial view and somewhat partisan conviction.[2] And it allows for more than one valid viewpoint. This is a weak form of impartiality. Alternatively, impartial can mean a single viewpoint that all rational persons could adopt under ideal conditions. This strong sense of impartiality renders participation superfluous. It leads to color blindness (as I will show)—and of course color blindness fails its goal if it perpetuates racism rather than racial neutrality. As an alternative, and one that accommodates a weak version of impartiality, I propose a notion of justice that emphasizes procedural issues of participation in discussing and deciding public issues. The justness of a just norm then derives from conditions that allow and encourage everyone affected by the norm to participate in its public deliberation. A just norm is one that all persons subject to it can freely embrace because the process from which it emerged was procedurally correct. In this sense proceduralism generates transparent and noncoercive grounds for citizens' cooperation with governmental authority. Procedurally established legitimacy derives from respect for the rules of argumentation that define the mode, the parameters, and the method of discussion. It does not presuppose some end or value prior to or independent of the goals in the instant case; it does not presuppose particular goals or necessary outcomes. The normative content it imposes is minimal and includes the norm of proceduralism itself; the norm of equality (all persons are treated equally by the procedure); of fairness (all persons are treated equally as a condition of the

fairness of the procedure); and of neutrality (no particular persons or groups are favored by the procedure).

The procedure itself can be beyond dispute but not its outcome: A fair process cannot guarantee a fair outcome. According to Stuart Hampshire, the "fairness of the actual outcome of a conflict will be evaluated differently, even though both sides recognize the fairness of the adversarial process" (1993:44). In other words, what it is for something to be a fair outcome may itself be a matter of dispute between contending parties. A dispute of this sort is not resolvable by procedural means.

If fair procedures could guarantee fair outcomes, they could simply substitute for public discussion in the sense that the result reached by the impartial decision maker would be precisely the result any impartial person would reach. So constructed, the impartial decision maker would then seem able to represent completely and exhaustively all persons affected by the procedure's outcome. In that case the decision maker might identify the fair outcomes without running the procedure; he or she could simply simulate it. We see again that a strong sense of impartiality renders political participation unnecessary and in principle does nothing to encourage participatory democracy. For example, such impartiality entails the political, social, economic, and moral insignificance of race, in the sense that the impartial decision maker could adequately represent any member of society regardless of his or her race. In a racist society, a stance impartial toward race is one that, by ignoring its social environment, facilitates racism's survival. As a strong form of impartiality, color blindness sustains the very racism it wants to reject.

2. Even as it is charged with carrying out the politics of impartiality, governmental authority—from bureaucratic administration to judicial opinion, from legislative enactment to executive enforcement—cannot be entirely impartial. To begin with, quite partial is that central feature of human life, the individual's deep embeddedness in his or her culture, in patterns of socialization, in beliefs and need interpretations, in group-specific experiences and political commitments. By contrast, in its strongest sense, impartiality presupposes an objective moral psychology; it assumes role-playing in a completely impersonal manner; it presumes the complete exclusion from one's performance of institutional roles of one's personal characteristics, personal life, and the particular circumstances of that life. And of course humans are not often impartial creatures, at least not in this thoroughgoing sense. Such impartiality is not possible when those charged with maintaining the public interest—bureaucrats, judges, officials elected and appointed—have no superhuman capacity to see and judge relevant matters from some perfectly detached "view from nowhere."[3] It is not possible when officials have no superhuman capacity to completely abstract from their multiple identities of sex, race, socioeconomic status, educational achievement, political persuasion, moral convictions, religious belief, and so forth. Nor is it

possible when they have no preternatural ability to ignore or deny their various affiliations with multiple groups (affiliations that in fact establish their identities). To be sure, individuals are capable of surpassing a completely self-regarding stance to communal life. Individuals are capable of some degree of other-regarding belief and behavior. Likely in all societies they are to varying degrees socialized into this capacity. But the other-regarding behavior of even the most selfless person cannot overcome the partiality of his or her views. To that extent he or she cannot be impartial in the strong sense of the term. And yet color blindness demands nothing less—even in a color-conscious society.

3. Impartiality applied in certain ways misses salient differences between dominant and subordinate communities. Standards of neutrality may in fact privilege one social group or sector over another, expectably to the advantage of society's strongest groups. These groups' experiences and perspectives are more likely to inform society-wide standards (or to inform them disproportionately) than are the experiences and perspectives of weak groups. Groups with the best access to cultural communication and political interpretation have the best chances of imposing their standards. They have the best chances of disseminating the values, experiences, and commitments that inform those standards. The very strength of their voices lends them a seeming self-evidence, even the appearance of neutrality.

Under these circumstances, other groups that assert their own standards, experiences, and perspectives then define themselves as deviant—which, technically, they are in the sense that the "impartial" norm that obtains is not *their* norm. Society perpetuates deviance when it allows expected behaviors of some subcommunities to reproduce, or allows dominant groups' expectations of subordinate groups' behavior to reproduce, constraining the latter continually to respond to dominant expectations. The member of a devalued group, says W. E. B. Du Bois, is "born with a veil, and gifted with second-sight in this . . . world which yields him no true self-consciousness, but only lets him see himself through the revelation of the other world. It is a peculiar sensation, this double-consciousness, this sense of always looking at one's self through the eyes of others, of measuring one's soul by the tape of a world that looks on in amused contempt and pity" (1996:364). "Double-consciousness" means that even as one sees oneself through the eyes of others, one can still see oneself through one's own eyes and thereby refuse the image projected by the dominant culture, reject one's stereotype, resist internalizing the imposed sense of inferiority. Double-consciousness is an acutely responsive form of vision, unlike color blindness that thinks itself impartial by ignoring the obvious (that color matters). In this sense, says Kimberlé Crenshaw, even as they disagree on the advisability of affirmative action

> liberals and conservatives who embrace dominant civil rights discourse treat the category of merit itself as neutral and impersonal, outside of so-

cial power and unconnected to systems of racial privilege. Rather than engaging in a broad-scale inquiry into why jobs, wealth, education, and power are distributed as they are, mainstream civil rights discourse suggests that once the irrational biases of race-consciousness are eradicated, everyone will be treated fairly, as equal competitors in a regime of equal opportunity. (1995a:xv–xvi)[4]

4. A notion of strict impartiality entails a rigid and impractical distinction between reason and affect. It constructs moral reasoning as if it were guided solely by the norms of discursive thought, quite free of other norms generated by emotional affect (think of moral outrage or humanitarian compassion), or by cultural inclination (consider definitions of boundaries between morally acceptable and morally unacceptable sexual behavior), or by specific needs predicated on particular historical experiences. In the latter sense, the Nineteenth Amendment to the United States Constitution (adopted in 1920) extends to women the right to vote even though the Constitution as unamended nowhere denies them the vote.[5] Even if logically otiose, the Amendment may have been culturally necessary as a means of political "consciousness-raising" for the American people (men and women alike), as a moral statement that the Constitution properly understood does not discriminate against citizens on the basis of sex. The amendment may have been necessary as a statement that Americans (including the Constitution's authors) misunderstood their Constitution over the preceding 133 years. The claim about sexual equality is more than a logical proposition; it is a moral appeal, and as such is not unattached to affect. It is not normatively neutral but normatively committed, as is any assertion of racial equality. Color blindness and color consciousness are competing models for achieving the goal of racial equality. Neither is normatively neutral; neither is affect-free.[6]

5. Impartiality understood formalistically has a logic that is unique not plural: Its legitimacy or validity lies in its putatively universal character, as a standpoint independent of particular persons or groups, independent of their specific attributes, concerns, preferences, and perspectives. Its legitimacy or validity also lies in its character as a standpoint that supposedly holds equally for all particular persons and groups.[7]

Speaking of objectivity rather than impartiality, Thomas Nagel offers a coherent alternative to this universalizing rationality, if, in the following passage, impartiality is analogized to objectivity.

> Reality is not just objective reality, and any objective conception of reality must include an acknowledgment of its own incompleteness. . . . In saying this we have not given up the idea of the way the world really is, independently of how it appears to us or to any particular occupant of it.

We have only given up the idea that this coincides with what can be objectively understood. The way the world is includes appearances, and there is no single point of view from which they can all be fully grasped. An objective conception of mind acknowledges that the features of our own minds that cannot be objectively grasped are examples of a more general subjectivity, of which other examples lie beyond our subjective grasp as well. (1986:26)

If, alternatively, impartiality is understood as the subsumption of particulars under a universal category, then, in Iris Young's well-turned phrase, "by seeking to reduce the differently similar to the same, it turns the merely different into the absolutely other" (1990:99). Consider: human intelligence takes many forms. The reduction of that diversity to one kind of intelligence (such as discursive reasoning in the sense of the scientific analysis of causal relationships in nature) depicts other ways of understanding the world (emotional, aesthetic, moral) as the other of intelligence, rather than as different kinds of intelligence.

Instead of subsuming particulars under a universal category, one might pursue the kind of intelligence appropriate to the experience or phenomenon one seeks to understand. (Even then, the most appropriate kind of intelligence may not allow one to understand the object of interest entirely or exhaustively.) In any case, impartiality cannot be the absolute measure of reality but merely one way to approach it: To "insist in every case that the most objective and detached account of a phenomenon is the correct one is likely to lead to reductive conclusions. . . . Reality is not just objective reality. Sometimes . . . the truth is not to be found by traveling as far away from one's personal perspective as possible" (Nagel 1986:27). In the treatment of human beings, impartiality so understood likely misses important differences among people, and among various social groups. Again (but now in the context of epistemology) we come up against the problem of impartiality as color blindness. This is the problem of ignoring race in a racialized society, as if claims about how persons in this or that sense are fundamentally the same were a means to protecting groups and individuals whose differences should not be predicates of oppression. These differences continue to be predicates of oppression, however, where they are ignored, denied, or elided.

THE CONSTITUTION OF GROUPS THAT MIGHT BE REPRESENTED PROCEDURALLY

To speak of race is to speak of groups; and to speak of groups is to identify both similarities (those similarities within the group that count in constituting the group) and differences (those differences within the group that are irrelevant to the group's identity, and those differences between groups that allow each group to define itself over against the other). In this sense difference and similarity are pendants. In its individual members, social integration inculcates shared cultural categories: Not all members of society are equally integrated; not all are integrated into all the same categories. Shared cultural categories allow many individuals significant space for individual difference (and to some groups at least they allow significant space for difference between groups as well). We members of this society share somewhat because to some extent we are similar; in part we are somewhat similar because socialization "norms" many of our self-understandings and many of our need interpretations. For this reason some of us are different from most of our fellow citizens: Socialization norms the dominant as dominant, and the subaltern as subaltern (even as some individuals sometimes can overcome the ways in which they have been "normalized"). What is plausible, understandable, or justifiable to ourselves as well as to others becomes so in part when it finds expression in our shared understandings. Take one subcommunity of shared understandings: The Catholic's "need" to attend mass or to confess to a priest is not for the Catholic an idiosyncratic need but a group-specific one. For the same reason, well-intentioned non-Catholics may not be able to regard the Eucharist as the spiritual need and point of identity for him- or herself that it is for many Catholics. By the same logic, what is plausible to some—that nonwhites are inferior to whites—is implausible to others. What then is justifiable to some (discrimination against nonwhites) is implausible if not outrageous to others (to nonwhites and to nonracist whites).

Through culturally generalized modes of understanding, people win access to their own particular understandings, to their individual need interpretations. Individuals express their innermost thoughts in a shared language through which even the most personal becomes communicable, in terms understandable across many if not all differences between sender and receiver. Communication operates through the generalized categories of thought and experience without requiring that sender and receiver be like each other in many ways and without requiring or guaranteeing that different receivers of the same message receive exactly the same message. Different persons do not receive exactly the same message because the content of many messages (especially in deeply cultural beliefs, whether philosophical, religious, or aesthetic) is not indifferent to the receiver. In the twenty-first century "our" Shakespeare is very different from the nineteenth-century version, and is hardly the Shakespeare of his contemporaries.

In a similar sense basic legal rights, such as those provided by constitutions, have specific meanings (or, more accurately, horizons of plausible interpretations) within the relevant political culture by virtue of ways of thinking and experiencing that have been generalized within that culture.[8] These cultures are available to outsiders precisely where outsiders can win access to the ways of thinking and experiencing presupposed by the Constitution and the particular rights it provides. (That interest is learning about other interpretive communities, in the sense given it by the anthropologist Clifford Geertz,[9] which is quite absent from the parochial members of the U.S. Supreme Court. The justices display little or no interest in the jurisprudence of Western European countries, even as Western European judges regularly study and cite holdings of their American colleagues.) General ways of thinking and experiencing facilitate group consciousness, and thereby common political reference points, some of which achieve representation in the legislature, and which must achieve representation if this or that group is to realize its place within the larger political community. My concern in the following pages is with group-based representation, and with procedural means to group-based representation. I will then turn to the logic of group representation, as I work toward a notion of race-based representation of minority interests.

BASIS FOR AN ALTERNATIVE MODEL OF GROUP SOLIDARITY

In a moment I shall introduce an alternative model of the relationship between individual and society. But first I briefly want to lay out my point of departure: Émile Durkheim's claim that, as socialized individuals, we have two consciousnesses at once. (I do not mean here what Du Bois describes as the double-consciousness of downtrodden people who contest the devalued group image of themselves.) One consciousness is "particular" and the other "universal": "one that we share in common with our group in its entirety, which is consequently not ourselves, but society living and acting within us; the other that, on the contrary, represents us alone in what is personal and distinctive about us, what makes us an individual" (Durkheim 1984:84).

Consciousness in these two forms corresponds to social solidarity in two forms. Durkheim's notion of 'mechanical solidarity' is analogous to the cohesion that links together "molecules" that cannot "move as a unit save insofar as they lack any movement of their own, as do the molecules of inorganic bodies" (ibid.). And his concept of 'organic solidarity' is analogous to living bodies in which "each organ has its own special characteristics and autonomy, yet the greater the unity of the organism, the more marked the individualization of the parts" (ibid.:85). Mechanical solidarity derives from similarities, "at its maximum when the collective consciousness completely envelops our total consciousness, coinciding with it at every point" in which our "individuality is zero" (ibid.:84), in which the individual "does not belong to himself" but is "literally a thing at the disposal of society," in which "personal rights are still not yet distinguished from 'real' rights" (ibid.:85). Organic solidarity by contrast derives from differences in which "on the one hand each one of us depends more intimately upon society the more labor is divided up, and on the other, the activity of each one of us is correspondingly more specialized, the more personal it is." Here the "individuality of the whole grows at the same time as that of the parts," where the whole of society "becomes more effective in moving in concert, at the same time as each of its elements has more movements that are peculiarly its own" (ibid.).

These two forms of social solidarity—by similarities and by differences—provide a basis for constructing a theory of group representation. In these terms I shall configure proceduralism: in the spirit of enlightened localism.

THE ALTERNATIVE: GROUP SOLIDARITY WITHIN SOCIALLY MARGINALIZED GROUPS

Mine is a model of solidarity within a subcommunity. Quite beyond either of Durkheim's notions of solidarity, my concern is to conceptualize the legal rights of socially marginalized or oppressed groups—at least in procedural areas such as group representation at the ballot box. For marginalized groups, solidarity by similarities is a means to agreement on the meaning and application of relevant group norms; to determinacy that can facilitate a group's goals of social and political inclusion; to demands for fairness in the organization of political participation. Solidarity by similarities facilitates a group consciousness Durkheim describes as "something totally different from the consciousnesses of individuals, although ... only realized in individuals," linking "successive generations to one another" yet without constituting the "entire social consciousness." Nor is it "coterminous with the psychological life of society"; it constitutes "only a very limited part of it. Those functions that are judicial, governmental, scientific or industrial—in short, all the specific functions—appertain to the psychological order, since they consist of systems of representation and action. However, they clearly lie outside the common consciousness" (Durkheim 1984:39).

Yet in other passages Durkheim closely associates communal with individual consciousness, as in the claim that the individual personality—one that has internalized general social norms—combines the individual and the communal ("they constitute only one entity, for both have one and the same organic basis [ibid.:61])." Durkheim posits in this "identity" between individual and community a "solidarity *sui generis* which, deriving from resemblances, binds the individual directly" to the group (ibid.). It generates collective or shared motives, some of which are relevant to the group's political presence in the public sphere.

I reject as vastly overdrawn the strength and uniformity Durkheim attributes to solidarity deriving from resemblances, such that difference can only be a threat to solidarity. For example, any act that "offends the strong, well-defined states of the collective consciousness" is criminal (rather than, say, provocative or critical or mind opening) (ibid.:39).[10] On this view, social norms defend similarity from all deviations, from difference: "[W]herever an authority with power to govern is established its first and foremost function is to ensure respect for beliefs, traditions and collective practices—namely, to defend the common consciousness from all its enemies, from within as well as without. ... Thus it partakes of the authority that the collectivity exercises over the consciousness of individuals, and from this stems its strength" (ibid.:42–43). At this point solidarity smothers difference;

group resemblance denies particularity; and solidarity from resemblances becomes oppressive. In the construction of group solidarity within a socially marginalized group, Durkheim's notion of solidarity is not useful; it conceives of solidarity as deriving from resemblances so strong among the members that all are homogenized into the group, such that their individuality may be lost. An alternative notion, allowing more scope for individual difference among members of a group, would be subcommunal consciousness of a voluntary constituency based on interest. Before showing how such consciousness can capture the kind of group able to deploy procedural means in pursuing their legitimate interests in a democratic polity, I will outline some of the ways in which it allows scope for individual difference.

For starters, individuals are not born, they are made.[11] The individual as socialized is a product of the groups that socialize him or her, including the family, the school, and the individual's socioeconomic stratum, as well as his or her ethnic and linguistic community. Groups are composed of individuals who, as a group, are socially prior to any one individual. Groups' shifting membership need not elide the respective identities of groups; nor need the diffusion of group consciousness over many individuals diffuse the intensity of group feeling. Identity and consciousness can abide even as one generation gives way to another.

Social solidarity, however, does not require profound or deep agreement between individual and collectivity, or among subcommunities. Social solidarity is possible at the "lower" or "more basic" level of a voluntary constituency based on interest. A constituency so understood is neither Durkheim's individual consciousness that internalizes norms of society, nor the common consciousness of all members of society. It is a limited form of group identification, based on affinity. Group identification is of course very important to individuals; members of oppressed groups experience sympathy for fellow members (just as members of socially privileged groups feel affinity for their peers). Affinity is a matter more of identity than of shared attributes—a matter more of how a group understands itself (and is understood by other groups) than of objective markers. It is a matter of imagination, of an imagined community, a notion to which I will return in the coda.[12]

For example, Hispanics in North America constitute not a racial group but an ethnicity, tied for many members to a shared socioeconomic status, and thence to shared experiences. Expectably this sharedness is differentiated within itself: The common history of Cuban Americans differs from that of Mexican Americans, even as the common history of Hispanic Americans differs from that of Asian Americans. Skin color exists within very wide chromatic ranges, such that dark skin for example is not what makes one an African American (as blacks with a light complexion know). And group identity abstracts from any number of characteristics of individual members, such as age and sex, social class, or national origin.

Different characteristics become salient in different contexts. Sexual identity may be salient: All women confront sexual discrimination and stereotyping, unequal wages for the same work as men, and (as mothers) inadequate day-care provisions. Or socioeconomic status may be relevant: Middle-class women dispose of more resources than poor women in confronting such problems. Or race or ethnicity may provide the classificatory principle: Women of color, or Hispanic immigrant women, may want to maintain racial or ethnic solidarity with their beleaguered community, even when this position (without their wishing it) tolerates patriarchy within that community.[13]

It follows that the citizen can be oppressed within any group, such as women who suffer discrimination within their own racial, ethnic, or religious communities because they are women. Social groups are not homogeneous even as they socialize individuals into membership. In powerful ways the individual's communal affinities inform his or her beliefs and goals, understanding of history, conception of self, and manner of expression. But even the most powerful affinities do not reduce the individual member to a mere vessel of communal beliefs and ways. And any member has aspects of identity quite beyond this or that communal identity.

PROCEDURAL MEANS TO PURSUING THE INTERESTS OF A VOLUNTARY CONSTITUENCY BASED ON INTEREST

I return now to the issue of racial inequality today. I shall explore subcommunity consciousness as an interest-based voluntary constituency with respect to African Americans seeking representation in the U.S. Congress though district elections. Assume, arguendo, that the group self-identifies in racial terms. Proceduralism—as the device that apportions participation on the basis of one person, one vote—can be deployed effectively in an enlightened localist way. Here the "local" aspects relevant to proceduralism include a specific group with a distinct social history under particular circumstances (in a country legally pledged to nondiscrimination yet in practice still beset by such indices of racial discrimination as the proportionally significant underrepresentation of black Americans in Congress). The link between the act of voting and the influence of that vote is not absolute: Some votes have more influence than others (such as votes cast as part of a voting bloc or votes cast by members of various kinds of majorities that vote as blocs). The right of one person, one vote entails no right to the equal influence of each vote. But one person, one vote cannot possibly imply the acceptability of gross disproportions in the relative influence of individual votes: In a democratic order worthy of the name, the logic of an electoral majority with a majority of influence cannot mean that the minority should have little or none. One person, one vote is most meaningful when the right to vote entails more than a merely formal right to be represented in the legislature (formal in the sense of representation by the electoral winner, regardless of who that turns out to be, and not by one's own candidate). Perpetual defeat at the ballot box and a perpetual lack of preferred representation renders voting politically impotent. Absent a robust link between representation and voting, voters have little incentive to participate. A robust link means equality of political access toward inclusion in political decision making, at the voting booth but also beyond, in the council chamber.

Inclusion means connectedness along several dimensions: Governmental decisions that enjoy broader consent have greater legitimacy. Governmental decisions that are shaped by more rather than by fewer groups and by more kinds of groups are more equitable. The more that governmental decisions are expressive of the individual's connectedness to his or her community, the greater his or her motivation to participate in the deliberation of public matters. Inclusion encourages connectedness of individuals to other individuals who share their interests on the basis of political leaning or socioeconomic status, of race or sex, of occupational group or geographic location. The individual takes these affiliations and interests with her or him into the voting booth, rendering voting a procedure for articulating and expressing group voices, hence group differences, hence group autonomy. Voting then facilitates institutions of group representation, as a procedure for including and hearing the voice of each group. This is proceduralism in an enlightened localist sense. It is my alternative: group solidarity on the basis of limited sharing ("limited" when compared to Durkheimian solidarity). This is solidarity at the level of subcommunity. Solidarity so conceived is a basis for race-conscious electoral districting. I shall develop this basis in subsequent pages, but should first like to anticipate some of the possible objections to the very idea of such a proceduralism.

ARGUMENTS FOR AND AGAINST RACE-CONSCIOUS PROCEDURALISM

A number of objections can be raised against this enlightened localist goal. One might argue that not being impartial or neutral toward this or that ascriptive characteristic of citizens negates the moral universalism at the heart of claims to political, legal, and social equality: the claim that all persons are morally equal, that all possess the same moral value. Even if one concedes that we "tend to assume that people's characteristics are a guide to the actions they will take" and that we are "concerned with the characteristics of our legislators for just this reason," it remains that the "best descriptive representative is not necessarily the best representative for activity or government" (Pitkin 1967:89). The insane person, the criminal, the alcoholic could each serve as a descriptive representative for members of the same category, but political life is unlikely to be advanced by such representation. And some observers will object specifically to the goal of a race-conscious construction of proceduralism. After all, the political use of race is always open to danger: It may be appropriated for racist ends; even if not so appropriated, it may only exacerbate divisions within a society already split along racial lines; it may be essentializing (treating all members of a group as indistinguishable exemplars of one basic type); it may imply the biological givenness of what in fact is a social construction.

As a biological phenomenon, race is uninteresting politically. As a political phenomenon, it is crushingly significant; stigmatism is a product of society and politics (where race exists), not biology (where, at the level of molecular biology, it does not). Further, race may ill capture the intended addressees of the label, above all because the "views of the black community are no longer monolithic" (Bell 1995b:16). With regard specifically to racialized group representation, one might argue that race-conscious districting distorts the logic of the legal right to vote: a right accorded to individuals not groups. On this view minorities as minorities have no special or particular right to electoral influence or legislative influence. Finally, even if one concedes the existence of good reasons for some groups to organize politically around their shared racial identity, one might object to the correlation of geographic district with racial identity; one might object to the notion that a given territory can "approximate" a given race: "Race-conscious districting, as opposed to racial group representation, may be rigidly essentialist, presumptuously isolating, or politically divisive. For example, different groups may share the same residential space but not the same racial identity. A districting strategy requires these groups to compete for political power through the ability to elect only one representative" (Guinier 1995:218).

These various objections to using proceduralism in race-conscious fashion boil down to three: that proceduralism so understood (1) essentializes its addressees (for example, as though there were the "black person as such"); (2) further fractures an already racially balkanized society; and (3) misconstrues information about the target group, or simply misses the relevant information altogether. Consider counterarguments to each.

1. Individuals are, to be sure, constituted by their group affiliations, but those affiliations hardly subsume the entire identity of individual members. All groups are composed of individuals who in various respects differ greatly from each other. Each individual has affinities with multiple groups, and any two individuals are unlikely to share all the same affinities. Affinities stand in complex relationship to each other (think of the politically complicated relationship between a person's sex and race, particularly in the case of women of color). That relationship is fluid (thus a black woman may identify primarily with other women in addressing sexism, but primarily with other people of color in addressing racism). An individual is not some "underlying substance to which attributes of gender, nationality, family role, [or] intellectual disposition" simply "attach" (Young 1990:45).

Group representation does not essentialize where groups are understood as interest-based coalitions with specific political goals: temporary coalitions that may dissolve, or that might constitute themselves differently once goals are either achieved or redefined. The importance of a specific category, around which to build a coalition, varies with time and context. Race, or sex, or class may be crucial categories in some cases, while age, or ethnicity, or sexual orientation may be more important in others. Salient identities and differences, deployed to facilitate a coalition for a period of time, need not inscribe themselves permanently in the electoral configuration. As Hannah Pitkin notes, "politically significant characteristics vary with time and place, and . . . the doctrines about them vary as well"; the "history of representative government and the expansion of the suffrage is one long record of changing demands for representation based on changing concepts of what are politically relevant features to be represented" (1967:87).

Positing a robust form of group identity, as a basis for a voluntary affiliation for purposes of electoral districting, need not essentialize the addressees and participants if group identity is understood as a coalition of interests that does not exclude the individual's membership in other coalitions, simultaneously or in the future. To say that African Americans as a group have distinct interests does not entail that all members have the same beliefs and commitments, or that only blacks can effectively represent blacks, or more generally that one identity (such as race) can or must subsume other, simultaneous identities (such as sex, social class, age, or status with regard to handicap). The point of robust group identity is not to deny other, simultaneous identities but to recognize that, on any number of political and social issues, the affected persons themselves should always be included among the authoritative interpreters and rule makers for that group. Because women are the victims of something like nine out of every ten rapes,[14] they should be included in groups with the authority to decide how to punish rapists, how to help victims of rape, and how to develop a culture and society that discourages and prevents rape. This approach does not essentialize women; it does not essentialize men; rather, it asserts that the primary victims, as the parties most affected, should always find substantial representation in the corresponding fora and institutions addressing that victimization. This approach does not exclude men from participation in addressing the problem of rape; it stands against the exclusion of women from participation. It implies a special interest on the part of women, takes seriously experiences specific to women, but does not entail that all women as women have all the same interests, experiences, convictions, or needs.

Finally, where race serves as a proxy for a group's political interests, it need not entail a permanent relationship between a particular race and particular interests. Group interests among black Americans have been forged through the experience of intentional discrimination across multiple facets of life. Race has played a significant role in American history and continues to be a significant factor across a number of social indices, including rates of longevity, quality of health care, educational opportunities, socioeconomic level, rate of victimization by violent crimes, and rate of incarceration. Under these circumstances the individual's race-based group identity may function as a political proxy for various social, economic, and political interests. According to Lani Guinier, "[T]o the extent that an overwhelming majority of group members experience a common 'group identity,' those who are group members are more likely to represent similar interests. Group members may also share common cultural styles or operating assumptions" (1995:215–216). In this sense identity construction is both defensive and aspirational. It seeks to protect the group's members against the kind of depredations visited upon it in the past and in the present. It aspires to a society in which defensive measures become unnecessary. In this case identity construction is contingent, not essentializing.

2. To recognize difference is not to deny universality; however, it is to deny viewpoint-homogeneity: the notion that ultimately there is but one valid viewpoint (which defines truth); or that there should only be one; or that, under ideal conditions, a community could find its way to a consensual viewpoint.[15] But the recognition of difference does embrace and facilitate universality in the sense of universal inclusion, of extending to all adult citizens (other than felons, persons suffering severe mental illness, and so forth) access to meaningful participation in the deliberation of society's public affairs. Proceduralism in a race-conscious fashion extends meaningful participation to self-identifying racial groups whose voices can never achieve expression in color-blind proceduralism and where their votes make little or no impression. In political and legal terms, precisely the recognition of difference can be (and historically has been) a predicate of universality (in the sense of universal inclusion). The long historical trend in the modern West toward extending to more kinds of persons the procedural means to legally equal citizenship has been a gradual process of recognizing this or that difference.

Yet the recognition of persons previously excluded on the basis of sex, race, ethnicity, economic status, or religious faith has not torn society apart nor balkanized it. For the same reason, the recognition of difference need not restigmatize groups historically devalued and excluded. On the contrary, if "oppressed and disadvantaged groups can self-organize in the public and have a specific voice to present their interpretation of the meaning of and reasons for group-differentiated policies, then such policies are more likely to work for than against them" (Young 1990:185).

Group-specific proceduralism need not be socially divisive if its raison d'être is the group members' inclusion in larger society: inclusion in its political process, and inclusion in the public sphere. Groups based on shared identities are potential coalitions, whether these identities are voluntarily embraced or imposed by others. Race may be a shared identity, one among many others. So far as racial identity can itself be an interest-based identity, racial identity can serve as a focus for some group-specific interests. But racial identity cannot so serve if it is a matter merely of chromatic identity; to be an interest-based identity is to be an identity in consciousness. Indeed, consciousness-raising is one means of transforming a "group-in-itself" (a group with identifiable interests of which the members are unaware, and who therefore do not identify as a group) into a "group-for-itself": a group conscious of its shared interests and able to pursue its corresponding political goals.[16] So far as group identity is interest-based, group representation encourages political engagement organized around issues rather than particular candidates. Candidates and particular political representatives come and go, but the issues remain, and are always larger and deeper than any particular political personality.

3. Racialized group representation need not distort information about local interests and needs. The aspiration to realize a government of the people compels a democratic society to consider the merits of the claims of all social groups, and in this sense local interests are elements in the mosaic of partial interests that cannot be irrelevant to the interest of the entire society. Determining that interest includes identifying and understanding the disparate partial interests that constitute it. Group representation increases the number of social interests that find expression at the public podium. It increases the level of participation by increasing the number of interests represented in the legislature. Legislative deliberation is strengthened by wider participation. Legislative decision is the more rational, one may hope, the more informed it is; the more legitimate, the more representative it is. The source of the legislature's information about the interests of society is important precisely because its accuracy cannot, in practice, be divorced from its sources. The inclusion of more relevant viewpoints provides more information, and information likely to be more accurate about the local levels of society and communities, given that the source is immediate rather than mediated. Finally, the presentation in the legislature of local viewpoints requires committed, diligent representatives; precisely group-based electoral districting can identify and select such persons.

PROCEDURALISM MODIFIED TOWARD GREATER CIVIC INCLUSION

Race-based discrimination in the United States has been a long history of state-supported or state-tolerated exclusion of black Americans (among other groups) from the public sphere, from political representation and electoral participation. Forms of exclusion range from socioeconomic deprivation, which can easily block the deprived group's entrance to social and political acceptance, to systematic exclusion from white public schools and white professional schools, to systematic exclusion from municipal employment and from service on juries. Forms of exclusion range from the refusal to appoint African Americans to municipal committees and boards, to elected officials unresponsive to the interests of black citizens. Exclusion ranges from barriers to the process of selecting a candidate, such as denial of access to candidate slating (through which candidates seek support from organized groups and alliances with other candidates), to excluding blacks from white primaries or even from the very franchise itself, either formally in the Constitution before the Fifteenth Amendment of 1870,[17] or through poll taxes and Jim Crow Laws thereafter, which effectively excluded blacks from electoral participation even as they enjoyed a constitutional right to cast ballots. Pamela Karlan describes African Americans at this point as "aliens in their own land, impotent to stop monochromatic legislatures from developing ever more oppressive forms of apartheid" (1989:183).

In the latter half of the twentieth century, the Civil Rights movement, together with decisions by the Supreme Court, as well as legislation such as the Voting Rights Act of 1965,[18] realized substantial measures of civic inclusion of black Americans, to the extent that victims of discrimination could now more reasonably turn to courts, to legislatures, and to the public sphere to seek further redress.[19] But voting remained racially polarized, with "white voters and black voters vot[ing] differently. Where blacks are a numerical minority, [white] racial bloc voting means that the political choices of blacks rarely are successful" (Guinier 1995:216). To remedy the problem of blacks as permanent losers at the ballot box, proceduralism in an enlightened localist sense can be employed to create districts, the majority of whose residents are black, such that the majority of voters who select the winner are black.

Proceduralism in this sense furthers the inclusion of black citizens in electoral and governing processes alike; it facilitates representation. Voters who can form their own electoral districts—on the basis of voluntary affiliation—become capable of robust representation. Voluntary constituencies constructed around shared interests are defined not only by shared attributes but more importantly by a shared identity, born of experience and interest, of social status and history. Constituencies then act as their own agent, representing themselves rather than being represented, passively, by others. They speak for themselves in the sense of selecting their own legislative representatives. They speak for themselves not as mere assemblages of individuals but as a shared consciousness. They speak for themselves not in the sense of Durkheimian solidarity but on the basis of a more limited similarity. They speak for themselves by "defining" themselves, and they define themselves by determining their electoral representation in the legislature. They define themselves temporarily, inasmuch as they can describe themselves only on the basis of shifting identities, interests, and affiliations. By contrast a group that is merely spoken for—in the sense of being represented in the legislature by a person or persons not of its choice, and not simply because its candidate lost but rather because the electoral process effectively precludes the group from putting forth a candidate of its choice—substantially lacks expression for both group identity and group consciousness.

A racial minority excluded by conventional electoral proceduralism from effective participation in the political process is geographically insular within an electoral district, deprived even of the potential to elect its own representatives.

Constitutional protections against dilution of a racial minority's voting strength,[20] as well as the Voting Rights Act of 1965, seek the inclusion of voices from the black community (among other minority communities) articulating concerns of that community in the electoral process and in elections and legislatures. In 1964 in *Reynolds v. Sims*[21] the Supreme Court repudiated the conventional proceduralism of making the effectiveness of a citizen's participation in the electoral process—the degree to which his or her vote can speak for his or her interests—dependent on the contingencies of geographic residence. The Court argued that the "right of suffrage can be denied by a debasement or dilution of the weight of a citizen's vote just as effectively as by wholly prohibiting the free exercise of the franchise."[22] In 1969 in *Allen v. State Board of Election*[23] the Court interpreted the Voting Rights Act through *Reynolds*. The act makes illegal any electoral practices that in effect disenfranchise citizens on the basis of their race. In *Allen*, the Court concluded that electoral procedures violate the Voting Rights Act when they effectively dilute the voting strength of racial minorities.

Under these circumstances, race-conscious districting, and single-member districting in particular (in distinction to multimember or at-large districting), uses geography as a proxy for the political interests of black residents. The authors of the U. S. Constitution configured politicized geography into the design, which deploys geography as a proxy for group interests in two ways: It structures the country as a federation of states, each of which constitutes a distinct unit of group representation; and citizens elect every state legislature, as well as both houses of Congress, from geographically defined districts. This political use of geography is immediately problematic and remains even at best a less-than-ideal solution. It is problematic, as we have seen, because it can be (and has been) used to discriminate against racial minorities. Housing markets, both private and public, have generated residential segregation by race, usually in the sense that, on average, black Americans have never enjoyed the same degree of residential choice as white Americans, in part as a consequence of differentials in socioeconomic status. Residential segregation here marks the exclusion of black interests, unless matched by race-conscious districting.

Geography without regard to race-conscious districting is an inappropriate category to improve the social and political position of African Americans if the context of the discrimination in question is more a question of identity than location: discrimination on the basis of who the voters are rather than where they live. If for example certain elected officials are unresponsive to the needs and interests of the black community, they will be unresponsive regardless of where that community is located; racial interest is then independent of geography. By contrast, "while urban and rural whites may have distinctive interests, those interests are inextricably intertwined with questions of geography. If the two groups were to switch locations, their distinctive interests would not likely travel with them. . . . Even if blacks were to be residentially dispersed (for example, by scatter-site housing) . . . this would not necessarily eliminate their distinctive interests" (Karlan 1989:188, n. 50).

These are significant caveats. Bearing them in mind, geographic proceduralism from the standpoint of enlightened localism provides an important means to counter contemporary racism and the residual effects of past discrimination. This standpoint turns segregated housing patterns around, transforming them into a representational proxy, thus providing black voters electoral control—choice and representation—as the capacity to initiate representation and to terminate it, to select one's own representatives and subsequently to retire them if warranted. By this arrangement black residents' political strength is no longer diluted by majority-white electorates. In some relevant areas, such as much of the South, the black community is already sufficiently concentrated to realize majority-black, single-member districts. In other relevant areas the "location of black neighborhoods may enable the court to provide the black community with political access by making it possible to draw single-member districts in which the black community may exercise effective voting power" (ibid.:212).

Note that, in this model, both "being" (when people are judged ascriptively in terms of what they "are," for example in terms of their sex or race) and "doing" (when people are judged in terms of what they "do," in terms, for example, of their profession) can serve as proxies for the political interests of a distinct group of citizens. Each offers a model of group association; neither entails anything about the content of the interests to be represented; both are procedural.

One model authorizes certain citizens to represent others with regard to formal requirements of age and residence and renders them accountable for their work as representative (with respect, for example, to reelection). Representation is then a matter of doing: the representative *acts* on the voter's behalf—*for* him or her. What matters, in this model, is what the representative does, not who he or she is. Some voters might well prefer a representative who is *not* typical of the district, in the hope that the best representative is more able, or more intelligent, or a better speaker, or is better connected (or even more moral or honest) than persons typical of the district.

An alternative model seeks an "accurate" correspondence between representative and constituents, not with respect to what the representative *does* but with regard to who he or she *is*. So conceived, representation is a matter of the representative standing for certain characteristics of his or her constituency. During the American Revolution John Adams claimed in this sense that the legislature "should be an exact portrait, in miniature, of the people at large, as it should think, feel, reason and act like them" (1851:205). Today Lani Guinier makes a related, but more particular, claim that "many racial minorities do not feel represented unless members of their racial group are physically present in the legislature" (1995:216). In this model the representativeness of each member is what constitutes representation: the legislature's composition is itself representation.[24]

Race-conscious districting is compatible with both models: Both locality and identity can be proxies for the political interests of a distinct group of citizens. Depending on the circumstances, each can be as effective as the other. It remains that any electoral proxy is less effective than a more direct form of localism, one that allows voters the opportunity to determine their interests directly, unmediated by a legislative group. But as long as the formal proceduralist model of one-person, one-vote disadvantages minorities, an enlightened localist political proxy offers itself as a viable alternative. Unlike the formal proceduralist model, it can realize politically disadvantaged citizens' electoral and legislative interests.

An additional way of coping with indeterminacy, one that does not compete with proceduralism but rather complements it, is pragmatism. Pragmatism is the second element in my proposed solution to the problem of normative indeterminacy. It forms the topic of the following chapter, which further develops the notion of an interest-based, voluntary constituency introduced here. In this chapter I attempted to make plausible a proceduralism sensitive to local conditions (in distinction to a proceduralism wholly impartial and neutral). In the next chapter I shall rely on a notion of relativism to show how pragmatism can reduce the indeterminacy of problematic legal rules, such as constitutional provisions mandating the legal equality of citizens.

CHAPTER 3

Coping with Indeterminacy through Pragmatism

An interest-based constituency is locally possible (in one locality, or in one constituency) by means of enlightened localism. And it is possible in the process of coping with normative indeterminacy: The indeterminant can be made determinate in pragmatic ways, and I shall show how these ways are central to enlightened localism. This chapter continues the discussion of law developed in preceding chapters but moves to the more abstract plane of legal theory, to examples of important norms in the public sphere (which, as a concession to the reader's patience, I offer in relatively short paragraphs). Here the central claim is that society can cope with indeterminacy—and with indeterminate legal rules in particular—by relativism not absolutism; by sensitivity to the local circumstances rather than insistence on universal and uniform validity or applicability; in short, by localism enlightened not parochial.

At chapter's end I shall take up once again the question of racial equality and, sustaining the conclusion of chapter 2, argue that pragmatist considerations in law and public policy also urge color consciousness, not blindness, as the most promising means in addressing racial injustice.

HISTORICAL ANTECEDENTS TO MY POSITION

My focus on indeterminacy recalls a particular strand of American legal history. In the 1920s and 1930s Legal Realists thought a great deal about indeterminacy, as have protagonists of the Critical Legal Studies movement since the late 1970s. The Legal Realists, and subsequently proponents of Critical Legal Studies, have been concerned with how to justify a judge's (or other person's) claim to have followed a particular rule. Members of both movements have contended that "case law always or typically underdetermines the rule that emerges from a line of cases, and that one can never be sure what rule(s) a judge has followed in reaching a decision, insofar as such contentions seem to rely on treating *rule* as a logical, linguistic, or psychological category" (Landers 1990:179). Legal Realists also advocated an aspect of what I have been calling "localism": "direct reference to the purposes of rules" is key to their "*wise* construction" and the only way "they can be applied to facts" with "consistency and determinacy" (Fisher, Horwitz, and Reed, 1993:167). Moreover, like me, some of the Legal Realists were influenced by pragmatism. Karl Llewellyn (1893-1962) and Roscoe Pound (1870-1964), for example, viewed legal rules as guiding decisions, not as rigidly controlling them. This is pragmatism in the sense of William James (1842-1910): where legal rules are guides rather than prescriptions.

But my position differs from that of both Legal Realism and Critical Legal Studies. Realism would solve the problem of indeterminacy by creating, through social science, increased certainty and judicial predictability. The Realists sought to provide certainty and predictability in judicial decisions. They were concerned with what they took to be the indeterminacy of legal rules, that "legal rules are not explanatory; [that] appeal to them in justification is circular; that [giving] judges . . . discretion in deciding cases annihilates any constraint a rule might supposedly have, yet a 'rule' that doesn't constrain is no rule; [that] rules are not sufficiently determinate to provide certainty about what the law is; [that] the relation between a legal rule and an individual judicial decision is unclear" (Landers 1990:186-187). Hence justifications given by judges of their decisions can only be circular, or else mere rationalizations. For example Felix Cohen (1907-1953) claimed that "every legal decision (particular proposition) can be subsumed under an indefinite number of different general rules. . . . Every decision is a choice between different rules which logically fit all past decisions but logically dictate different results in the instant case" (Cohen 1933:35-36).

But many of the Realists were ambivalent, contending that while rules are subjective, standards of justice are objective, that while "values are subjective and arbitrary," "objective standards of justice and the pubic good" exist, standards the law "should strive to advance" (Fisher, Horwitz, and Reed 1993:169). Thus the Realists rejected, as unscientific, the analysis of legal doctrine, that is, the formal explication of legal rules and their interconnections. Only the pragmatists among the Realists rejected empirical science as an inappropriate model for the study of legal phenomena. I argue—in some ways like Critical Legal Studies—that indeterminacy inescapably defines some law; for example, although adjudication leads to predictable results, these results cannot be derived wholly or importantly either from a system of legal rules or from judicial process but only from the influence of extralegal factors.[1] But Critical Legal Studies theorists then abandon all hope that adjudication can ever be certain or predictable, that it can be anything other than deeply fraught with indeterminacy. Pragmatism offers the possibility of a less pessimistic conclusion. I refer to a further presupposition of pragmatism that rules can be guides to decision, but never rigid prescriptions, and at best a means to standardize growth and improvement through human experience.[2] To be sure, two of the Legal Realists—Karl Llewellyn and Roscoe Pound—viewed rules in just this way. Pound inferred from William James's pragmatism that rules cannot be rigid and precise prescriptions that refer to unambiguously defined, closed categories. Rather, rules function as flexible guides to behavior and are always open to interpretation and modification.

MY VERSION OF PRAGMATISM

I will begin developing my version of pragmatism by offering a positive account of the nature of normative knowledge possible in an indeterminate world. I shall then repeat the offer, but this time with respect to normative principles. In both cases I shall argue for a specifically pragmatist account of truth, knowledge, and guides to behavior. Pragmatism is a form of relativism, and I will be at pains to distinguish my account of relativism from that of a currently pervasive, and very different, kind of relativism: that of postmodernism.

To define pragmatism broadly is necessarily problematic. Although we must not slight significant differences among related authors, debates over who is, and who is not, really a member of school X or movement Y easily become ponderous exercises in scholasticism. I construct a pragmatist social theory in the sense of offering a specific version of a tradition not sharply delimited in terms of beliefs, methodology, or canon. *Pragmatism* is an umbrella term sheltering diverse perspectives, some of which may not agree with each other. To speak generally of pragmatism is necessarily to construct one version of it, much as I will in this chapter.

Recall the historical origins of the term *pragmatism*. Charles Sanders Peirce (1839–1914) arrived at the term through Immanuel Kant's (1724–1804) distinction between "practical" and "pragmatic" (Kant 1991). Moral norms are practical when a priori. By contrast, rules of art and technique are pragmatic when derived from and applicable to experience. The practical, says Peirce, is a "region of thought where no mind of the experimental type can ever make sure of solid ground under his feet." By contrast, pragmatic expresses a "relation to some definite human purpose," an "inseparable connection between rational cognition and rational purpose" (1905:163).

In chapters 1 and 2 I argued that in many cases norms are indeterminate in meaning and application. I seek now to show how a pragmatist approach is conducive to creating determinate answers, that is, to creating durable agreements on, and recognition of, binding meanings of otherwise indeterminate norms. To determine the meaning and application of a norm is to render it usable and to associate it with predictable consequences. To create determinate answers is either to generate new social norms or to sustain existing ones.

Similar to the kind of proceduralism I developed in chapter 2, pragmatism allows members of a community to avoid intractable questions of ultimate foundations, absolute truths, and universal validity.[3] (I will return to the issue of universalism in the coda.) It can avoid these questions because, in support of norms, methodologies, or justifications, it appeals to nothing beyond our practices. It does not deny the existence of a mind-independent reality; it emphasizes that any discussion and description of reality is possible only relative to some conceptual scheme. It rejects the notion of a single, complete, true description of reality: There are many, and many competing, conceptual schemes that seek to describe reality. Pragmatism rejects the notion that reality identifies itself; it claims rather that we know reality only as it exists for us, that is, in terms of whatever conceptual scheme we employ.

And yet pragmatist thought is rooted in action not consciousness. The environment for cognition is not consciousness per se but problems related to action (Joas 1993:95, 198). Pragmatism offers a foundation for understanding society as a normative order, with respect to how norms guide the behavior of its citizens.

I reject one common understanding of pragmatism: as the appeal to standards of efficiency or standards of satisfactory performance. This understanding entails a kind of irrationalism. If action as such is taken to be the goal of human behavior, without regard to the thought or goal that the action attempts to realize, then behavior would seem to be less than rational. By contrast, pragmatism, as I define it, is a kind of rationalism, a rationalism of and in action. It is rational because it is "self-conscious," that is, it refers to itself critically, is self-referential in the sense that it can correct itself. It can place any claim within itself into question, and so displays the rationalism of fallibilism.

Enlightened localism understands democracy as a kind of pragmatist localism. On the one hand, democracy involves cooperative activities aimed at sustaining contemporary situations or bringing about new ones, in light of social needs and guided by communal bonds. On the other hand, democracy presupposes the equal autonomy of moral agents. The authority of the community, while external to the moral agent, is nonetheless rationally acceptable to him or her because it rests on grounds that advance the agent's purposes.

Pragmatism in this application emphasizes a cooperative construction of truth, in distinction to the lonely Cartesian ego passively receiving a truth that derives from outside and beyond that ego. A cooperative construction of truth does not require the like-mindedness of the participants and other affected persons. Through language, different minds can communicate among themselves without necessitating like-mindedness. Social order, like linguistic communication, does not require an external authority; both are possible through the activities of the participants themselves. The notion of political democracy presupposes this claim: Language, like democracy, is dialogical not monological. Dialogue need not reduce the differences among the participants to sameness. Indeed, only through dialogue can relevant differences be identified and sustained. Dialogue—collective interpretation, decision making, and adjudication—does not entail social conformity of the participants or other concerned persons. In this way a democratic or self-regulating society can respect many differences, and many kinds of difference, among people involved and people affected.

Fallibilism is inherent to relativism for two reasons: First, any proposition may be true if the category or sphere or universe to which it applies is adjusted adequately. People tend to make only the minimal adjustments necessary to maintain a situation as close to the previous status quo as possible. Hence relativism need not be inherently destabilizing socially. Indeed, some adjustments are likely to be conducive to social stability, given the widespread disinclination to adjust one's categories or areas of application.

Second, we call "true" those propositions that allow us to make sense of information; we call "true" those propositions that allow us to create and sustain a structure of meaning within the flux of experience. We call "false" those propositions that crumble in the face of experience. "Truth" and "falsity" are human posits; in the long run, in many cases, true propositions may be more likely than false ones to unify human experience and belief and to render them coherent. Thus, with regard to consequences for coherent belief and for harmonizing conviction and behavior, a true proposition may have consequences for the holder in the long run more powerful than the consequences of a false proposition. To be sure, errors can sometimes unify experience and belief, just as falsehoods can sometimes satisfy humans as much as truth can sometimes dissatisfy them—especially in the short run.

NORMATIVE KNOWLEDGE POSSIBLE IN AN INDETERMINATE WORLD

I develop my version of pragmatism in terms of the following propositions, some of which overlap. None is particularly controversial within the pragmatist tradition broadly understood.

TRUTH IS NOT A MATTER OF CORRESPONDENCE

Pragmatism rejects the correspondence theory of truth, a theory of Cartesian ambitions for certainty according to which a true proposition corresponds adequately with putative "facts."[4] Adequation between the cognizing mind and the cognizable world is determinate in the sense that cognition reports more or less objectively and faithfully on a reality independent of mind (Margolis 1986:xvi). Each of the following theses constitutes a specific way in which pragmatism rejects a notion of truth based on the metaphor of a cognitive copy of an external reality.

TRUTH IS A PROPERTY OF LANGUAGE AND A CONVERGENCE OF OPINION

Even if truth itself is immutable, our estimation of it can only be variable. Pragmatism does not equate being with belief in the sense of what is, is what is believed to be. Rather it claims tautologously (and hopes for the reader's good humor) that what is believed to be is believed to be as it is believed to be—and not as it is independent of belief (Prado 1987:13). An undistorted inquiry into a matter cannot be defined without circularity because our only checks on the methods of inquiry are our beliefs about the correctness of their results. To say that a proposition is true is to not to say how things are "in themselves" or "as such," but how things are believed to be.

Although belief and the language in which we express it usually refer to reality, we cannot know for certain the reach of that reference. Truth, then, is a property of language and not the reality to which language refers. We do not know if and how a sentence "connects up" with reality, but we can know if and how a sentence is true within a language. Here I commit to a coherence theory of truth.

To act in everyday life we frequently need guidance from some notion of truth, whether or not cognitively and psychologically satisfying. Whatever conception of truth we employ has practical consequences. These practical consequences are features of the way we order our lives, individually and communally. A pragmatist conception of truth recognizes both the practical necessity of some conception of truth—in a sense, people "need" truth to cope with daily life—and the limitations of human certainty. Such a conception is fallibilist and consequentialist; it justifies belief within domains of discourse we provisionally accept because we find them useful in coping with life in the vernacular. If humans can know no absolute truths, then at best they can know only warranted belief. Human behavior is belief-guided not truth-guided. The constitution and reproduction of a political community (through moral and legal arguments, and through public policy) is possible only with recourse to belief. Truth, understood as a property of language not reality, is the convergence of opinion under counterfactual conditions that cannot be satisfied. Truth does not transcend belief.

Of any belief we may ask, How is it justified? Understood minimally as one aspect of social organization frequently involving normative claims backed by coercive enforcement, law involves peculiarly social justifications. Any definition of a democratic polity excludes a legal system in which norms could be legitimate even if their justification were purely private or idiosyncratic; the justification of socially legitimate norms can only be social, and a social justification is a shared belief. Even if the simple fact of being shared might lend a certain credence to at least some beliefs, that credence is always fallible. John Dewey (1859–1952) makes just this point.

> Every proposition concerning truths is really in the last analysis hypothetical and provisional, although a large number of these propositions have been so frequently verified without failure that we are justified in using them as if they were absolutely true. But, logically, absolute truth is an ideal which cannot be realized, at least not until all the facts have been registered . . . and until it is no longer possible to make other observations and other experiences. (1968:24)

What justifies shared belief? Like any enterprise charged with regulating social order on a daily basis, social norms are oriented toward action, not truth—which is why normative disagreement demands a response practical, not theoretical. Pragmatism, too, is belief-oriented: Its orientation toward behavior, and toward the consequences of behavior, is itself guided by belief. But pragmatism seeks "acceptable" action, whereas many nonpragmatist approaches seek justified true belief. The pragmatist and nonpragmatist alike embrace belief, yet each embraces a kind of belief distinct from the other, and each by a different means.

By pragmatist lights, means are "adequate" if they meet their predetermined goal; the goal defines "adequacy" in any given instance. When pragmatism accepts the goal, it does so only provisionally. It proceeds from the goal and seeks the best means toward its realization, yet does not renounce or forfeit the possibility of rejecting or revising the goal in other instances. At any time it can place its presuppositions into question. Yet no more than any other approach, pragmatism cannot place into question all of its presuppositions simultaneously. Action (in the sense, for example, of trying to achieve one's goals) is possible only if some relevant matters or concerns are not placed into question. Given an Archimedean point, everything other than that point can be placed into question. Nondogmatism in any discussion is possible only if at least one point of dogmatism is allowed, on the basis of which alone we can proceed nondogmatically. Because the standpoint itself can always be questioned, it enjoys a warrant not absolute but merely provisional, ever attendant on the next provisional warrant. Pragmatism provides no absolute way of knowing; indeed, it denies the possibility of absolute knowledge. It seeks to provide a way of knowing conscious of its own limitations, able to identify its own aspects of dogmatism. The degree of dogmatism in nonpragmatist ways of knowing may be greater to the extent that such theories tend to involve a greater number of presuppositions because they constitute more complex theories—more complex because more ambitious, more ambitious because intended to answer what pragmatism sees as intractable questions of *ultimate* foundations, *absolute* truths, and *universal* validity.

A Peircean theory of truth—a true proposition is one that would be accepted in the long run by the community of inquirers if inquiry were temporally unconstrained—provides no assurance that we possess the truth. Counterfactual arguments like Peirce's are regulative not descriptive: They may regulate behavior but they are never empirical descriptions of it because inquiry is always constrained, temporally and otherwise. Correspondingly, the absence of consensus at any given time does not make impossible a right answer to a difficult normative question; rather, it means we do not yet know whether a particular answer is, in fact, the right one—a particular answer can be correct without our yet knowing it to be so.

All Claims to Truth Are Fallible (Including This One)

No inquiry provides infallible results. This presupposition follows immediately from the pragmatist rejection of a conception of truth that transcends belief. Pragmatism understands itself merely as one belief system among others. This presupposition—no inquiry provides infallible results—follows also from pragmatism's rejection of a notion of truth determinable by appeal to a reality independent of our beliefs about reality. According to Dewey, "no judgment of fact can ever be completely verified. Any experiment involves a new risk in the very process of resolving *a priori* doubt. But this does not mean that judgment and experimental testing get us nowhere, or that we might as well have tossed . . . a coin to decide" (1922:349). Empirical knowledge is rational as a self-correcting effort that can always place into question any of its presuppositions. To do so, pragmatism does not require a foundation independent of itself.

Truth Is Generated by Experience, Consequences, and Action

We judge a belief to be true if it proves to be a successful guide to action. Like all the theses I am attributing to pragmatism, this one provides an alternative to the correspondence theory of truth. Truth then expresses not a cognitive representation of reality but an enhanced capacity for action within a specific environment (Joas 1993:19).[5] This proposition dovetails with the claim that pragmatism is guided by consequences that concern the satisfaction of desires.

To say that pragmatism is consequence-guided is not to equate it with what might be called "actionism." The claim that we are guided by consequences is the claim that we are guided more by the future than the past. To claim that pragmatism is consequence-guided is to say it draws no distinction between principle and policy in the following sense.[6] Principles are concerned with consistency over time, a concern that always looks backward. From a pragmatist perspective principles are important inasmuch as a "given legal arrangement is what it does, and what it does lies in the field of modifying and/or maintaining human activities as going concerns" (Dewey 1941:77). In this instrumental sense—the sense that norms such as law should serve human needs, not frustrate or ignore them—pragmatism is forward-looking. Legal pragmatism, in particular, is forward-looking in Benjamin Cardozo's sense that "not the origin, but the goal, is the main thing. . . . The rule that functions well produces a title deed to recognition" (1921:102-103). Continuity with the past or status quo is not desirable in and of itself but rather for the consequences entailed by continuity. Pragmatism values the past as a means to an end.[7] In this sense William James defines truth as the "expedient in the way of our thinking much as the good is the expedient in the way of our behavior" (1975:127-128).

Pragmatism is concerned with consequences related to the satisfaction of desires and to the nature of belief as affected by those desires and their satisfaction. The "classical" pragmatists Peirce and Dewey agree on this point. Peirce thinks it "best for us that our beliefs should be such as may truly guide our actions so as to satisfy our desires; and this reflection will make us reject every belief which does not seem to have been so formed as to insure this result. . . . [A]s soon as a firm belief is reached we are entirely satisfied, whether the belief be true or false. . . . [W]e seek for a belief that we shall think to be true" (1992a:114-115). Dewey, following Peirce, suggests that the meaning of a proposition follows from the proposition's practical consequences.

According to Dewey, James does not treat reasons, thought, and knowledge with contempt, or regard them as a "mere means [of] gaining personal or even social profits. For him reason has a creative function . . . which helps to make the world other than it would have been without it. It makes the world really more reasonable; it gives to it an intrinsic value" (1968:25-26). To be coherent, pragmatism must be able to distinguish truth (however plural, partial, uncertain, and changing) from falsity, just as it must affirm the goal of seeking truth. Pragmatists must have just as much reason as moral realists to accept the meaningfulness of questions of justice and the coherence of questions of truth. Correspondingly, legal pragmatists should be able to advise judges and others responsibly from a pragmatist perspective.

Truth for pragmatism is created, and it is created not individually but communally. It is a social belief created experimentally, through inquiry into the process of resolving problems as they present themselves to the community. Resolving problems, satisfying needs, and achieving goals generate impetus for inquiry, but do not provide the criterion of truth by which the success of that resolution, or satisfaction, or achievement can be measured or defined. Just as the resolution of many problems or the satisfaction of some needs is, for any community, an ongoing process, never completed, so, too, is truth an ongoing process, one ever dependent on future experience, open always to revision, correction, rejection, and replacement. Truth of this sort may be called "opinion" but only insofar as opinion is something tested by experience and experiment. It is never merely wishful thinking.[8] James identifies true ideas as "*those that we can assimilate, validate, corroborate, and verify. False ideas are those that we cannot.* That is the practical difference it makes to us to have true ideas; that, therefore, is the meaning of truth, for it is all that truth is known as" (1975:3).

NORMATIVE PRINCIPLES POSSIBLE IN AN INDETERMINATE WORLD

Principles Are No Prerequisite for Normative Behavior

Even where enduring consensual values do not exist, or may exist yet always escape identification, advocacy is not rationally groundless or unavoidably partisan. This last proposition reflects a pragmatist perspective on principles, specifically on principles of *internal* compromise—the compromise *of* a principle in distinction from a compromise *about* principles. According to Ronald Dworkin, to enter into an internal compromise is to "endorse principles to justify part of what [one] has done that [one] must reject to justify the rest" (1986:183-184). On this view, normative principles are always matters of internal integrity or internal unity, and any norm that compromises such integrity is immediately unprincipled (and to be rejected on that basis). If in a particular case, for example, social justice and fairness were not matters of internal integrity, then internal integrity would morally trump justice and fairness. In that case a society dedicated to racial equality would violate that commitment if it employed race-conscious means toward racial equality, even if justice and fairness could not be brought about by race-blind means. Affirmative action with respect to admission to colleges or professional schools or in the granting of governmental contracts might be means to racial and ethnic equality in the long run but, if in the short run they treat different groups of citizens differently (on the basis of race or other forms of minority status), then as internal compromises with the norm of legal equality across racial and ethnic differences, they must be rejected as unprincipled.

Pragmatism sees things differently: To adhere strictly to principle—that is, not to enter into an internal compromise—may sometimes bring about an outcome that is normatively worse than acting in an unprincipled manner. Parties to a conflict of irreconcilable norms can pursue a mutually satisfactory compromise without compromising themselves or others. Integrity-preserving compromise is possible in normatively conflicted circumstances. In cases of "factual uncertainty, moral complexity, the need to maintain a continuing cooperative relationship, the need for a more or less immediate decision or action, and a scarcity of resources" (Benjamin 1990:32), the strongest of normative convictions may be compromised without thereby compromising the moral integrity of the compromiser. Thus the argument for color-conscious public policy in a racist society compromises the norm of strict civic equality of all citizens, regardless of the color of their skin. The argument compromises that norm in the short run, as a means to realizing a just society, one in which color blindness could be practiced without (unintentionally) perpetuating racism. The moral integrity of the compromiser is not itself compromised, inasmuch as race in the United States, for example, continues to influence citizens' opportunities, experiences, and life chances. Color-conscious public policy is then deployed as a means to realizing in fact what today, certainly for many black Americans (among other citizens), is merely a promise: the fundamental equality of all citizens.

Integrity-preserving compromise excludes instances in which none of the conflicted circumstances obtain—or when the relevant parties do not agree they obtain. Compromise turns on the existence of something shared, something commensurable: shared perceptions of, and judgments about, certain conflicted normative circumstances. In some acute differences—perhaps over race, religion, sex, or rankings of personal values—many people may not share perceptions and judgments. Their incommensurable perceptions and judgments may preclude any compromise.

A pragmatist approach does not reject all principled explanations of how a normative order constrains or generates social behavior. For example, race-conscious means toward racial equality, even as an internal compromise of the principle of strict equality in the form of color-blind treatment of all citizens under all circumstances, is not unprincipled by pragmatist lights. By pragmatist lights, race consciousness is morally justified precisely as an effective means to racial equality and is justified only to that end, and is unjustified wherever it cannot contribute to that end, or once it no longer contributes thereto. Its proper use is principled in this sense.

Individuals in legal and other institutional settings do not always, or necessarily, use principles or rules as practical guides to behavior, however. Where we cannot be sure what a rule means, there we cannot be sure that we have altered it either; the social world sustained intersubjectively by human beings is an interpretive one. But for purposes of normative critique, public policy, or law, the deeply hermeneutic nature of the social world is not always or necessarily a problem.

Pragmatism does not conclude that, in normative contexts as elsewhere, principles don't matter. They certainly do matter, but they matter as one among a number of factors affecting the kind of norms we actually get in practice. Pragmatism emphasizes that some of the regularities we observe in everyday life, and in legal or other normative systems, are not necessary consequences of adopting a given regime of principles. In those instances, no theory, rule, or principle constrains particular normative opinions—at least not in the powerful sense of constraining adjudicators to decide similar cases similarly or any given case in just this or that way.

Finally, someone who interprets and applies principles does not always comply with them in the sense of preserving their current usage intact. Sometimes he or she "complies" with them by altering the way they were understood previously. Participants and other affected persons may have no alternative but to alter them, inasmuch as principles sometimes can be interpreted and applied in no other way. This, too, is a pragmatist approach.

Social Order and Belief Are Possible without Determinate Foundations

Consider now the pragmatist proposition that determinate foundations, as posited for example by moral realism or natural law, are unavailable to humans. This proposition requires that pragmatism explain how social order, and belief, are possible without determinate foundations, and how social change is possible under the conditions of habit-reinforcing stability that pragmatism identifies in its explanation of social order and belief.

Social order. Pragmatism assumes that human society is not the expression of some underlying natural order, that social arrangements are not rooted in some logic of social development, and that current institutions do not reflect a higher rational or practical necessity than past institutions. It assumes that the social world is held together by the mundane patterns of everyday life.

The force of stability in human societies cannot be overestimated. Routine promotes predictability, for example where people are able to conduct their affairs without fear of dramatic and sudden change. Extant social practices are valuable precisely in that they may contribute to stability and predictability. In this sense, a legal system generally contributes to social stability.

Our situatedness in history and culture makes our stabilized condition neither arbitrary nor fully malleable (Gadamer 1972). We are born into custom, language, and history; only later do we consciously appropriate such givens. Whether or not we can appropriate them, we cannot fully escape them. If we do not decide what is right, or true, simply by some free-floating act of will, then our historical and social embeddedness, its constitutive power over us, is not arbitrary. Embeddedness fosters predictability.

The patterns of everyday life need not be the imposition of the few on the many; they may simply be the "mode of existence best suited to the overwhelming majority of the human race" (Galston 1987:759). Stability in some social contexts can be liberating and facilitative, in others, confining and oppressive. A legislature that continually altered institutional arrangements governing decision making would quickly find itself unable to make any substantive decisions whatsoever. Citizens can address political and social problems of a quotidian nature only once they have decided the basic political organizations that can first provide an institutional means for treating problems.

Quotidian patterns have a certain prescriptive aspect: They direct activity along defined courses and rely on finite stocks of knowledge that change only infrequently. As such they limit the range of theories available to the individual for understanding the world and for planning activities. One pattern of vernacular life is routine. Routine promotes individual security by minimizing drastic alterations to the status quo. It promotes some of the qualities often associated with the rule of law: predictability over time as well as checks on discretion and caprice. Routine finds expression in legal doctrine, which may not constrain judicial behavior in the ways it is often thought to. Doctrine does not always require judges to reach the results they reach; often it is sufficiently ambiguous or internally contradictory to justify almost any result. Doctrine includes principles as well as arguments. Arguments ground principles and sometimes provide grounds for criticizing particular principles. Yet many principles would be useless were they not ambiguous. Thus the Ninth Amendment to the U.S. Constitution, adopted in 1791, states: "The enumeration in the Constitution, of certain rights, shall not be construed to deny or disparage others retained by the people." It has no specified content but is not therefore useless. In 1965 in *Griswold v. Connecticut*[9] Justice Arthur Goldberg interprets it as a rule of construction authorizing courts to enforce unspecified rights (such as a right to privacy in matters of sex and procreation, including the purchase and use of contraceptives).

Often we can use principles only because we can cope with ambiguity as an aspect of everyday life, including our collective social life under the Constitution. For example we might amend a principle if it yields an inference we are unwilling to accept (Goodman 1983:67).[10] Thus in 1995 in *United States v. Lopez*[11] the Supreme Court struck down a federal statute barring the possession of a firearm in a school zone. The statute was based on the constitutional right of the federal government to regulate interstate commerce.[12] The majority opinion argued that Congress could not reasonably have thought that gun possession in schools had a substantial effect on commerce, hence that the Constitution's clause on commerce could not support a right of the federal government to regulate firearms in schools. In response to this case, and to avoid the inference that Congress had assumed a plenary national police power (allowing the federal government to regulate matters until now left to the discretion of local authorities), Congress added a requirement providing: "It shall be unlawful for any individual knowingly to possess a firearm that has moved in or that otherwise affects interstate commerce at a place that the individual knows, or has reasonable cause to believe, is a school zone."[13] We might say that legal doctrine does not compel specific answers so much as it provides an approved language for discussing a given conflict's issues. Doctrine provides scope for coping with ambiguity, and with indeterminacy; it determines the scope of conversation, not its outcome.[14]

Routine is often a prerequisite for economic welfare. Patterned behavior is equally important at the level of individual identity: Our identities as persons are constituted largely by learned paradigms of behavior. We learn in certain contexts then project what we have learned into other contexts. Success in doing so requires that relevant individuals (teachers and students, projectors and receivers) share something. If individuals do not share objective transcendental principles, then perhaps they share something like a way of life. To follow a principle is to participate in a way of life. In this sense Ludwig Wittgenstein associates "*comfortable* certainty," something that "lies beyond being justified or unjustified," with the "inherited background against which I distinguish between true and false" (1973:pars. 94, 357, 359).[15] In this sense, to follow a principle is to generate predictability. The sort of predictability generated here is not the sort that derives from the unproblematic application of determinate principles, rather, it is the type that derives from following the conventions commonly observed in the way of life in which an indeterminate principle is embedded. Convention is why legal justifications can be final even if fallible—why, in the words of Justice Robert Jackson, majority opinions of Supreme Court justices "are not final because [they] are infallible," but "infallible because [they] are final."[16]

Normative principles can be both indeterminate and predictable. In the lapidary language of systems theory, "normativity is nothing but counterfactual stability" (Luhmann 1989:140). By protecting expectations, some normative principles relieve us from having to learn through disappointment and to adjust our behavior accordingly. Predictability offers the prospect of anticipating conflicts, withstanding them, sometimes even resolving them.

Pragmatism need not appeal to a normative system's putative internal characteristics to allow us to predict how given normative principles will affect us. To view a principle as something indeterminate is to locate the predictability of its results not only in alleged inherent characteristics of the normative order but also in extra-normative influences on that order. From this perspective judicial decisions are explainable in part only by reference to criteria outside the scope of a judge's formal justifications: by reference to the social and historical context in which the judge operates. That context, the social world, displays many short- and medium-run regularities, including regularities in the interpretation and application of legal principles. Routines are recurrent patterns of economic, political, and governmental activities that tend toward self-preservation. Mundane routines contribute to the cohesion of social order and the endurance of a system of social roles and ranks for members. Individuals constantly produce, alter, and maintain patterns in their ordinary efforts to cope with the world and to manage their daily lives. Regularities in a legal system are part of what constitutes its specifically systemic character.

Regularities in the social world involve the prosaic routines of life in the vernacular as an ubiquitous set of discernibly similar social practices across time and space, with some degree of systemic form (Giddens 1984:24). Yet not all the regularities we observe in daily life or in systems of normative principles are a necessary consequence of adopting a given regime of rules. In some cases the given system of principles could have generated a somewhat different set of stabilizing conventions leading to different results: for example, because the facts to which the principles apply may be interpreted differently, each interpretation leading to a different set of conventions. What, for example, are the facts concerning racism? If one believes that race consciousness is inherently, unavoidably racist, then one would likely support solely color-blind forms of public policy, generating a corresponding set of conventions (a public university concerned with increasing the presence of racial minorities in its student body might then admit the top ten percent of the state's high school graduating class, on the assumption that this ten percent will capture more than a few minority students). If one believes that race-conscious public policy need not be racist and can be an effective means to overcoming racism, one might support direct forms of race-based affirmative action in university admissions.

Even though a set of principles can generate more than one set of stabilizing conventions, it remains that all of them are stabilizing: They all contribute to social stability, even if in different ways. Why in any given instance we get one set of conventions rather than another can be explained in terms of contingencies that lie beyond the sphere of normative phenomena. Extra-normative contingencies determine the outcome of normative principles that must function in pragmatist fashion given their lack of ultimate epistemological foundation, coupled with the practical need in everyday life at some point to terminate theorizing and to act.

Belief. If determinate foundations for belief are unavailable, how, then, is belief possible? We have seen that pragmatism points to routines and settled contexts. Members of social groups tend to adhere to similar views of the world and of proper action in that world, yet adherence does not require a high degree of coherence. After all, patterns need not be external constraints on individuals, and individuals may not often feel themselves constrained by some all-inclusive pattern. In a large sense, for example, modernity is not only about differentiation and the cheek-by-jowl coexistence of lustily competing views; some degree of normative homogenization is also a feature of life in the modern world. Various integrative forces, institutions, and practices contribute to the convergence of cultures, including the global capitalist economy, science and technology, popular culture, and educational systems that create links and mobility, for example between the educational institutions of the various nations of the European Union. And similarities in lifestyle and consumption patterns continue to grow rapidly worldwide. But these phenomena do not issue in monolithically identical communities and societies and are simultaneous with increasing diversity. Under these circumstances neither majorities nor minorities may feel themselves constrained by some all-inclusive pattern. And within a given society or community, routines and settled contexts may take on an apparent "truth" and "reality" not easily altered. In this sense I earlier claimed that the patterns of everyday life need not be the imposition of the few on the many.[17]

Some settled patterns may even allow for the "adherence" of persons who disagree with those patterns at some level. For example, with respect to having to tolerate a public policy or judicial holding that violates a group's ethical self-understanding, a just solution to a problem may distribute "ethical hardships" unequally among the relevant groups. Sometimes some citizens are called on to tolerate other citizens whose behavior they find morally reprehensible. Such tolerance need not violate the integrity of the moral beliefs of the tolerant. Even as they are called on to recognize the law, citizens who reject the idea of legalized abortion may continue to abhor morally the legally permissible behavior of citizens who perform or undergo abortions. One doesn't become "deviant" if one tolerates legal behavior that one nonetheless considers "deviant"; a law doesn't "constrain" individuals who reject the behavior it permits in the sense of forcing the objectors to embrace what they reject at a moral level but must tolerate at a legal one.

Belief, understood as habit or consciousness bound to the present moment, is not immune to new information, different contexts, changed perceptions, or whatever else might lead to doubt. Given our predisposition to maintain or preserve our system of belief as much as possible, we readily accommodate experience that contradicts or ill fits the system by reevaluating the experience, perhaps subsuming it in some other part of the overall system (Quine 1963).[18] Nor is belief in this sense blind to its own consequences insofar as it may well be conditioned by them: Belief is a habit whose practical validity is determined by its capacity to satisfy particular needs.[19]

Social change. Pragmatism must explain how social change is possible despite the conditions of habit-reinforcing stability it posits. Because our estimation of truth can only be variable, pragmatism is attuned to how meanings and applications shift. In part they shift because the meaning and application of principles depend on context; they shift as contexts shift. Thus, in one context, a principle of political equality may emancipate an ethnic, racial, cultural, religious, or other minority from the dominant one (a political equality tantamount to disregarding many natural and social differences). The principle that all religious faiths be treated equally may generate the demand that the state neither favor nor disfavor any particular religion (or religionists over nonreligionists). In another context, the same principle of political equality may pressure a minority to assimilate itself to the majority in ways that elide differences important to the minority. The principle that all religious faiths be treated equally may generate the demand that a religious minority forsake a certain practice (unless the principle is misused as a means to discriminate against a particular—and most likely socially marginal—religion, such as prohibiting ritual animal sacrifice practiced by members of the Santeria faith in a predominantly Christian community in a secular political culture).[20] In fact the context in which principles are interpreted and applied—the social world—displays many short- and medium-run regularities, including regularities in the interpretation and application of principles.

Social change occurs when the patterns, or portions thereof, cease to accomplish practical tasks or generate psychologically satisfying understandings. Patterns can be exogenously inadequate, for example in the face of new technology, migration of cultures, events of nature, or when external coercion alters existing patterns or imposes new ones. Patterns can also be endogenously inadequate. As long as they are usable, commonsense theories generated by individuals need be neither systematic nor necessarily consistent with each other, nor consistent across discrete areas of practical activity. Social change is driven by changes in the relative usability of patterns, at least as much as by the introduction of new or modified worldviews or ideologies.

A pragmatist theory of moral knowledge can explain the normative sphere's empirically observable disorder, internal contradiction, and indeterminacy without having to conclude that a particular normative order is illegitimate, indeed incapable of legitimacy or any other notion of normative coherence. Pragmatism can show how indeterminacy need not be debilitating to social order, indeed how indeterminacy can allow for predictability and thus need not threaten the possibility or legitimacy of social norms. It can show how indeterminacy provides some of the flexibility social norms need to function in the first place. It allows us to see how indeterminacy, in a moderate version—distinct from the postmodern version I treat in the following section—does not reduce normative systems to chaos. Pragmatism can do this because it does not exclude the possible validity of individual norms despite their ambiguity and consequent fluctuation in meaning. Nor does it preclude legal notions such as equal treatment and justice through law.

PRAGMATIST RELATIVISM IS SUPERIOR TO POSTMODERN RELATIVISM

Determinacy marks a belief in the existence, for a given norm, of a "correct" meaning or "proper" application and, correspondingly, of a "right" answer to any given normative question. Indeterminacy refers to the lack of determinate knowledge of what some norms mean and of how they should be applied in specific instances. By no means are all legal rules indeterminate, but those which are tend to be ones of significant consequence for the lives of millions of people. On the one hand, the mundane traffic rule "stop on a red light, proceed on a green one" is highly determinate. The correlation of "red" with "stop," and "green" with "go" could be changed without consequence, in the sense that nothing in the world would change if all drivers and pedestrians adopted the change and together followed the rule "stop on the green light, proceed on the red."[21] On the other hand, the Fourteenth Amendment's guarantee of legal equality ("nor shall any State deprive any person of life, liberty, or property, without due process of law") is highly indeterminate. With respect to race, does legal equality mean, for example, "separate but equal" facilities for different races or does it mean "separate is always unequal"? The Fourteenth Amendment itself does not, cannot, tell us.

A pragmatist jurisprudence directly confronts the phenomenon of indeterminacy. It regards legally relevant behavior and belief as products of their particular social and historical context, not of innate or otherwise transcendental knowledge (as natural law has often been understood to assert)[22] or established authority (as analytic jurisprudence maintains). Today only one other type of jurisprudence embraces indeterminacy in this strong sense: what I shall construct as "postmodern jurisprudence." Jean-François Lyotard distinguishes postmodernism from any "metadiscourse appealing to some grand narrative" (1984:xxiii)— for example, the linear progress of science. From this distinction we can derive an initial definition of a postmodern jurisprudence: It views legal determinacy as one of the false "grand narratives" of the European Enlightenment.

Both pragmatist and postmodern jurisprudence eschew any kind of transcendental foundation or principled approach for which meaning is "closed," unique, or otherwise strongly determinate. This similarity is so striking that one wonders, Is a pragmatist jurisprudence postmodern (or a postmodern jurisprudence pragmatist)? In fact various authors regard some types of postmodernism as compatible with some types of pragmatism. Pierre Schlag (1989:1223, n.109) regards pragmatism as the peculiarly American form of postmodernism. Lyotard views "language games" from a postmodern perspective as "heteromorphous, subject to heterogeneous sets of pragmatist rules," and concludes—contrary to modernist claims—that not all speakers can come to agreement on which rules or "metaprescriptions" are universally valid for language games (1984:65).

I, too, will identify several affinities between pragmatism and postmodernism. Yet I shall argue that, at least with reference to their respective jurisprudential implications, they are more different than similar—and that in coping with the problem of indeterminacy, pragmatism is superior to postmodernism.

Pragmatism and Postmodernism Are Both Antifoundationalist

One similarity between the two approaches has emerged already: Both accept a strong version of the indeterminacy thesis[23] and both reject notions of ultimate foundations for systems of norms. The "right" meaning or "proper" application of indeterminate norms is open at the levels of practice and consciousness. For an indeterminate legal norm, we cannot know with any finality which nonlegal norms should guide its interpretation and application, or even might best guide its interpretation and application.

Pragmatism and Postmodernism Are Both Localist Not Universalist

Pragmatist and postmodern notions of law agree that, even if the determination of "correct" meaning or "proper" application is impossible by appeal to some putatively universal standpoint, it might yet be possible by appeal to some local standard. A standard is local if available only in the community concerned, or valid for that particular community but not for all communities, or valid on one or more occasions but not all. Unlike universal standards, local standards are ad hoc, discontinuous, and sometimes inconsistent.

The notion of local determination can accommodate the fact that the historical development of any contemporary legal system (with respect, for example, to extending rights to more groups, and more diverse groups, within society) is discontinuous, indeed often internally inconsistent. Such discontinuity and inconsistency follow from the ad hoc nature of determining meaning and application. Although such similarities between pragmatist and postmodern notions of jurisprudence are significant, they hardly render these notions synonymous. In fact the differences are greater than the similarities. I shall consider the following six.

Localism need not be parochial. For both pragmatist and postmodern jurisprudence, legal and other norms are a form of cultural practice. Cultural practices are historically specific, contingent, and ungrounded except in terms of other, prior, contingent, historically specific behavior. Michel Foucault, a leading theorist of postmodernism, concludes that each cultural practice has its own criteria for truth and falsity, its own institutional sanctions (1980:112-113, 131, 133).[24]

We reach a different conclusion from pragmatist presuppositions: that legitimation cannot be plural, each instance of legitimation warranting its own constitutive norms, with practitioners legitimizing their own practice. Otherwise legitimation is parochial. A postmodern localism is parochial in the sense that its moral scope is so limited as to be incapable of claiming validity across disputes or among communities. But if one appeals to local standards as the final moral arbiter, to whose locality is one appealing? The constitution of local standards is as problematic and subject to contestation as the constitution of universal standards. Moreover, how likely is it that every member of a community or group helps determine local standards? How likely is it that every member agrees with all other members as to what those standards are? If disagreement occurs and adjudication is only local, then adjudication would appear impossible because, from the local point of view, every claim would be equally valid. Pragmatism embraces localism as does postmodernism, but pragmatism does not embrace the notion of plural legitimacy, to which I turn under the following rubric.

Normative critique is possible even under indeterminate conditions. Both types of jurisprudence allow that legal and nonlegal norms can be indeterminate in meaning and application. A postmodern stance concludes that the indeterminacy of norms precludes the very possibility of social and legal critique or, more precisely, critique is possible only as something normatively idiosyncratic or wholly subjective. But pragmatism allows for the still viable, if sharply restricted, modernism of what I have developed in this book as enlightened localism, a notion of "decentered" critique of a society, community, social institution, or social role. *Decentered* means that critique, whether of an entire society or of a single statute, starts from norms immanent in that society or legal system (immanent, hence "centered") but goes beyond them as well, becoming decentered. In exceeding them, critique neither ceases being situated nor starts being universal (an idea I will return to first in chapter 4 with respect to social critique and then in the coda with regard to politics without universalisms). I term such a localism "enlightened" to distinguish it from parochial forms of localism such as we observed, under the previous rubric, in the respective postmodernisms of Foucault and Lyotard.[25]

By contrast, postmodernism cannot exceed the radical subjectivism of parochialism or "centricity." J. M. Balkin proposes a nonparochial postmodernism yet can do so only incongruously, via a notion of "transcendental deconstruction," an oxymoron akin to a "universal localism" (1994:1142). Transcendental deconstruction turns on a "conception of values that 'go beyond' the positive norms of culture and convention" and "attempts to reveal the mistaken identification of justice with an inadequate articulation of justice in human culture and law" (ibid.:1139). Less ambitious is Steven Winter's assertion of postmodernism's humanism in its insistence on the Promethean prowess of human agency: Norms are a house we actively build for ourselves, rather than one we must passively inherit and simply accept and occupy as given in all its features (1992:806). But even here the point remains: If values need no warrant outside and beyond themselves, then the moral narrowness of unrestrained subjectivism prevails; critique would be crippled by its own parochialism.

I would make the same argument with respect to the term *decentered*, which is central to both types of jurisprudence. Winter's understanding of the term simply precludes the possibility of critique: The "dominant discourse" of Western culture and history "affirms the subject as an originary, self-directing agent. To undermine *that* discourse is to decenter the subject" (ibid.:799). In fact to "undermine that discourse" is to undermine the very possibility of critique: Critique by an other-directed agent (someone not in control of him- or herself, a heteronomous agent) is not critique but mimicry (which is never critical) of whoever or whatever controls the agent. But the pragmatist notion of a decentered standpoint is a condition of critique, not its elimination. A standpoint can be decentered and still aspire to nonparochial forms of localism.

Nonparochial localism presupposes what might be called "weak objectivism," a type of objectivity defined "by contrast to the 'subject,' or unreflective and unsorted beliefs and preferences people happen to have." Objective is that which has "passed certain tests of reflective scrutiny . . . that need not have anything to do with extra-human or extra-historical standards of value" (Nussbaum 1994:201). A weak objectivism comports with a pragmatism that doesn't exclude the possibility that moral beliefs can be objective. Weak objectivism refers to nonabsolute objectivity which, again, is compatible with the pragmatist view that judicial decisions can be given objective grounds for the most part but not grounds that will be morally legitimate always and everywhere. Weakly objective norms are applicable locally, not universally.

Feminist perspectives have shown particular sensitivity to those aspects of postmodernism that defeat critical intentions. Linda Nicholson and Nancy Fraser, for example, conclude that Lyotard's postmodernism allows for a merely "anemic" social critique because it precludes analysis of categories such as race. Postmodernism's rejection of large-scale approaches to oppression (Lyotard's "grand narratives") renders it incapable of recognizing women collectively as an oppressed group. Postmodern antifoundationalism precludes institutional analysis and cannot, in terms of postmodernism, support social and political movements whose goals postmodern thinkers may otherwise share (1988:87-89).[26]

Autonomy is possible even under indeterminate conditions. Postmodern theory is a radical form of skepticism.[27] It claims that anything sayable in language can be explained or elucidated, but only explained or elucidated—it cannot be criticized discursively or rejected rationally. Pragmatism by contrast claims that the strategies we employ in disparate discourses are groundable in the linguistic practices embodying them (if solely these). It claims not that radical skepticism can be articulated coherently (it cannot be) but, rather, that certainty is possible, if only in a limited or narrow sense, namely as a certainty constructed through linguistic conventions within particular discourses.

Postmodernism urges that no standpoint of rational, discursive critique is possible because postmodern society in many respects is totalitarian, if not politically then at least cognitively, in this way narrowly constricting human agency or what many postmodern authors refer to as "discourse." From this perspective, law and legal institutions appear to be nothing but monolithic instruments of oppression. Only a "postmodern theory of justice allows otherness to survive and to become a theoretical space through which to criticize the operations of the law's ceaseless repetitions." Postmodern ethics is antitotalitarian because it is sensitive to the uniqueness of each individual, unlike the "totalizing influence of politics and law" that homogenizes individuality and reduces distinctions (Goodrich, Douzinas, and Hachamovitch 1994:23-24).

Pragmatism need not draw such politically debilitating conclusions from indeterminacy. It can employ the Wittgensteinian trope of "language games" to explain law and politics in terms less sinister. As a social institution in part generated by and through language, law appears as a collection of language games. If the language of law is not monolithic, then institutions of law need not be monolithic; the very heterogeneity of legal language games points to the possibility of heterogeneous legal institutions.

The local determination of legal meanings and applications generates heterogeneity because by definition different localisms differ from each other (if only in location). Decisions in the interpretation and application of laws do not imply totality or unity; they can be made according to an idea of multiplicity, diversity, or plurality. Pluralism of this sort allows for the very autonomy Lyotard dismisses as impossible; it allows for the modernism of self-determination, for the "unencumbered interplay of different perspectives and the competing demands of different interest groups" (Ehrenreich 1990:1188). Bruce Ackerman (1980:41-42) and Judith Shklar (1964:vii-xi), among many others, associate pluralism with democracy. Pluralism is a form of indeterminacy, and democracy a form of self-determination. Indeterminacy so understood is not the carrier of heteronomy and foil of autonomy posited by some postmodern authors.

Of course the premise of multiple language games does not by itself entail our autonomy to choose among them. That conclusion follows only from the additional premise of an autonomous, self-directing subject who can choose. This is an explicitly pragmatist premise, indeed one that highlights pragmatism's distinctly modernist cast. Modernism in the sense of the European Enlightenment places individual autonomy at the very center of its conception of the good life, or good society, but also of a possible life and possible society. From a postmodern vantage the subject is but a contingent, passive incident of the ongoing language games in which it participates, such that the multiplicity of language games implies not the subject's autonomy but its dissolution as a coherent entity. The postmodern subject is more a dependent object than a self-determining subject.

The same conclusion follows from a postmodern understanding of power as all-pervasive domination. According to Foucault power is in play in every social association and connection, even at the basic level of language use: "[I]n human relations, whatever they are . . . power is always present" (1988:11; see also 1978:92–97). Political discourse for postmodernism is necessarily systematically distorted (Feldman 1993:2245, 2265) because prejudices and self-seeking interests immediately constrain the possibilities and parameters of dialogue, much as traditions preclude, exclude, or destroy some prejudices as well as some interests and their carriers.

Stanley Fish offers an alternative reading of Foucault, one that retains an element of individual autonomy. Here power is never concentrated in a single person or place but rather is distributed throughout a community or institution. No one is simply an object of power. Everyone is also, potentially, a subject exercising power, for the exercise of power is a two-way street (if not a multilane highway) where the effectiveness of one person's or one group's power depends on the affirmation of that power by other persons or groups: a relationship of perhaps skewed, always alterable reciprocity. The configuration of power relations is subject to "innumerable nodal junctures at which a shift in emphasis and pressure can lead to a system-wide readjustment or even to a system-wide breakdown" (1994:189).

But this reading confuses the normative presupposition of Foucault's analysis of power with the analysis itself. The analysis concludes that individuals "are not only [the] inert or consenting target [of power]; they are always also the elements of its articulation[,] . . . the vehicles of power, not its point of application" (Foucault 1980:98). The analysis presupposes political autonomy and individual sovereignty: A society as a whole, as well as the groups and individuals composing it, ought to be self-determined. This presupposition of Foucault's discussion of power—a type of knowledge independent of power relationships—is at war with that discussion inasmuch as the analysis itself rejects any possibility of realizing the presupposition. The presupposition is useful only as a foil, a counterfactual impossibility, since Foucault so thoroughly identifies knowledge with power.[28]

Contrary to Fish's reading, Foucault is not explaining the constitution of subjectivity so much as its elimination. In this respect Foucault is representative of postmodern thinking. Winter argues that "postmodernism's decentering of the subject is not the same as its obliteration" (1992:814), yet he describes nothing less than the subject's extinction: the postmodern self is deprived of agency, becoming an effect of power rather than its agent (ibid.:794).[29]

Law does not require self-delusion. Pragmatism has long observed how patterns of human behavior in society engender regularities in the social world. Regularized patterns of behavior contribute to the production and reproduction of social systems, but they also constitute resources for the exercise of free will: Without routine and habit, individuals on each occasion would need to think from scratch.[30] Much human behavior, and not just complex intersubjective behavior, would be impossible if it had to be continually reinvented. A readily available cognitive pattern (any commonsense theory, for example) simplifies experience to manageable proportions, imposing order on an otherwise stochastic series of events.

Fish, marrying a pragmatist conception with a postmodern one, contends that legal actors must behave pragmatically in bad faith, in sustained and complex acts of self-dishonesty, given humankind's frailty in capacity both moral and epistemic (1990:1468). The institution of law pretends that justification in the interpretation and application of laws is independent of the particular goals and self-seeking behavior of legal actors. In reality, however, legal justification is dependent on just such goals and behavior. Law engages in sham and pretense: It describes partisan programs as the natural outcomes of nonpartisan imperatives, makes self-centered goals appear decentered, and misrepresents limited, parochial, idiosyncratic goals and behavior as objective and universally valid. To do away with this carapace of bad faith and subterfuge would do away with law itself.

Contrast this view with a more straightforwardly pragmatist one in which individuals and groups seek to understand their world in a manner pragmatically efficient, say, by formulating ad hoc theories. Because individuals probably theorize only to the extent (subjectively) necessary to make sense of a situation or to achieve some end, and because they rarely, if ever, have reason to consider the overall consistency of their various ad hoc theories, they may easily hold internally contradictory views (Gellner 1970). But a contradictory mix of views is not the same as the mass self-delusion postulated by Fish.[31]

By pragmatist lights, when judges convince themselves and others that their decisions are dictated by law—when judges engage in the pretense of constraint—they do so not necessarily as an act of willful deception, nor even necessarily to deleterious social or legal effect. A public announcement of the contingency and heterogeneity of value would probably be of no operational consequence to anyone. Awareness of contingency doesn't allow one to master contingency; knowledge of an inescapable condition doesn't free the knower from the inescapable.

Judges and other legal actors behave pragmatically; in an indeterminate world, law would be impossible otherwise. The pragmatic functioning of the law does not require self-delusion among judges and other legal actors, or within a community of citizens.

Justice is singular not plural. At the level of language as well, a pragmatist jurisprudence entails a modern, not a postmodern, notion of justice. In the legal sphere, as in so much of social life, individuals are bound together through language. Law is codified, interpreted, and disputed via language; language provides the sole medium in which legal disputes can be conducted within a social system. This bond is not of a single thread, however, but like a woven fabric, made up of many pieces of thread. It is formed by the intersection of an indeterminate number of language games, perhaps obeying different rules (as the postmodern theorist Lyotard [1984:40] also maintains), yet most more or less coordinated, somehow, with most of the others.

Both pragmatism and postmodernism contend that each language game may have its own presuppositions and goals, different from those of every other language game. As we found earlier, both approaches support a notion of localism. But then they part ways: A pragmatist jurisprudence leads to a conception of justice that can only be singular, while postmodernism entails a notion of plural justice. Lyotard claims that, in a postmodern world, "most people have lost the nostalgia for the lost narrative. It in no way follows that they are reduced to barbarity. What saves them from it is their knowledge that legitimation can only spring from their own linguistic practice and communicational interaction" (1984:41). In short: Legitimacy is plural.

Yet how can the idea of a multiplicity or diversity distinguish, for example, between a "just" decision and an "unjust" one? How can we decide justly according to a multiplicity, a plurality of justices, a plurality of language games, with no one game dominating the others? Can justice be plural? Jean-François Lyotard and Jean-Loup Thebaud, speaking not of law in particular but of knowledge in general, can propose the "justice of multiplicity" only paradoxically: by insisting on a universal and therefore singular value, namely the singular justice of each game (1985:100). In attempting to resist the imperialism of the allegedly colonizing perspective of modernism, Lyotard actually reproduces it as the universal value of each game (Weber 1985:103–104).

To claim, with Lyotard, that each game is entire unto itself—that each game is its own universal value—entails in practice that all interpretations and applications are metaphysically equal, because each is beyond the critique of the others. For each game, then, normatively "anything goes," in which case normatively nothing matters—and one coherent set of values, for example intolerance, racism, sexism, or xenophobia, are no more or less desirable than a very different but also coherent set of values, for example tolerance, respect, kindness, or solidarity. We could no longer claim a capacity to identify evil; we could merely identify "tastes" dissimilar to our own, as preferences that might be judged substandard (different from our own) but never evil (morally unacceptable).[32]

Unlike Lyotard, Jacques Derrida, another major theorist of postmodernism, claims that justice is addressed always to events and persons in all their singularity (1990:949). Yet he presupposes the very transcendentalism that postmodernism, like pragmatism, cannot presuppose: transcendental justice. He argues that the meaning of justice must—as an ethical imperative—transcend individual acts of legislation, cases of judgment, and existing codifications of law that might bring about justice in concrete instances: The "responsible interpretation of the judge requires that his 'justice' not just consist . . . in the conservative and reproductive act of judgment. . . . [F]or a decision to be just and responsible, it must . . . be both regulated and without regulation: it must conserve the law and also . . . suspend it enough to have to reinvent it in each case" (ibid.:961). By itself, this proposition might seem to express the indeterminacy of law, an indeterminacy that sometimes requires judges to go beyond the printed word, beyond the four corners of the page, if they are to understand and apply a law. But Derrida intends more, much more, indeed an "infinite 'idea of justice,' infinite because . . . irreducible, irreducible because owed to the other, owed to the other, before any contract. . . . This 'idea of justice' [is] irreducible in its affirmative character" (ibid.:965). At this point, transcendentalism contradicts Derrida's assertion of legal indeterminacy, that "[e]ach case is other, each decision is different and requires an absolutely unique interpretation, which no existing, coded rule can or ought to guarantee absolutely" (ibid.:961).[33]

Interestingly, justice can be singular for a pragmatist jurisprudence as well, although in a somewhat different sense. Each language game—each local group or community—may have its own conception of justice. The differences among the various localisms are important from a local standpoint. The grand narrative of epistemic and normative determinacy, the overdrawn modernist urge to definite and distinct meanings and exclusively appropriate applications of legal rules, insists that differences among localisms be elided, that what is true for one localism should be true for many, perhaps all. This is a false universality, false because imposed from outside each localism, one that simply ignores, denies, or represses the differences among the various localisms. For example, two different communities might have different levels of tolerance for pornography. A false universality would impose on both communities the same definitions of pornography and the same standards for deciding between what shall and what shall not be allowed in the community. An enlightened localist approach would allow each community to apply its own standards to itself. Consider a different example: A significant number of immigrants to France, Britain, and Germany today come from Muslim countries. A false universality would prescribe the same instruction in religion for all children in schools that require pupils to receive "religious instruction" (instruction in Christianity, in other words). By contrast, an enlightened localist approach would support a religiously neutral framework in terms of which a variety of religions (including Islam) might be taught in a thoughtful manner. Correspondingly, it would allow Muslim pupils to be exempted from Christian-oriented collective worship, just as it would provide for collective worship among Muslim pupils. In this context it would also reject any "universalism" imposed from within the minority group. Thus it would insist that Muslim parents' wishes be respected (parents, for example, who would not wish to separate themselves or their children from the conventions of the schools); it would insist that Muslim parents not be manipulated by local imams or political personalities who campaign among parents.[34]

Similarities among the various localisms are also important, and are so from the pragmatist vantage of what might be called "singular justice." If we spoke Ronald Dworkin's (1977) language we might say that each local justice is a particular "conception" of justice, whereas singular justice refers to the "concept" of justice. The notion of singular justice may be used to adjudicate among the various local justices, and does so first by identifying the similarities among them. Unlike Dworkin's notion of concept, singular justice is not what Lyotard calls a grand narrative of Enlightenment rationalism, something claiming transcendental validity. Singular justice is indeterminate, itself a product of deliberations. Ideally, such deliberations would be as public, and as inclusive of the community, as possible. Deliberations might lead to provisional definitions of the singular justice that can adjudicate among the various local justices of disparate groups or communities (and their incommensurable language games).[35]

Justice is more than simply authority. Pragmatism and postmodernism agree that if justice has no fixed content, justice cannot be determinate. Both hold that an indeterminate concept of justice can nonetheless be normatively regulatory. Such a concept can regulate behavior yet not, as Lyotard and Thebaud urge, by defining law as that which simply must be respected (1985:84–85). This definition mocks the notion that justice refers to anything other than authority as such. If *just* simply means authority, then we lack criteria by which to distinguish normatively acceptable forms of authority from unacceptable ones. Although a concept of justice needs no fixed content to be coherent, a postmodern concept of justice—authority *simpliciter*—is normatively incoherent. If authority were hopelessly politicized, then the ultimate grounds of law could only be force. Legal and other normative disputes are resolvable by rational rather than forceful means only if we can make judgments of fact, and of value, more or less free from our parochial interests.

Justice conceived as simply authority is a conception of arbitrary content. Arbitrary does not mean "chaotic" in the sense of "lacking discernible patterns" or "unprincipled," or even "unjustified" or "unfair." When predicated of justice, it refers to the application of a rule to a concrete situation, or to a judicial decision that appeals to a rule, where that application or decision is guided at best by nothing more than a concern with power—with creating, conserving, applying or otherwise husbanding power.

Derrida reminds us of Lyotard by asserting that "justice is not necessarily law ... [but] become[s] justice legitimately ... by withholding force or rather by appealing to force" (1990:935). Similarly, Fish (1994) maintains that law is a matter ultimately of force. Against this politically and morally defeatist conclusion, enlightened localism understands justice as more than authority *simpliciter*. Authority is up for grabs insofar as access to the material and other resources for "grabbing" are distributed more equally than unequally. And yet enlightened localism also understands justice as less than objectivism, as justice created intersubjectively, through discursive disputations within a legal community. Unlike conventional jurisprudence, enlightened localism does not seek ahistorical or transcendental or otherwise enduringly determinate guides to legal interpretation or application.

Justice can derive from the pragmatist notion of a nonlocal, decentered critique of a legal community or society. Justice of this sort entails a critical optic that adjudicates among real alternatives. It adjudicates on explicitly normative grounds without being petrified by intractable problems: In an indeterminate world, and amid the multiplication of worldviews characteristic of complex modern societies, ultimate grounds are unavailable, and complete systemic consistency appears impossible. Justice of this sort furnishes an enlightened localist way, not a postmodern one, of coping in politics with indeterminate norms. With respect to its indeterminacy, law may be viewed plausibly from a postmodern perspective; with regard to legal justice, the postmodern perspective is morally incoherent. For purposes of realizing justice through law, or even theorizing about justice, postmodern theory fails when it would prescribe legal justice or any other normatively regulatory idea. To this end we still need modernist theory. Yet we need it in a modified version, modernism as a type of nontranscendental Enlightenment rationalism. We need a rationalism that is enlightened because nonarbitrary, and nontranscendental because pragmatist.

As an example of coping with legal indeterminacy through the pragmatist approach of enlightened localism, consider the question of affirmative action in university admissions. Indeterminate is the meaning of *legal equality* of applicants when related to the question, What properly are the social goals of higher education? What contributions can universities make to the society that supports them? If their social purpose is educating those students with the strongest academic records and standardized test scores, then legal equality does not entail affirmative action. If the social purpose is, in addition to educating those students with the strongest records and scores, working toward social (and not just legal) equality by providing (among other things) for a more racially diverse cohort of students than would be possible without affirmative action, and in this way breaking down racial stereotypes, as well as providing role models for minority as well as majority youth, then legal equality encompasses affirmative action. Pragmatic in this calculation is a matter of tailoring: How closely need a given preferential treatment fit with the social purpose that justifies it? A relatively tight fit recommends itself if the criteria for decision are unambiguous and uncontroversial, for example specific technical competence (a plumber, a physician, a professional basketball player). A relatively loose fit might be acceptable when the criteria are more open to disagreement, as in cases of scholastic admission (academic merit alone, or merit plus geographic diversity, or racial diversity, or diversity in life experiences?), or the giving of governmental contracts (strictly to the lowest bidder, or to higher bidders who are members of racial or ethnic groups strongly underrepresented as recipients of governmental contracts?), or the distribution of broadcasting licenses (should the government attempt to provide for a variety of group voices or are such efforts condemned to essentializing racial, ethnic, or other characteristics of presumed group-based identities?).

In this context the pragmatic calculation about justice might include a decentered perspective on the beneficiaries of preferential treatment. *Decentered* then means judging members of the group by standards not defined solely by the group itself. Thus members of a historically oppressed group should not be considered somehow morally virtuous solely because they have suffered discrimination. Hence individual group members should not be allowed to free ride on the efforts of other members who actively engage in combating discrimination against the group. The pragmatic calculation about justice might also include a decentered perspective on groups, individual members of which might be disadvantaged by programs of preferential treatment. Thus white Americans might appreciate the extent to which, collectively, they have (in most cases unintentionally) benefited from various advantages that follow from a national history of racial discrimination, such as possessing the kind of "cultural capital" needed to do well on standardized exams, some of whose questions reflect experiences that some minorities are unlikely to have had (will many inner-city minority youth be as familiar with the word *yacht*, on a multiple-choice vocabulary exam, as youth from the white suburbs?).

Finally, the pragmatic calculation about justice might also include a decentered perspective on the social institutions that arrange and dispense programs of preferential treatment. Thus institutions from the government to universities to law firms hiring recent law school graduates should not construct the beneficiaries of preferential treatment as monolithic, undifferentiated, "essentially" all the same—as if there were no tensions, debates, disagreements, controversies, and struggles within the minority communities themselves. Minorities within minorities should not be silenced or ignored by social institutions contributing to efforts against racial injustice. And such institutions should not define, for minorities themselves, how best those minorities should fight racial injustice. And they should not allow members of an oppressed group to oppress others.

From the perspective developed in this chapter, no point in society, no group, no public policy, no legal interpretation is immune from critique or critical examination. The social use of ascriptive identity may be judged in this spirit: negatively when ascriptive identity serves as a tool of oppression, positively when self-identifying groups deploy it as a means of group solidarity and mutual support, in response to social injustice. The pragmatist claim here is: Consequences matter, and public policy, like judicial interpretation, legitimately may be considered with respect to consequences. This critical approach leads to the following chapter, which develops an enlightened localist conception of social critique. Social criticism is linked to the pragmatist concerns in Charles Anderson's sense: "Perhaps the most distinctive feature of pragmatic liberalism then is the proposition that the performance of the diverse functional associations that make up our society is a matter of public concern and that participation in them is a form of public responsibility and an act of citizenship" (1990:3). As the next chapter will show, social critique is central to a democratic society and constitutes an irreplaceable form of public responsibility. Ideally all citizens would be social critics, as an act of critical citizenship. In fact, all of the remaining chapters—each a specific application of localism without parochialism—suggest forms of pragmatic liberalism: through social critique (chapter 4), by means of public policy (chapter 5), but also in law and morality (chapter 6).

PART III

THE SOLUTION:

LOCALISM WITHOUT

PAROCHIALISM

CHAPTER 4

Enlightened Localism in Social Critique

Pragmatism and proceduralism each contributes to coping in politics with indeterminate norms. The pragmatist element in any enlightened localist approach is relativism, in distinction to universalism. The proceduralist element is fairness through variable (because context-dependent) participation of citizens in the public sphere; it distinguishes itself from participation on the basis of strict or formal neutrality. Together, as the basic components of my solution to the problem of normative indeterminacy, pragmatism and proceduralism provide means for a society to render norms determinate. It does so in ways that promote greater civic inclusion of all citizens; a theory of enlightened localism is a democratic theory.

This chapter treats the first of three sites for applications of the theory of enlightened localism, of coping in politics with indeterminate norms. (Additional scenes are certainly possible, but within the covers of this book, at least, I will confine myself to these three.) Social critique in this vein is animated by both the proceduralism worked out in chapter 2 and the pragmatism elaborated in chapter 3. Even as I identified critical forms of both pragmatism and proceduralism in those chapters, the critical potential of enlightened localism flowers most fully in the fertile soil of social analysis and commentary. Critique is essential to the process of making political and social progress. By identifying problems of groups, of communities, and of society as a whole—and by doing so in ways persuasive to all citizens[1]—critique contributes to the possibility of positive social change. Enlightened localism can be dynamic instead of static only if it can contribute to social progress, and social critique is central to this effort as a means of identifying and analyzing problems and opening up perspectives on possible solutions.

The diagnostic evaluation of society, particularly societies of moral diversity or cultural heterogeneity, immediately raises the question, What are the appropriate standards of evaluation? After all, to treat social and political questions normatively is to treat them in terms of "rightness" or "justice" or other norms of normative correctness. The claim to correctness is a claim to moral authority. Yet normative correctness can only be a matter of interpretation, of judgment; to judge is to interpret (unless we suppose the existence of objective and necessary criteria of correctness—a supposition I will discuss later). The application of norms is itself a matter of judgment, one ever problematic because ever contested by a variety of mutually incompatible answers to the question, What is the source and validity of the norms that an individual or group actually employs, of the norms that a community or society should employ? In some cases the application of norms is made further problematic by indeterminacy. At the end of this chapter I will return to the question of a color-conscious response to racial injustice. There I shall consider a critique of color consciousness that advocates class consciousness as a more appropriate guide to public policy. The question there, as at the very beginning of this chapter, is, If the relevant social norm is indeterminate, how can a society decide what it entails?

The problem of indeterminate norms poses itself only in the context of significant determinacy, in the sense of social stability and cultural assumptions. Social systems in most liberal democratic states display great stability over time and a largely unchallenged validity at any given time. In these pluralist societies many citizens display an uncomplicated allegiance to that union with only minor differences in the levels of their allegiance. But that stability cannot be located wholly or even mainly in what might be taken to be the determinate quality of social norms, where determinacy makes possible normative principles that are more or less transparent, consistent, and rational. I shall argue that social stability on the basis of a critical understanding of society—where citizens' allegiance is based on free and rational consent to social arrangements they understand and find to be just—is possible without recourse to social norms determinate in the strong sense of requiring someone following them to act in a particular way.

First, however, I would note that, to someone who regards social norms as epistemically and normatively determinate, the thesis that many socially significant rules and norms in fact are indeterminate will imply the impossibility of critique, at least on the basis of indeterminate norms. If the indeterminacy of this or that norm derives from the fact that it is contingent in meaning and application, or that it is inherently incomplete, or that it contains inconsistent premises, or that it operates in some social contexts but not others, or that it does not admit of formal procedural or otherwise impartial application, then one might draw one or the other of the following conclusions.

1. If indeterminate norms cannot justifiably judge or evaluate a group or community or society, then only determinate norms can provide a basis for critique. Yet determinate norms, as we saw repeatedly in previous chapters, tend to be less socially significant than indeterminate ones (the determinant norm "stop on a red light, proceed on a green one" is less socially significant than the indeterminate norm "all citizens are legally equal"). If it is to be nontrivial, critique requires socially significant norms.

2. If the relevant nonlocal norms (what I shall call "decentered" norms) are indeterminate, by what norm can any group, community, or society justifiably be judged or evaluated other than by a norm immanent to that society? Under the circumstances of normative indeterminacy, internal norms (norms "centered" in the practice or community or society under examination) would appear to be the only norms

that might find acceptance within a community or society. At the same time, those norms probably would be unpersuasive to any standpoint outside or beyond that community's contingency, incompleteness, and inconsistency. For if a society can be considered solely with regard to its own (contingent, incomplete, inconsistent) criteria, then solely a local critique of any given society would seem possible. Therefore on the one hand, the application of norms external to society or community would not be persuasive, because they would be arbitrary, and they would be arbitrary because they would be unrelated to the specific society or community to which they were applied. On the other hand, the application only of norms internal to society is unlikely to be critical because they will simply confirm existing understandings, practices, and prejudices. And if in this way they simply confirm the status quo, they do so on an uncritical basis. Here we follow a recipe for parochial localism: critique solely from a standpoint "centered" in the object of critique itself.

Both of these conclusions defeat the purpose of critique. I shall argue in this chapter for a different conclusion: That the indeterminacy thesis does not imply that social critique can only be normatively idiosyncratic, subjective, or individualistic. I shall argue that a nonlocal, decentered critique of a particular society or a given community is possible to the extent that critique employs intersubjectively generated standpoints that are both decentered epistemically and potentially or virtually (but never actually) universalist in their normative claims. I mark off a middle ground between localism and universalism, what in this book I have developed as enlightened localism.

I proceed in eight steps: I articulate a notion of critique as something more than localism but less than universalism (a topic I return to in the coda). I then develop a notion of social criticism as critique from a decentered standpoint. Third, I discuss the relativism of critique and, fourth, critique as a form of postempiricist persuasion. Fifth, I examine critique as a form of proceduralism. Sixth, I again argue that critique is not empiricist. I then propose critique as a form of pragmatism and, finally, examine the situatedness of critique.

CRITIQUE: MORE THAN LOCALISM, LESS THAN UNIVERSALISM

We cannot defend social arrangements by analyzing their individual and social consequences solely in light of local traditions, values, and practices. Where local community values are the sole values to which one may appeal, there parochialism becomes a necessary predicate of "good." Different values within a society or community tend to be homogenized, or at least locally sanctioned values appear to minorities and outsiders as monolithic, even though in complex modern societies communities are likely to be heterogeneous in a variety of ways. If communal values are not available for criticism by noncommunal values, then they cannot be available for criticism to anyone inside the community who might want to challenge them. If solely an immanent perspective is valid, then any dissenting member of the community by definition holds a standpoint unacceptable to the rest of the community because all minority norms and viewpoints within the community are immediately intolerable simply by definition of their minority status.

Nor can particular ways of life be justified by appealing to the beliefs, norms, and ideals embodied in the cultural conventions and practices of the very society that is the focus of moral contestation. From the moment moral rules, boundaries, and hierarchies are contested, the contestants exceed merely local critique inasmuch as the act of discursive contestation itself minimally implies a shared belief in procedures of argumentation and standards of adjudication—procedures and standards that are potentially universalist.[2] If particular social norms and ideals can be justified only ethnocentrically, simply because they promote the kind of society "we" happen to value and want to perpetuate, simply because it is "our" society, then no outsider could justifiably oppose slavery in the American South when slavery was still legal (except, of course, the slaves themselves, but as slaves they are immediately excluded from the "we" anyway). Nor could any insider oppose a repressive regime, current examples of which can be chosen from almost any part of the globe. If we cannot provide compelling reasons for the kind of society we want, beyond saying that it is our society from whose conventions and history we take our identity, then the status quo is good by definition—good simply because it exists, because localism can only point out different perspectives but not judge among them. Localism is morally and politically problematic for other reasons as well. If all differences were recognized by law, then all established hierarchies, desirable or undesirable (by whatever criteria), would be beyond normative critique.

Nor can the "view from nowhere" (Nagel 1986) serve as a foundation for norms because claims and counterclaims can be evaluated only if we assume the existence of a reality beyond all discourse about reality (as the empirical referent of discourse) and only if we assume the possibility of a decentered access to reality. Nor can the view from nowhere serve as the normative basis of ethics, politics, or law, because communal norms that privilege the conditions and perspectives of some members of a community may be inequitable and oppressive to other members.[3] Yet if a community or society appears to be homogeneous, the conditions leading to that apparent homogeneity probably are neither fixed forever nor totally stable now. If a community or society considers its own social, political, or moral judgments and actions to proceed from contingent conditions and perspectives, the community or society can avoid assigning dominant status to what may be the merely particular conditions and perspectives of its judgments and actions and can avoid blending out the claims of other conditions and perspectives.

Suppose norms are a form of cultural practice, and cultural practices are historically specific, contingent, and ungrounded except in terms of other contingent, ungrounded, and historically specific behavior. Can each cultural practice be allowed to have its own unquestionable criteria for truth and falsity, its own institutional sanctions?[4] No, it cannot; otherwise the notion of contingent, historically changing, and culturally variable norms simply licenses the cynical thought that "who will do what to whom under the new pluralism is depressingly predictable" (Lovibond 1989:22). Legitimation cannot be plural, each instance of legitimation warranting its own constitutive norms, with practitioners legitimizing their own practice. After all, if one appeals to local standards as the final moral arbiter, to whose locality is one appealing? The constitution of local standards is as problematic and subject to contestation as is the constitution of universal standards.[5]

CRITIQUE FROM A DECENTERED STANDPOINT

The alternative to a local standpoint is a decentered one. A decentered standpoint is possible within the pragmatist approach I developed in chapter 3. A pragmatist route seeks an explanation that will satisfy some particular need or desire or interest. This need or interest is itself the internal standard by which to evaluate the approach. But not all other standards, including external ones, are therefore irrelevant. Conflict among competing approaches can be adjudicated if noninternal criteria exist with which to adjudicate—even if those criteria are ad hoc (indeed, given the indeterminacy thesis, they can only be ad hoc). Only then is adjudication possible not merely within any one approach but among different approaches. Otherwise there would be as many "truths" as approaches because each approach would have its own truth irrelevant to, and not criticizable by, all others. Truth and normative standards would be plural.[6] By this approach, universal standards or justificatory strategies could be theoretically unconvincing; politically or morally they could not be compelling.

If the criteria by which we evaluate the truthfulness, accuracy, and ethical standards of a statement, theory, or social criticism are nothing but the consequences of that statement's social and political aims, we regress to the prior question: By what criteria can we evaluate those consequences? If these criteria can only be local—the interests of a particular social group or the critic's own community—then pragmatism can only be ethnocentric. But where criteria can be extralocal, pragmatism can be decentered. Pragmatism appeals to consequences for criteria of evaluation. Insofar as consequences also need to be interpreted in a process that is ad hoc, pragmatism would seem to be an inherently ethnocentric approach. In fact pragmatism is neither inherently ethnocentric nor inherently decentered; it can be either. But only a decentered pragmatism can conceive of a society or community tolerant of diversity, disagreement, and minoritarian views. It offers us a means of keeping private concerns from blinding us to public concerns, of preventing narrow interests from blinding us to broad ones, of discouraging parochial considerations from blinding us to cosmopolitan ones.

The decentered alternative to localism is a standpoint somewhere between the individual's idiosyncratic perspective and the world entirely outside, a perspective more extensive and general than the former, less absolute and transcendent than the latter. Socially constructed knowledge is not the only alternative to transcendental knowledge, just as the autonomous subject freely choosing whatever he or she pleases is not the only alternative to universalism. An analysis not transcendental might be historical; justification not universal and unconditioned might be restricted and partial, yet without being subjective or individualistic.

Language is used subjectively (because it can only be used and understood by subjects) yet is itself objectifying, universalizing, generalizing. (When we say "green," we assume the listener will understand the same "green" even though no two patches of the color are exactly the same.) The activities of describing, analyzing, and criticizing are always homogenizing; human language cannot describe, analyze, and criticize without universalizing. Whether one describes behavior in a particular culture, such as a specific business or religious practice, or "world-historical" processes such as the development and spread of modern capitalism or secularization in the modern age, one homogenizes or generalizes. Human language can lay hold of culture or community only as something more than an indeterminate ensemble of narratives too complex, heterogeneous, and fleeting to be portrayed as a whole. It can grasp the individual only as something not too complex, heterogeneous, or discontinuous to be capable of coherent representation in terms of identity, selfhood, and subjectivity.

Consider two sorts of statements: One type seeks to realize self-interest, as when a white person says, "Black citizens are morally inferior to white citizens (and therefore whites justifiably benefit from racial inequality)." The other type sort seeks to describe a state of affairs or point of view, as when a white or black person says, "Black citizens are treated as though they were morally inferior to white citizens, when in fact they are not (and therefore whites who benefit from racial inequality do so unjustifiably)." By itself, a localist standpoint cannot distinguish statements that seek to realize self-interest from statements that seek to describe a state of affairs or a point of view.[7] In a racist community, for example, the first claim might appear as an objective description of a state of affairs, not a justification of the self-interest of racists. The second claim does not express the self-interest of either race, but in a racist community it might be regarded as expressing the self-interest of black citizens. Yet in everyday life, competent social actors reasonably claim to understand this difference and to discern the particular circumstances when one or the other type of statement would be more appropriate. The fact that the two types are sometimes confused or conflated, or that statements of self-interest and statements oriented to describing a state of affairs sometimes coincide or stand in ambiguous relation to each other, does not detract from the validity of the distinction. Only if the distinction is valid can we identify confusion, overlap, ambiguity, and manipulation in the first place.

The very process of mutual understanding that produces a decentered standpoint creates a normative or interpretive context distinct from the particular perspectives and self-seeking urges of concrete, socially and historically embedded human beings. A racist community will not regard its racism in the same way that a nonracist community will regard it; the self-interested nature of the racist community's racism is a parochial localism beyond which some members of the community may not be able to go until they assume the decentered standpoint distinct from that community's self-serving justifications of racism. An extra-personal standpoint may arise from, yet be free of, deep interpersonal experiences. (From the internal standpoint of the racist community, profiting from racial equality either does not appear to be profiting or, if it does, it appears as morally justifiable; at the same time, someone who profits from racial equality may realize at some point the unjustifiable nature of that profit and either be willing to act in morally unjustifiable ways or come to reject racism.) An extra-personal standpoint can evoke generalized or extra-particular standards. Only by invoking such standards can one make one's argument available (sometimes even persuasive) to others who stand outside one's own social group or community. For example, the nonracist can make his or her standpoint available to the racist by invoking standards the racist will understand, such as notions of human worth and dignity, and suggesting that if the racist can understand how such notions apply to him or her, they might also apply to members of groups he or she discriminates against. Further, only intersubjective norms of inquiry, only arguments available to such "outsiders," can identify socially significant problems, clarify different understandings and misunderstandings within a community, and identify and address disconfirming findings. Thus racism appears as a problem only from the standpoint of the nonracist community; racism will appear as a problem within the racist community itself only when nonlocal standpoints can be made plausible to members of that community.

Objectivity is possible in both relatively unstable and relatively stable communities. A community in which assumptions are widely shared and firmly in place will be more stable than one in which assumptions differ, where agreement must be negotiated repeatedly. Yet even in a community of widely shared assumptions, communal stability is a contingent matter, one that can always be upset because the objectivity of social critique is not a function of the critique's relation to the external world (in the manner of natural science). The objectivity of social critique is cultural objectivity. Objectivity in a cultural sense refers to homogeneity: The more uniform a culture, the more "objective" its standards—but solely from a perspective internal to that culture. No matter how unified a culture is internally, its standards are not thereby objective for other cultures. And if negotiation is necessary within a nonuniform culture, it is all the more necessary among different cultures. The expression *different cultures* refers just as well to the distinction among communities and other subgroups within any one society.

For reasons epistemological as well as normative, social actors continually need to engage in dialogue with one another. Only a self that can sometimes look beyond its sovereign subjectivity will be able to recognize already existing relations of reciprocity. The decentered subject—the person who assumes an enlightened localist perspective more general than his or her original idiosyncratic perspective, yet less absolute than the entire world beyond—is not antithetical to relations of reciprocity but, rather, is the very condition of such relations. The decentered subject is the very condition of intersubjectively generated and always revisable standpoints that are both decentered epistemically and potentially universalist in their normative claims. To the extent that these standpoints are possible, the normative indeterminacy of the social world does not preclude the possibility of its critique.

THE RELATIVISM OF CRITIQUE

Such standpoints are relative. According to the relativist position, the world is continuously changing and various and may be understood in a variety of plausible ways (though, of course, one cannot adopt all understandings at the same time and still be self-consistent). Like every other position, the relativist one is contingent. But a contingent position does not deny the existence of an external reality because the possibility of knowledge presupposes an external reality that can be known to some extent, if not absolutely. This presupposition does not provide any noncontingent access to that external reality. If the process of knowing is contingent, but presupposes an external reality, then one knows only contingently. At best, relativism can ground itself only contingently, not absolutely. Like any other position, it seeks self-stabilizing confirmation and seeks to avoid self-destabilizing contradiction. But it does so without ever being able to achieve a final or ultimate or noncontingent confirmation. The standpoint of relativism is itself relative; knowledge of the contingent, itself contingent. Yet a relative standpoint nonetheless can possess explanatory power, and contingent knowledge of reality is viable knowledge nonetheless. We can ask of any narrative, scientific or otherwise, "Is it true?" and "How do we decide if it is true?" Although we cannot answer these questions definitively, we can put forth and criticize answers we find plausible and explain why we adopt the explanations and narratives we in fact adopt and why we change those we change, and our answers need not be conclusive in order not to be pure fiction or false consciousness. Pragmatist epistemology evaluates conflicting perspectives by asking about their social and political consequences (which have to be interpreted in an ad hoc manner). A perspective may be evaluated according to criteria from precision to conceptual economy, from enhancing predictability to advocating social values or ways of life. This epistemology cannot itself adjudicate among these various ways of evaluation except pragmatically, hence contingently.

Again, human societies as a whole, and groups and individuals within them, regularly judge or prioritize epistemic standards that include empirical adequacy, explanatory comprehensiveness, quantitative precision, empirical predictability, logical coherence, conceptual economy, aesthetic appeal, practical efficacy, and moral acceptability. Individuals, groups, even whole societies disagree about epistemic standards, and revisions and qualifications of these standards are part of the "normal activity" of judging such standards. Although no such judging will ever be conclusive, uncontested, or satisfactory to everyone concerned, in a cultural sense such judging is necessary to human life. It is both useful and meaningful to enough people over long enough periods to sustain both the belief, and the desire to believe, in the possibility of "correctly" judging normative and epistemic standards. The apparent impossibility of ever achieving that kind of "correctness" (which may not exist) does not vitiate the strength or coherence of the belief in the possibility of correct judgment. In fact, the belief may have a regulative function without which the practical, ever-present necessity of making judgments could not be discharged.

But a world without absolutes need not be one where norms can be nothing other than force. If knowledge is simply equated with power, then communication and understanding are unlikely because if power and desire are the sole basis for knowledge, then knowledge is impossible. If the subjective and objective dimensions of knowing are sundered, neither is possible; if impersonal understanding and personal knowledge cannot be bridged, then decentered knowledge is unlikely. If all knowledge and discourse is merely an ethnocentric projection, then no knowledge or discourse can be a tool of social critique (*pace* Richard Rorty).[8] Epistemologically there would be no possibility of offering anything like a cogent critical standpoint regarding social realities. To claim that all knowledge and discourse is an ethnocentric projection is to conflate knowledge and power, thereby enthroning the reign of self-interest. Advocacy of change or reform could not have any but a self-interested basis. Self-interest alone would provide the rationale for making discriminations about the world and its consequences for our lives, and for debating our various understandings and theories about that world. Self-indulgent and grossly partisan points of view would be the sole ones imaginable; knowledge and action would be possible only as manipulation.

For these reasons a viable normative system must be able to entertain criteria of truth distinct from its own. To entertain alternative criteria of truth is to reject reductionism, to employ a form of relativism (and, as I argued in chapter 3, pragmatism is one form of relativism). The claim to relativism is, in part, a claim that no single normative system exhaustively grasps an object domain, and that no social criticism can sustain a claim to encompass totally, to explain wholly, any phenomenon.

CRITIQUE AS POST-EMPIRICIST PERSUASION

To endorse particularist interest as the primary criterion for evaluation is to rule out the possibility of understanding, and therefore cooperation, among individuals and among groups. If particularist interest is the sole criterion for evaluation, then relations among individuals and between groups can rest solely on force, never on reason. Social science would be impossible, and human interaction doubtful, if a person of the X race (or religion, nationality, age, sex, or political persuasion) could not apply nonlocal standards to persons of the Y race (or religion, nationality, age, sex, or political persuasion).

To abandon the search for epistemological access to reality in a direct, mirroring sense is not to renounce the search for impersonal criteria of evaluation. To abandon the goal of a single ahistorical standard of truth is not to deny the very possibility of truth; a proposition can be true even if no procedure exists for demonstrating its truth in such a way that any rational person must freely acknowledge that truth. Alternatively, truth might be defined as negotiated, consensual agreements, in principle revisable at any time. Then the sole test for our theories and interpretations cannot be "facts" but, at best, something like their coherence with the rest of our beliefs.[9] The activity of interpretation is then one not of demonstration but of persuasion. The persuasion of discursive arguments, as well as the rational criteria they imply, can only be subjectively compelling: they flow inside schools and traditions, with more the movement of a conversation than the progress of a rational proof or an empirical test.[10]

Persuasion, like so many other means of reasoning, comes in different forms. One distinction among others is that between an empiricist and post-empiricist foundation for persuasion. Three features of Mary Hesse's (1980:172-173) account of natural science, when reformulated as social theory, resonate with a theory of enlightened localism toward coping in politics with indeterminacy.

First, data ("facts") are not detachable from social critique because what count as data are determined in light of some interpretation, and the facts themselves must be reconstructed by the lights of interpretation. Social critiques are not models externally compared to society in some hypothetico-deductive schema but are the way facts themselves are seen. For the social critic, social meanings are determined by the critique itself; meanings are constituted by theoretical coherence, not correspondence with facts.

Second, the validity the social critic asserts of his or her theory is internal (or ultimately circular) because what counts as facts are constituted by what the critic's theory says about the interrelations of facts. Different critics' accounts of the same event are highly variable and context dependent.[11] Hence we cannot use what critics say as evidence for what society is "really like" but need instead to consider the methodologically prior question, How are critics' accounts of action and belief socially generated?[12] After all, normative critique is underdetermined by evidence. More than one critique can fit the same facts; put differently, empirical evidence does not provide conclusive grounds for accepting or rejecting any one critique. Where critique cannot be rejected or accepted on the grounds of the evidence brought to bear on it, the critic has great leeway in her or his choice of norms. If a variety of nonlogical and possibly social influences affect the choices critics make,[13] then we must put social explanations of critique prior to logic and evidence and seek to explain the content of critique as far as possible in social terms.[14]

Third, normative judgments in social criticism are not more arbitrary than in scientific theories; they are subject to empirical appraisal yet are underdetermined by facts. Because theories are underdetermined empirically, and empirical accounts are theory laden, theories may be justified on value-related grounds. Scholars of the natural world then invoke the pragmatist criteria of successful prediction and control; scholars of the social world must look as well to ethical values and political goals. Increased knowledge about social life does not usually translate into increased control over the social world. Greater understanding of society might generate greater technical control over institutions, increasing the "rationality" of behavior with regard to specific needs, but this hardly redeems the Enlightenment promise of generating ever-greater autonomy by spreading reason to all corners of society. Anthony Giddens notes how modern social life is characterized by its self-reflexivity; he stresses the importance of what he calls the "reflexive monitoring of conduct," which refers to the "intentional or purposive character of human behavior," as a "routine feature of human conduct" that "does not imply that actors have definite goals consciously held in mind during the course of their activities" (1994:56). Here

> reasons and intentions are not definite "presences" which lurk behind human social activity, but are routinely and chronically . . . instantiated in that activity. The intentional character of human actions is not to be seen as an articulation of discrete and separate "intentions," but a continuous flow of intentionality in time; and not to be treated as a set of conscious states that in some way "accompany" action. Only in the reflexive act of attention are intentions consciously articulated: normally within discourse. (ibid.:39–40)

But self-reflexivity cannot reduce the numberless unintended consequences of social life.[15] We should not conclude that no stable, knowable social world exists but, rather, that knowledge of the world itself contributes to its unstable or mutable character: Knowledge is not certitude.

Willard V. O. Quine (1963:42, 44) asserts that any proposition can be held true if we make drastic enough adjustments elsewhere in the related system, and conversely, that no proposition is immune to revision. Epistemologically, the respective "myths" of physical objects and gods are on the same logical footing. In neither case can justificatory procedures be anything other than conventions (and therefore contingent); we choose among procedures according to our various interests and purposes.

CRITIQUE AS A FORM OF PROCEDURALISM

Enlightened localism confronts the problem of epistemic indeterminacy also through proceduralism (which I developed in chapter 2). For Stuart Hampshire epistemic indeterminacy is the problem that every individual and every social group to some extent is "blind to many of the injustices of its time, because its own culture and education, supporting a particular way of life, represents embedded and distinctive features of a way of life as unavoidable features of human life in general" (1989:59). In the ways it is neutral, proceduralism can rise above such parochial localism. Consider the following six ways.

First, procedures are neutral toward many of the various competing normative worldviews. They do not "infect" or influence the particular moral convictions or the moral sources of individual motivation they treat. In the case of political liberalism this means that, in Cass Sunstein's words,

> Government is above all respectful of the divergent conceptions of the good held by its many constituents. People are taken as they are, not as they might be. Modern government has no concern with souls. Although electoral processes are ensured, no special premium is placed on citizen participation. Self-interest, not virtue, is understood to be the usual motivating force of political behavior. Politics is typically, if not always, an effort to aggregate private interests. It is surrounded by checks, in the form of rights, protecting private liberty and private property from public intrusion. (1991:4)

Most liberal theories today are proceduralist at least in the sense of embracing democratic deliberation and rejecting such forms of proceduralism as lotteries, mere voting or bargaining, or the nondemocratic sovereign favored by Thomas Hobbes (1588–1679).[16]

Second, with respect to law this means that authoritative interpreters and appliers of legal rules should approach them more as procedures than as purveyors of values. One then argues that courts should approach the constitution as a kind of formal framework, which, while dedicated to certain "thick" norms such as democracy, should proffer few others. In this sense John Hart Ely reads the American constitution as concerned chiefly with "procedural fairness in the resolution of individual disputes" and with ensuring, through procedure, "broad participation in the processes and distributions of government" (1980:87). So understood, the document contains few substantive values. To the political process it leaves the embracing or rejecting of all other values. The idea here is that a procedural approach to legal rules leads to impartial decisions through the application of legal rules, and that a legal decision is valid because of the formal or nonsubstantive means by which it was derived. We then determine the constitutionality of, say, the distribution of social goods on the basis not of distributional outcome but of procedural correctness (ibid.:136). Normative commitments would be disputed (and some eventually chosen over others) in the public sphere and through the political process, by citizens or by their democratically elected representatives—but not by courts of law. Instead judges would ensure the procedural correctness of the political process, by such normatively thin norms as openness, representativeness, and transparency. Even where a diverse community cannot agree on many substantive normative issues, it might agree on minimal procedural standards that might provide basic mutual respect at a formal level. The norm of respect might then take the procedural forms of due process and equal representation. On this basis proceduralism can contribute to the settling of normative disputes, and to the regulation of life under conditions of normative disagreement, where proceduralism requires a collective capacity to solve collective problems on an ongoing basis, rather than a capacity dependent on enduringly stabilized, consensual agreement. (We see that political agreement through procedure is a matter more of community than of individuals. Because we can measure success or failure in solving social problems only by reference to the affected community, some level of communal agreement is an expectable feature of success.)

Third, proceduralism can rise above parochial localism in the form of social integration in normatively neutral ways or, at least, in procedural ways. Stable social interaction does not require that people share normatively thick motives if they share normatively thin procedures. Groups and individuals need not share some map of substantive norms in situations in which they "can integrate their behaviors into reliable systems . . . without extensive motivational or cognitive sharing" (Wallace 1970:35). Social integration does not depend on—and would be impossible in complex modern societies if social integration required—substantial normative sharing, as in the claim that a community's integration depends on what Émile Durkheim (1995) calls the community's "common sentiments."

Fourth, proceduralism offers a means to the formulation of public policy under conditions of moral diversity. To be sure, some people have needs that can be articulated only in very substantive terms, such as religious fundamentalists. Proceduralism precludes such perspectives, and the needs they express, not as such but only as bases for public policy in a liberal democratic society. Seyla Benhabib rejects this enlightened localist approach and calls for a "moral-transformative process" through which "new needs and interests, such as can lead to a consensus among the participants, emerge" (1986:314). Her alternative allows normatively substantive perspectives to guide public policy but only as long as they are held by everyone (and her approach imagines a public discourse that might engineer such consensus). William Connolly, by contrast, rejects the "demand to *ethicize* or universalize [our] entrenched contingencies on the grounds that they [can] flow from a true identity" (1991:174) even if, as in Benhabib, that identity is created, not found. His approach politicizes normative and other differences under the assumption that public policy inevitably involves hard choices regarding which perspectives should be promoted, and which discouraged, and that participants should struggle politically for the success of their particular thick perspective over the perspectives of competing groups. By enlightened localist lights, proceduralism does not seek, like Benhabib, to transform a whole community or society at a deeply moral level but, rather, to facilitate cooperation among people who continue to disagree at that level. And it does not presuppose, like Connolly, that endless struggle is ultimately in the best interests of all participants but, rather, that diverse populations are best served by the stable social peace of enlightened localist agreement, as long as that agreement does not intrude on personal commitments of participants equally prepared not to foist these commitments on others.

Fifth, proceduralism can be critical when it can generate unmanipulated results. The notion of unmanipulated may itself be contested, but it is rationally contestable only from a standpoint itself claiming to be unmanipulated (which standpoint then provides the standard by which to identify manipulation). Contestation is no rejection of the notion of unmanipulated but a dispute as to whether, in any given instance, people are in fact practicing such scrutiny, as a means to accuracy and consistency, corrigibility and transparency, and as a means to participation by or representation of all relevant persons. A critique of unmanipulated scrutiny relies on presuppositions compatible with proceduralism: that human knowledge is always fallible and ever revisable in light of new arguments, experiences, or knowledge; that the process of arriving at rational convictions depends on free argumentation; that participants and other affected persons must themselves be open to argument; that participants should make arguments in good faith, and attempt to give unprejudiced consideration to opposing arguments, and should be open to persuasion by the rationally better argument. These propositions do not prescribe specific contents but only the normative conditions for those contents.

Finally, proceduralism works by abstraction, and abstraction can cope with difference. Standards, for example, vary among societies just as they vary among groups; they vary within cosmopolitan societies, and within the same subgroup at different times. Differences of this kind do not defeat proceduralism because of proceduralism's robust capacity for abstracting from the particularities of situation, issue, dispute, and person. Proceduralism abstracts citizens from some of their prescriptive identities, aspects of their social and economic circumstances, and many of their substantive normative beliefs. In this way it can uncover or create possible grounds of agreement, grounds predicated on the participants' abstract legal and political equality.

"To abstract," then, refers to generating conditions of neutrality. To advocate neutrality, however, is not to commit to complete and absolute neutrality. In a logically banal sense, to advocate neutrality is not to be neutral about neutrality. Quite beyond banality is the claim that even if proceduralism cannot appeal to norms claiming universal validity, it must appeal to some norms nonetheless—even as it disregards others. The procedural resolution of conflicts within the polity—and more generally in the day-to-day social integration of individuals—requires of proceduralism certain normative assumptions that all persons related to each other as legal equals must make. In other words, typically we would find a mix that would include both the procedural framework for voting or making other decisions of public concern and such nonprocedural values as the worth and dignity of the individual and the desirability of group and individual self-determination.

Precisely an enlightened localist approach to proceduralism is sensitive to problems with some of these values. Thus the procedural norm of equality is problematic not least because of its double-edged nature. A procedural approach to securing equal treatment may overemphasize similarities and pay insufficient heed to differences. The political equality that may emancipate an ethnic, racial, or cultural minority from the dominant one (a political equality tantamount to disregarding many natural and social differences) is the same equality that may pressure a minority to assimilate itself to the majority in ways that elide differences important to the minority. Consider the demand that a religious minority forsake a certain practice (such as ritual animal sacrifice practiced by members of the Santeria faith in a predominantly Christian community in a secular political culture)[17] or that a cultural minority abandon traditional aspects of identity (for example, ethnic Koreans born and raised in Japan must assume Japanese names if they wish to gain Japanese citizenship). Sometimes equality is paired institutionally with similarity (similar social class, same race, sex, and so on) and inequality with dissimilarity (the view, say, that different social classes are politically unequal, or that women and men are socially unequal, or that the races are unequal to each other in intelligence). And under circumstances of social inequality, equality through procedure can lead to substantive inequality, for example in the argument that racial segregation does not violate the norm of racial equality (the claim, in other words, that separate can be equal): Thus in 1896 in *Plessy v. Ferguson*[18] the Supreme Court deferred to the usages, customs, and traditions of a good portion of the American populace in 1896, above all its racism.

CRITIQUE IS NOT EMPIRICIST

Enlightened localism is not empiricist. On its approach, facts are theory laden, and what we take to be evidence is shaped by our theories and their constituent concepts, other related conceptual schemes, and our normative presuppositions. Knowledge is not a matter of representations that stand in privileged relation to reality. Willard V. O. Quine and Wilfred Sellars make clear why an account of the nature of knowledge can be, at most, a description of human behavior.[19] Following Quine and Sellars, Richard Rorty argues that epistemic authority is to be explained by reference to "what society lets us say" rather than to inner, privileged representations or discourses, whether of the natural or social sciences. "[N]othing counts as justification unless by reference to what we already accept.... There is no way to get outside our beliefs and our language so as to find some test other than coherence" (1979:186). We cannot justify claims to truth or knowledge other than by appealing to specific social practices developed over long periods of time.

We cannot arrive at ahistorical standards of rationality and objectivity because no permanent criteria or procedures exist to which all disputants could appeal univocally for adjudicating arguments.

The respective ideas of Hesse, Quine, Sellars, and Rorty are anti-empiricist or post-empirical in tenor. Post-empiricism includes the notion that theory-neutral observations are impossible; that systems of deductively linked laws cannot be the highest ideal of scholarly explanation; that science itself is an interpretive endeavor to which problems of meaning, communication, and translation are immediately relevant.[20] Post-empiricism rejects the Cartesian duality of objectivism and relativism. The proposition that no neutral algorithm exists for choice among theories[21] does not imply the irrationality of science; scientists make discursive arguments to support their approach and conclusions over competing ones. These reasoned arguments are based on extended communities of inquiry developed over extended periods of time. Appeal to scientific criteria is no less a matter of persuasion than are appeals to nonscientific criteria.

On the other hand, the post-empiricist approach cannot, by itself, address such crucial questions as, To which social practices are we to appeal? How do we discriminate the better from the worse? Which ones need to be discarded, criticized, and reconstructed? Granted the absence of any transhistorical criteria, do other criteria exist for criticizing, evaluating, and improving or abandoning our practices? In short, even though post-empiricism properly stresses the ethical and political factors that inform social science, it provides no means of assessing competing values. To overcome this take-it-or-leave-it quality of post-empiricist thought, I shall offer under the following rubric a pragmatist account of how competing values may be assessed (and probably are assessed in many concrete instances).

CRITIQUE AS A FORM OF PRAGMATISM

Critical reasoning, to some extent, is always bound to authority in the sense of ascertaining the lines of authority in previous critiques, in normative rules, and in analogies, as well as in normatively "accredited" sources that may have issued citable pronouncements—and then cobbling and rationalizing these "authoritative" materials to the critic's purposes, intuitions, and beliefs. Yet if authority were hopelessly politicized, then the ultima ratio of norms could only be force. Disputes between "groups that want to make inconsistent kinds of world" (in the words of Oliver Wendell Holmes [1961:36]) would be resolvable by rational rather than forceful means only if epistemological contents, as well as normative ones, can be provided apart from the self-interest of any particular group or individual. If such contents cannot be evaluated in a relatively impersonal and rational way, then social criticism is possible on the basis of force alone.

But the reduction of norms (or the reduction of morality or rationality) to force renders norms impossible. In a world of epistemic indeterminacy, rationality and morality are possible, if only in the thin sense allowed by pragmatist theory. The thesis that the social world is epistemically and otherwise indeterminate does not lead, ineluctably, to solipsism. If no rule is determinate, "true" propositions about the world are still possible because "reality" can be determinate even if our knowledge of it cannot. Although we will never know in any ultimate sense whether a particular proposition is true, the less-than-ultimate ways in which we can postulate truthfulness are very often adequate to serve us pragmatically in coping with the world on a daily basis. Even if most of our shared beliefs are not true in some final sense, at any given moment we cannot know otherwise. And if most of our beliefs are true in this sense, we often have no compelling reason to entertain alternative worldviews that cast doubt on our current beliefs, especially those held on a community-wide basis. (The social critic, of course, may be the exception to the rule; he or she is typically dissatisfied with current beliefs and may be suspicious of any number of beliefs held on a community-wide basis.)

To use such community-wide paradigms, we need not know everything about them, as is suggested by an observation about the more formalized and rigorous field of natural science:

> Scientists work from models acquired through education and through subsequent exposure to the literature often without quite knowing or needing to know what characteristics have given these models the status of community paradigms. And because they do so, they need no full set of rules. The coherence displayed by the research tradition in which they participate may not imply even the existence of an underlying body of rules and assumptions that additional historical or philosophical investigation might uncover. (Kuhn 1970:46)

From a pragmatist stance, the social world is rational not because it has some ultimate foundation (it does not) but, rather, to the extent that it can place any of its rules in question (though of course not all of its rules at the same time).[22]

This pragmatist notion of truth challenges Rorty's concept of 'objectivity' as nothing more than conformity to current norms: The "historicist sense that this century's 'superstition' was the last century's triumph of reason, as well as the relativist sense that the latest vocabulary, borrowed from the latest scientific achievement, may not express privileged representations of essences, but be just another of the potential infinity of vocabularies in which the world can be described" (1979:367). Rorty posits a more or less homogeneous, unified, consensual set of norms, but no such homogeneity, unity, or consensus can be shown to exist. It is the case, however, that insofar as individuals, groups, or communities share a language (or at least one translatable language) and some aspects of a way of life, those individuals, groups, or communities are likely to share some standards of meaning and value. To agree (at least partially and sporadically) on standards of meaning and value is to possess (at least partially and sporadically) preconditions for the possibility of agreement on some normative questions.

Moreover, perhaps some forms of moral and practical reasoning are shared, especially if such forms are not specialized or do not require specific training. Stuart Hampshire, for example, maintains that "methods of adjudication and arbitration and negotiation are the outward equivalents of the methods of thought that everyone employs to some extent, and in proportion to his or her rationality, in inner debates" (1989:54). Similarly, Richard Posner argues that "there is no such thing as 'legal reasoning.' Lawyers and judges answer legal questions through the use of simple logic and the various methods of practical reason that everyday thinkers use. Because of the law's emphasis on stability, the scientific attitude is not at home in law" (1990a:459).

A pragmatist theory can explain the social world's disorder, internal contradiction, and indeterminacy without having to conclude that a society or community is normatively illegitimate, indeed incapable of legitimacy or any other notion of normative coherence. Normative indeterminacy need not threaten a society's or community's possibility or legitimacy. Perhaps it even provides (and explains) the desirable flexibility that a social system needs to function in the first place. Yet normative indeterminacy does not preclude the very possibility of social critique, nor does it preclude the possibility of a social or otherwise nonimmanent critique of any particular community or society. Even though they are nonfoundational, the pragmatist notions of truth, objectivity, and validity do not imply normative nihilism. On the other hand Posner (1990b) and Rorty (1982) rightly conclude that pragmatism has no inherent political valence. This conclusion does not mean, however, that if pragmatism is normatively neutral, then all fallibilistic, pragmatist critique of the social world is impossible. Critique presupposes a standard against which something is criticized; yet to be normatively neutral does not mean not to have a standard. Nor does it mean to suspend the standard the critic would otherwise employ. It means that the particular standard employed in any given instance is contextually given, according to consequentialist considerations. A pragmatist critique has no transcendent standards but rather situational, local ones.

THE SITUATEDNESS OF CRITIQUE

Pragmatism can reject both a metadiscourse articulating the criteria of validity for every first-order discourse and a naturalized epistemology that merely describes the status quo and surrenders all normative claims, for a notion of a situated social criticism that can account for its own possibility. On the one hand, the view of the social critic is never the view from nowhere in particular but always the view of an individual or group situated somewhere, in some culture and society and historical context. On the other hand, no single set of constitutive criteria exists in terms of which all complex social practices may be understood. Situated criticism must not assume that the norms of a culture are so univocal and noncontroversial that the critic can appeal to them unproblematically, without first having to evaluate them critically. Even if situated criticism is sensitive to the essential constructedness of culture and the need to examine cultural norms critically, that examination is itself culturally and historically situated. Criticism and its self-clarification are situated and do not require foundationalist thought claiming to articulate the ahistorical and transcendental criteria of their validity. Situated criticism does not preclude general norms but rather emphasizes that these, too, are situated.

To be sure, 'situatedness' is a problematic concept. On the one hand it cannot mean "parochial," that is, merely the individual's or group's or community's standpoint. On the other hand, it offers itself as a critique of universalism: A standpoint disconnected from local understandings is problematic because it is potentially manipulative of the local community, of its culture and understandings. Situated critique must be more than parochial and it can only be less than universal. Yet how can standards be internal to a society or community yet also properly critical of that society or community? A critic who is connected to local understandings, a critic who lacks an external standard, may not have sufficient critical distance from the society under scrutiny. A universal normative standpoint recommends itself as distanced and potentially critical but is probably impossible to derive. It cannot be derived even from what appears to be almost universal prohibitions against certain types of behavior (deceit, unrestricted killing by members of one's own community, incest, betrayal, rape, gratuitous brutality). Systems of norms, such as cultures and legal systems, are more than prohibitions.

Just as normative systems are partly shaped by prohibitions, so the critique of normative systems is partially shaped by current moralities. But if critique of the status quo can begin from principles internal to the status quo, it must also go beyond those principles if it is to be properly critical. Social critique of a local morality can begin with standards immanent in that morality, but it must exceed them as well. In exceeding them, critique neither ceases being situated nor starts being universal. It does not cease being situated because it cannot escape the conditions of collective life, including those (like parochialism) that discourage critical perception. And it does not begin being universal for the same reason. Critical distance, yes, but not absolute distance in the sense of "outside," "independent"; detachment, perhaps, but radical detachment is no prerequisite for social criticism. The unanswerable question is, How much distance is critical distance? But at least we know that the calibration of critical distance is fine, not rough; that it occurs in "centimeters," not "meters."[23] As an example of how this scheme actually works, I shall return to the question of racial equality in the final pages of this chapter.

It may be that the thesis of epistemic and normative indeterminacy is not "economic" for everyday purposes because it suggests that the world is much more complicated, and that we humans are much less in control of it, than we probably imagine on an everyday, commonsense basis. It may be that, in many instances, individuals and groups and even whole societies function more efficiently (or at least less stressfully) in situations of perceived clarity and control. But although a social theory must take into account the self-understandings and beliefs of participants, its validity need not depend on agreement with those self-understandings and beliefs. My notion of pragmatist critique seeks to explain how, if the indeterminacy thesis is valid and yet few participants accept it, social criticism is nonetheless possible.

The question remains, How can we know that a decentered, relativist, pragmatist, and detached approach to social critique is not just another form of localism? Facets of Michael Walzer's work provide a foil (in many ways sympathetic) against which I can formulate a response. His concern that critical distance not become radical detachment leads him to a social criticism that is contextualist and experience-near. Such critique wants a critic so involved that he or she would be a virtual participant in debates internal to criticized social practices, or contested community norms, or legal texts calling for interpretation. For Walzer engaged criticism is nonetheless criticism from a certain distance: "Criticism does not require us to step back away from society as a whole, but only to step away from certain sorts of power relationships within a society" (1987:60). He counsels both proximity and distance, as in his notion of justice as a search for principles internal to each distributive sphere (here we have proximity), yet allowing no one's standing in a given social practice to be undercut by his or her standing in some other practice or in some other institution's power structure (here we have distance, or at least an external reference) (1983:19).

But Walzer doesn't see that the line between distance and detachment is indefinable. If that line is indefinable, then forms of criticism cannot be distinguished from each other (as he suggests) in terms of their practical effectiveness in bringing about social change: "Success in criticism has more to do with the place or standing of the critic than with his theory of society or political ideology" (1988:x). Walzer cannot support his notion of critical internalism by appeal to competent participancy—a critic's "place or standing"—for how does a critic determine which effects are the results of power and which are not? A critic concerned with consequences need not require that he or she already share something in common with the participants in the practices or institutions under examination; rather, the critic may attempt to create shared points of moral or cognitive concern. Engaged criticism need not approximate participation in existing societal practices, institutions, or traditions. It loosens itself from those facets of practices, institutions, or traditions inflected with power by entertaining competing claims about those practices and traditions. Some of the claims may well be external to the participants' standpoint.[24]

Nor does the possibility of social critique depend on the findings of social scientific research, theoretical or empirical. If normative critique could not proceed without first achieving epistemological accord, neither critique nor research would take place. We need no secure epistemology or normative theory from which to sally forth and analyze the world. Nor does social criticism consist, as Walzer contends, entirely in "elaborating existing moralities." Internalism becomes self-defeating when critique leads critic into an infinite regress of ever-smaller circumscriptions of culture and identity, with ever-slighter capacities or critical self-scrutiny. Internalism fails by Walzer's own lights if it merely legitimizes the "easy comforts of being ourselves" (Geertz 1986). Internalism threatens to trap the critic within the resources of his or her own cultural particularity, whereas social critique in an indeterminate world is possible only as a self-reflexive, hence self-distanced and not radically internalist exercise. Self-distance and self-reflection provide a hedge against the possibility that a decentered, relativist, pragmatist approach to social critique might be simply one more form of localism.

Let us return now to the example that I employ throughout this book: the question of racial equality, specifically with respect to African Americans today. This chapter provides ways of moving beyond epistemologically and even politically debilitating forms of relativism—ways neither foundational nor dogmatic but, rather, pragmatist and decentered, intermediate rather than absolute or relative. To be sure, this position is self-limiting in holding that there is no one right approach, no one single answer to questions of social criticism; enlightened localism is still localism.

An enlightened localist approach seeks direction through several questions: First, What need or interest is to be satisfied? If the answer in this context is legal equality and social justice, then with respect to color-conscious public policy citizens must ask themselves, How does race explain social distinctions in America today? Can race function as a surrogate for either culture or identity? What role does race play in the formation of individual identity? These questions point up the fact that "race" is in many ways an indeterminate category; its effective meaning has to be constructed, under different circumstances, with respect to different questions. Race, however conceived, might always be differently constructed (after all, race is nothing but a social construct). With respect to racially preferential treatment for black Americans, the construction of race is motivated by the consequences of a history of slavery and other forms of race-based oppression. The construction of race here takes its departure from a history that has created a role for racial identities. On the other hand, race should not be so constructed as to undermine individual freedom and equality: Individuals should not be reduced to their racial ascription, even as race is considered a factor in legitimate public policy. Nor should race be constructed as the same phenomenon for all racial groups, in the sense that different groups have different moral claims for taking race into account with respect to decisions affecting individuals. Different groups have different moral claims for race-conscious public policy.

Second, how might a critic generate a decentered standpoint distinct from particular perspectives or self-seeking urges? With respect to the dominant racial group in America, the critic might note that social norms of individual freedom and equity have never functioned in color-blind fashion: not during the Second World War in the internment camps of Japanese Americans and Japanese nationals (but not Italian Americans and Italian nationals, nor of German Americans or German nationals); earlier, not in the extermination of the indigenous population "discovered" by European colonists; not in the kidnapping of Africans and their removal and enslavement in the British colonies, and the legal and cultural institutionalization of slavery in the U.S. Constitution as adopted in 1797; not in the restriction of legal naturalization to persons of the white race from 1790 until 1952.

With regard to disadvantaged groups, the critic might be concerned with not creating a culture of victimhood. She or he might consider, identify, and object to ways that preferential public policy places different groups in competition with each other, in competition for benefits and status, in competition that could only be decided by somehow "weighing" the suffering of different groups against each other, by somehow calibrating authenticity and intensity of collective degradation and discrimination.

With respect to all of the different groups composing society, the critic might generate a decentered standpoint for each by asking of each (and then comparing the answers), If society isn't color blind, can the government be color blind without disproportionately advantaging members of some racial groups and disadvantaging members of others? Can race-conscious public policy be compatible with norms of equality and freedom? Does race play the same role in the formation of, say, African American cultural identity as in the formation of, say, Asian American cultural identity? Indeed, to what extent does any racial group share a "common culture"? And even if certain features tie disparate members of a racial group together, What, if any, role should race play in the constitution of individual identity? To what extent should the government treat the individual in terms of his or her group membership (and which group memberships should count, and which intersections of which memberships—for example, class and race, or race and sex, or all three, if not others)?

Third, an enlightened localist approach seeks direction by asking, What relations of reciprocity already exist (for example, between members of the same socioeconomic class, across all racial differences)? Might these relations suggest a critical stance located beyond localism (for example, racial identity), yet this side of universalism (for example, without treating all persons in all groups as fundamentally the same, regardless of racial or economic differences)? With regard to racial groups in America, the critic might ask if socioeconomic class rather than race should guide public policy. If race does not have the same meaning for all racial groups, might class have the same meaning for all members of a particular socioeconomic class? Does middle-class status have the same meaning for different racial groups? What about class divisions within racial groups?

On the one hand, black Americans are residentially segregated to a much greater extent than European ethnic groups, whereas Asian and Hispanic groups are more likely to share a neighborhood with whites than with members of their own racial or ethnic group. To the extent that place of residence correlates with levels of cultural capital (including quality of public schools and other public facilities, as well as level of personal security), middle-class status does not offer the same benefits to African Americans as to other groups. And if the black middle-class is on average poorer than its white counterpart, if much of it is more recently arrivé than members of the white middle class, then the children of black middle-class households would seem to face greater obstacles to reproducing that status in the next generation than children of the white middle class.

Race does not operate in the same way for all groups; neither does class. Distributing social benefits on the basis of class not race would remove one of the black middle class's most important means of support. A universalist approach that sought to apply the same concepts, criteria, or categories to all members of a diverse society cannot possibly be fair to all citizens equally. The critic, seeking already existing relations of reciprocity among different groups (in the sense for example that members of different races may share interests as members of the same socioeconomic class, just as members of different socioeconomic classes may share interests as members of the same race), will have to evaluate race differently than class and will have to make distinctions among races within socioeconomic classes. While a critical stance must be located beyond the localism of any one group, it must also be located this side of universalism.

The following chapter continues the quest for an enlightened localist response to indeterminate norms. Whereas this chapter examined ways of coping with indeterminate norms in social critique, the following one looks for ways of coping with indeterminate norms within communities: in the very concept of community, in communal values, in communitarian aspirations. It considers the problem of achieving even a minimal normative consensus around which citizens might integrate themselves: agreement in the form of public policy. It considers how an enlightened localist policy might be constructed within one community (on questions of compulsory education) as well as among different communities (on questions of immigration).

CHAPTER 5
Enlightened Localism in Public Policy

Public policy is the second of the three settings in which I explore, by means of practical application, an enlightened localist theory of coping in politics with indeterminate norms. The preceding chapter explained how social critique in an enlightened localist vein displays elements both procedural and pragmatist. This chapter, which continues the argument for critical forms of proceduralism and pragmatism, makes a procedural argument for organizing public policy, asserting a general preference for levels more local than less. It considers qualifications and limits to this procedural modus operandi and shows how it operates with respect to issues of education and immigration. This chapter takes a pragmatist route to the communities for which public policy is formulated and to which it is applied. A pragmatist approach to community proceeds, in the face of wide differences among communities and deep diversity within some communities, by sensitivity to the local circumstances rather than insistence on dealing with community in ways universal and uniform. A pragmatist method proceeds by relativism not absolutism; by localism enlightened not parochial.

The centrality of community to human sociality guarantees it a plethora of meanings. Notions of community extend from governmental communities with civic or national identities to local communities centered around family and neighborhood to any number of other groupings bound by shared interests—from trade unionists to hobbyists. Conceptions of community span the horizon from merely the numerical majority of members to paternalism (community coercion may help individuals achieve their goals or lead morally better lives) and communalism (the quality of community life is the proper metric by which to judge the quality of any member's life). The concept of community is easily indeterminate. In application it is also ambivalent—that is, it can be anonymous or intimate, oppressive or liberating, sometimes neither, sometimes both.[1] Some analysts locate the source of communal values in family, school, and neighborhood.[2] Yet the practical meaning of each of these, too, is deeply indeterminate and sometimes oppressive or parochial or otherwise objectionable.

No less indeterminate is community as ideal: As communitarian aspiration, it seeks to integrate the individual yet also to secure for him or her some measure of autonomy. Autonomy of the person stresses individual choice within the community, whereas integration of the individual into the community stresses communal membership over individual identity. Membership may sometimes undermine individual choice and perspective. A strong emphasis on autonomy may reject the moral particularism of nonindividualist conceptions of community. Thus a curriculum for the all-black Ujamma schools once proposed for New York City espouses a notion of Afrocentricity that understands itself as distinct from, perhaps even defying, the norms of the European Enlightenment. Following another nonindividualist conception of community, some Muslim parents in France and England today demand, for their children in public schools, *halal* (religiously sanctioned) food and the *hajib* (the veil for women).

This definitional indeterminacy betrays a deeper, more intractable problem: The normative indeterminacy in almost any notion of political or social community. Normative indeterminacy is particularly acute in the context of public policy because policy's perceived legitimacy, even moral authority, often rests on appeals to a "community" supposedly guiding policy makers. One or the other notion of community underlies much policy and many of its judicial and political interpretations; each distinct vision of community would provide policy with its own particular normative basis. The nature of that normativity lies at the heart of the problem of community in contemporary cosmopolitan societies. It also lies at the heart of the solution, as we will see.

If the relevant norms of one community differ from those of others (or, within one community if the norms of some members differ from those of other members), how might members of one community engage members of other communities in discussion oriented to understanding, or even in practical cooperation? Might normative discourse sometimes bridge normatively distinct communities? Can members adjudicate normative disputes if they do not participate in much of a common way of life? Can they adjudicate disputes if they do not share many common values? To the extent that the state is constitutive of communal norms, these questions are relevant to public policy. They are relevant insofar as community is somehow constitutive of norms of public policy, where some conception of community provides policy's normative source or aspiration or where community provides the constituency that public policy would serve. If public policy is a carrier of communal norms, then it properly functions to "articulate and enforce at least some of the obligations recognized in and by the community."[3] Community then enjoys a right to promote within itself its own standards and values.

Yet normative discourse, the resolution of communal problems, and other forms of cooperation often enough are unlikely, if not impossible, among normatively distinct clusters within a community, or among normatively disparate communities. Recourse to public policy in a community's promotion of its own values and standards makes political legitimacy a function of that body's self-understanding. Often communal self-understanding has a normative component. Any one community's normativizing approach to public policy places into question the possibility of legitimate legal relations among different communities. At the extreme, the interpretive community—perhaps whatever community currently holds power—does not extend beyond its self-definition. The interpretation that obtains may do so not because of its rational persuasiveness or normative authority but simply because of the dominant community's coercive power.

In complex modern societies a fundamental problem of communal politics concerns the difficulty of achieving even a minimal normative consensus around which citizens might integrate themselves. The problem has multiple sources. In revolutionizing communication and transportation, for instance, the historical forces of industrialization, urbanization, and commercialization expose the individual to ever-greater and always changing varieties in ideas, values, and ways of life. Beliefs and forms of behavior of groups and individuals then mutate, often spontaneously, unnoticed (and often unobservable) by participants. Lack of consensus also derives from the structure of modern life in which the individual is a member of different communities, such as family and work, religious faith and secular society, or even communities of ascriptive characteristics so often problematic socially and politically, such as race (as we have seen repeatedly in the course of this book), but also sex, ethnic identity, and religion. Simultaneous membership in these various communities makes conflicting demands on the individual and generates tension among communities (and sometimes within the individual as well).

I will examine public policy's difficulties with indeterminate community with respect to a couple of illustrative issues: the indeterminate relationship of state and community, exemplified in competing interests between the state and parents whose children are compelled to pursue a state-approved curriculum; and the indeterminate relationship of the state between communities, represented by contending interests between would-be immigrants to a community and the citizens already resident there.

PARENTS' RIGHTS OVER THE CURRICULUM OF THEIR CHILDREN'S EDUCATION

Think of indeterminacy in the state's role within a community. Should parents have legal rights with regard to the compulsory education of their minor children, and if so, within what limits? "Does parental authority stop at the schoolhouse door or reach within to particular decisions about textbooks read, topics discussed, materials used?" (Burtt 1994:53). In this arena as in many others, public policy in modern states obliges citizens to heed laws mandating various types of behavior (as well as disallowing other types). Examples include prescribing the use of seat belts, prohibiting most psychoactive drugs, and withholding Social Security premiums from wages. Public policy does so in the conviction that compulsion of this kind is in the best interests even of those citizens who take exception to the putative wisdom of such measures (that it leads to their personal good, but also to the common good). The American government limits the authority of parents to decide in such areas as child labor,[4] teenage marriage,[5] severe physical deprivation,[6] abortion and access for minors to contraceptives[7]—and compulsory education.[8] Legally sanctioned parental control extends to areas of medical care and custody rights—but not to the sphere of education. The state (through public schools) has legal authority over the curriculum, to insist on its educational vision over alternatives, such as those favored by deeply religious parents.

To be sure, state and parents likely share some interests, and they probably agree on the idea of governmental restrictions in many areas of parental authority. Consider parents who reject a school curriculum that encourages a child to question its parents' religious or other convictions, but may agree to governmental restrictions on parental authority over minor children in such areas as labor, marriage, and abortion. For its part, the state will be disinclined to grant parents the legal right to pick and choose courses for their children on the basis of the parents' religious convictions. The state may well seek not to offend parents' religious beliefs in noncurricular matters (which, while never as important as the content of the curriculum, may be important nonetheless). But the state will be prepared to so offend on curricular matters; the parents' religious sensibilities cannot override school requirements that their child follow this or that particular course of instruction.

Still, parent–state disagreement on this or that particular course of instruction takes place in the context of broader agreement that benefits social stability and political legitimacy even in the face of partial disagreement. Of course the liberal state will hardly accommodate parents whose illiberality rejects civil tolerance of other faiths and worldviews, and who teach their children accordingly. But are many religious parents so extreme? According to Shelley Burtt, "Religious parents and secular schools share the end of an education in the basic skills and virtue of liberal democracy" (1994:620).[9] Indeed, an entire society as well as its disparate communities have an interest in compulsory education to ensure that subsequent generations are not left in ignorance. They have a general interest in curriculum as a means for individuals to attain minimal levels of literacy, to become effective citizens, to share democratic values, and to be cognizant of their state and federal political rights.[10]

Curriculum is also a means to encourage citizens' economic self-reliance, productivity, and law-abiding behavior. In *Wisconsin v. Yoder*[11] the Supreme Court recognized the state's strong interest in compulsory education, yet found that interest, as *parens patriae*, not sufficiently significant to curtail the parental exercise of religious freedom. The freedom in question was that of Amish parents who, on the basis of their religious convictions, would have their children end all formal education after the eighth grade. The court found that the training Amish parents provided in lieu of high school encouraged Amish children in just the ways mentioned.[12] It concluded that exempting the Amish from the compulsory education law would pose little threat to the state's interest underlying the requirement of compulsory education. Here parents opposed to exposing their children to secular or other beliefs challenging the parents' religious convictions (as well as children opposed to being so exposed) may nonetheless agree with the state that compulsory education is desirable insofar as it provides literacy, numeracy, and other basic skills.[13] Given such agreement, parental objections to secular, public school curricula should not be reduced to some desire to replicate the narrow-mindedness of one generation to the next, or to a reactionary nostalgia for some less pluralistic past.

We may expect agreement between state and parents in another more fundamental area: the need to provide for those not yet competent to decide for themselves. Yet agreement here may be too general to be of practical help. First, we confront the always contestable definitions of *incompetence* and the incompetent individual's *best interests*. The goal of providing for the good of the incompetent must be balanced against the rights of those being helped: the right not to be helped, or not to be helped too much (when help becomes harm). Second, states and parents may agree that some compulsory education is good but may well disagree on the number of years necessary. Or they may disagree as to the best or appropriate curriculum during those years. And although state and parents may agree that persons not competent to decide for themselves need others to decide for them, each may decide differently for the particular persons in question.

IMMIGRATION AND RIGHTS OF CITIZENSHIP

As a second illustrative issue, reflect on the role of the state among communities: in an international context with regard to the right of residence. Should the rights of citizenship be available to almost anyone who desires them, or primarily only to those born into them? Should only the minimal restrictions necessary for public order—restrictions necessary for the maintenance of legal and social rights of citizenship—serve as criteria to select among candidates for citizenship, or should those criteria include, say, the preservation of the host community's present cultural fabric? Consider the competition of interests: Those already resident might define their needs to include the preservation of a particular way of life, or maintaining employment opportunities, or containing local population density. Those seeking residency might identify their interests as the pursuit of a better life, or cultural and economic alternatives, or perhaps refuge from political or religious oppression at home. In the largely nondemocratic relations among nations, agreement cannot be based on what John Rawls calls "generations in a more or less just constitutional democracy" (1981:1). But even here, would-be residents and present residents share some interests. Even as would-be residents argue for permission to immigrate into a particular community, they may well share the present residents' belief in the right of communal self-determination. Even though disagreement might quickly follow from possible criteria for selecting among applicants (for example, to political refugees our community says yes, but to economic refugees, no), agreement is also possible. Would-be residents and present residents alike might agree on criteria such as respect for all immigrants equally as autonomous human beings, capable of citizenship regardless of their geographic origin, racial and ethnic characteristics, cultural background, moral commitments, or conception of the good.[14]

Bear in mind some of the normative differences between emigration and immigration. Michael Walzer regards them as "morally asymmetrical," suggesting that states are like voluntary associations, possessed of the right to refuse admission to all nonmembers (even if those already admitted, such as resident aliens, still have a right to naturalization) (1983:40). Voluntary associations may allow its members unrestricted exit but likely will not allow nonmembers unrestricted entrance. States are hardly voluntary associations, of course, but they are similar in that they restrict entrance much more than exit: Rights of immigration are always unlikely because the provision of rights as well as the redistribution of wealth, resources, burdens, and benefits make membership valuable and scarce. Rights of emigration, by contrast, follow from any system based on the consent of its members.

In this sense Albert Hirschman (1970) elaborates a theory of "repairable lapse" in which conditions might be reversed in response to members' dissatisfaction. Discontented members either voice their dissatisfaction to the authorities directly or through general protests or exit the organization, community, or society. But with regard to the exit option, Hirschman merely assumes what, if extended to immigration, cannot be assumed: a place willing to accept the immigrant. In other words, a right to leave one country cannot be exercised, or exercised fully, absent a right of entry into another. But if one state is obliged to allow exit, are other states then obliged to allow entry? Does a right of emigration entail one of immigration? What Walzer sees as asymmetry might instead be a badly skewed symmetry: A right of emigration may burden one state (it might burden the state of exit with such problems as "brain drain"), whereas a right of immigration could burden any number of states (it might burden all states "targeted" by would-be immigrants with problems of cultural incompatibility between the host and immigrant communities). A further skewed symmetry: Initial membership in a particular state is arbitrary, whereas immigrant membership is chosen (even if the degree of freedom may vary from immigrant to immigrant).

However we answer these questions, imagine that current residents and would-be residents alike agree that, given the international significance of migration and the interdependence of states, the admission of aliens cannot be an untrammeled discretionary power within the exclusive domestic jurisdiction of states. We might base this argument on a specific version of reciprocity, namely, mutual benefit. Or we might argue that the stronger is morally obligated to aid the weaker. We might argue that countries with relatively abundant land and resources therefore bear a moral obligation to accept immigrants. Reciprocity so construed may imply certain obligations on the part of the country of origin (such as cooperation with potential recipient countries in discouraging illegal immigration). Both sides might agree that although a state has no duty to admit all aliens seeking entry, it has a qualified one to admit aliens when they pose no danger to the public safety, security, general welfare, or essential political and economic institutions of the recipient state. But even if both sides should agree at this point—even if they should agree that immigration problems require international solutions that inevitably place limits on sovereign discretion—neither side thereby agrees on specific solutions. Agreement that a community has a qualified duty to admit aliens provides no guidance in deciding whether these particular would-be immigrants should be allowed entry into this particular community at this time—or whether this specific community has a right to refuse these aliens, but not those. Here again we confront the problem of indeterminate norms in the form of criteria of selection.

Despite grounds for at least some agreement among contending parties, both examples readily exhibit disagreement. To overcome disagreement we need to answer the question, How in the context of widespread normative dissensus is any normative agreement possible? My answer applies the concept of enlightened localism. First, a policy on any given issue should prefer the more local to the less local, with the individual usually but not always viewed as the most local unit of all. Second, a policy is enlightened if it is a critical alternative to parochial localism. Thus civil rights still trump local practices and preferences, despite deference to local communities on a wide range of normative issues. Civil rights, because they are broader than local rights, are relatively "cosmopolitan" in comparison with the "parochialism" of local rights. Rights applicable locally may not be generalizable to the population as a whole.

Enlightened localism offers a broad, pluralistic notion of citizenship and other forms of communal membership. In this way it is well positioned to capture the normative heterogeneity so characteristic of modern societies. It might also withstand the inevasible strain between the individual's commitment to one worldview yet feelings of loyalty toward another. It might capture the unavoidable tensions between the multiplicity of settings necessary if different kinds of people are each to pursue what each understands, and differently understands, to be the good life.

We can examine in our two issues the application of enlightened localism to indeterminacies in public policy. I shall consider three indeterminate dimensions of policy, each a significant factor for both issues: the dimension of boundaries, of citizenship, and of rights.

THE INDETERMINATE DIMENSION OF BOUNDARIES

Matters of civil rights belong at levels of policy less local. Because they are inherently general or nonlocal in their claims to validity, propositions of civil rights contradict themselves when they vary by location. A public policy of enlightened localism might apply nonlocal standards or perspectives to egregious local cases of unacceptable practices harmful to groups or individuals, to citizens or resident aliens, because such practices very likely are beyond interpretive doubt, at least regarding their harmful nature legally defined. Thus in many countries and cultures the enduring problem of racism requires special consideration with respect to the role of nonlocal public authority. The principle of the child's best interest fails when it separates her or him from children of other races. It fails because it denies to the excluded person not only the equality of equal citizenship but fundamental respect as well. (It also damages the privileged person because the biased exclusion of others may impoverish him or her in ways cultural, cognitive, and moral.) On the one hand, racism calls for a local response, at a level where any remedy or its failure will be experienced directly by the primary participants. On the other hand, the social engineering of behavior—motivating citizens to behave in ways in which they are disinclined—defines a central function of nonlocal compulsion. The imperative that all families accept racial integration invokes a nonlocal principle to guide local behavior. In this sense civil rights are nonlocal: They require some localities to accept unwanted rules or otherwise to behave in ways rejected by the local population. As we have seen, a public policy of enlightened localism is open to such nonlocal imperatives and does not thereby contradict itself.

Matters of preference not impinging on the individual's civil rights (nor on those of others in the community) can be decided at levels more local. Take the issue of parental control over curricular choices in the child's school. Enlightened localist policies might define local community in terms of boundaries neither political nor geographic but rather pedagogic: in terms of educational purpose and perspective. Pedagogic community is constituted by shared interests, possibly including families of many different neighborhoods with differences in socioeconomic status, ethnicity, and so on. Members of the same geographic neighborhood who do not share the same pedagogic vision might join with members of other neighborhoods closer to their educational preference (ideally through free and voluntary busing).

Rights and obligations of citizenship concern various nonlocal levels of authority. Developing political and cultural citizenship is a vital concern of compulsory education, even as education is, in practice, a fundamentally local responsibility. Nonlocal interests in local education likely concern enforcing compliance at the local level, or nonlocal demands for equality of citizenship, or remedying specific failures and abuses at the local level. On enlightened localist grounds, nonlocal intervention in local education might be justified only when the child's civil rights require defense against prejudice or negligence at the local level. In that case prejudice and negligence would be defined nonlocally, and local definitions in conflict with nonlocal ones would be rejected.

We can expect nonlocal levels of public policy to respond to certain concerns or needs on which more local levels may not place a high priority, or where they might be recalcitrant with respect to nonlocal demands. On the other hand, it is precisely local levels that must respond to needs often ignored at nonlocal levels, such as language training for immigrants to the local community. Nonlocal levels focus more on ensuring universal access to basic education, for example toward realizing citizenship and, through increasingly advanced education, more thoughtful understandings of citizenship. The local level, by contrast, more appropriately focuses on incremental improvements in local education: education that responds to the specific needs of *these* specific children and *those* particular adults.

The spatial metaphor of enlightened localism entails normative boundaries. Normativity in any concrete and practical sense involves boundedness. Like spatial boundaries, normative boundaries may be open or closed. From the standpoint of enlightened localism, which eschews all forms of normative universalism except civil rights, a normative claim's validity depends at least in part on its formulation within a particular community's shared convictions or understandings. Within shared convictions means "within closed normative boundaries." On the other hand, both education and political participation can enlarge the participant's moral horizons by expanding the community's shared normative convictions or cultural understandings. Both education and political participation might well open normative boundaries. In short, normative boundaries may be closed or open. I shall examine each in turn.

NORMATIVE BOUNDARIES THAT ARE CLOSED

Autonomy is a norm central to education and immigration alike. As we earlier saw in this chapter, autonomy as a norm to guide communal organization is indeterminate. Consequently, community as an ideal is indeterminate because it seeks both to bind the individual to society and to provide him or her some degree of autonomy from society. How those two competing goals might be balanced with each other remains in question. As a norm or rule, autonomy concerns a particular aspect of sovereignty for communities and states. It also concerns an aspect of self-determination for minors subject to compulsory education. As a rule it finds expression in a guiding principle of enlightened localism: the more local trumps the less local (except in cases violative of civil rights, where personal autonomy invariably trumps communal autonomy). Autonomy involves normative boundaries that are closed, not open.

The value of autonomy in public policy is problematic. In compulsory education, after all, the child, its parents, or its educational counselor might not share this value. When they do not, they may regard the nonlocalist model as intrusive, as imposing "foreign" norms that are insensitive, perhaps contrary, to local ones. An autonomy characterized by completely closed boundaries defeats enlightened localism because it denies localism a base for engaging perspectives that reject the norm of autonomy. Consider: A family is no undifferentiated monad but a group of highly specific individuals not all of whose needs and interests can possibly agree or coincide; inevitably, some will block others or otherwise compete for satisfaction. Identity of interest with respect to material nurture differs significantly from identity with respect to cognitive and emotional nurture. The principle of acting in the child's best interests must therefore recognize the nonidentity of at least some interests between child and family. Within the family the child is a part of a larger whole, as any notion of familial integrity implies. Parental choice and child's interest cannot always coincide, and when they do not, favoring parental choice may sometimes harm the child. Because parental preferences are not necessarily or always best for the child, enlightened localism rejects completely closed boundaries in favor of boundaries closed only partially.[15]

Whereas civil rights favor the state–child relationship over the parent–child filiation, a policy of enlightened localism favors parents over the state: The more local generally trumps the less local. But not always; hence the preference for partially closed boundaries over ones completely closed. The immaturity of children, and their likely lack of relevant knowledge and experience in many of the contexts of daily life, as well as their underdeveloped capacity for identifying and articulating their own interests, renders them dependent for guidance on parents or on the state (if not on some institution between the respective levels of parent and state, or guidance shared between parent and state). Depending on its measure or degree, the immaturity of a rights-bearing child may vitiate or even defeat the child's autonomous realization of those rights (at least until she or he acquires greater knowledge, experience, and communicative competence). On the other hand, to recognize the best interests of the child is to recognize the nonidentity of interests among children of different ages, hence to distinguish standards of autonomy with respect to age and other plausible criteria of maturity. Such distinctions do not simply extend to younger children degrees of autonomy reasonably extended to older ones.

Increasing a school-age child's autonomy entails lowering the age at which some degree of independent choice begins. But increased autonomy for the child may be accompanied by extending parental involvement in the child's choice, indeed beyond points at which it may currently end. A higher-level student might be allowed to decide which subjects are electives (other than English, math, science, and history, and students might still choose from multiple offerings within these areas where available) or whether to elect vocational or academic education (or within academic education, whether to emphasize natural science or the humanities and the social sciences). At the same time, parents might participate in school choices beyond points at which they may now halt, for example with regard to curricular choices in the local schools (for instance, in the selection of some of the books read in language arts class, or in the selection from among competing texts about history, or how to approach instruction in religion or politics or human sexuality).

Consider the curricular concerns of deeply religious or fundamentalist parents. Like many nonfundamentalist parents, fundamentalist parents likely are concerned to transmit some of their most deeply felt convictions to their children. As public institutions, public schools generally strive to be religiously neutral (or, at most, vaguely mainstream theistic in their expression, as in the motto reproduced on American currency: "In God We Trust"). Burtt argues that American secular culture is materialistic and, as such, offends deeply religious parents who seek to "protect" their children from corresponding influences. The parents pursue a normative orientation different from that of secular culture (to "supply the child with the resources necessary to live a righteous life, to prevent as far as possible the corruption that can follow from too early or too overwhelming temptation to sin" [1994:63]). Burtt fails to see that precisely the secular nature of American culture provides a major source of religious tolerance (flowing from popularly accepted views such as the desirability of a separation of church and state). And she fails to observe that the robust materialism of American culture has hardly dampened religiosity in America. The argument she articulates as an authentic perspective of some deeply religious parents is weak because simplistic: It cannot discern that what it takes to be the enemy of religious faith could equally well explain how it is that America is such a hospitable place for persons of religious belief.

The kernel of truth in this argument is not that secular culture precludes religious faith, but that more conservative types of faith are challenged by competing secular views whose strength feeds on the political egalitarianism, and Enlightenment rationalism, typical of modern liberal constitutional states. Thus in societies such as the United States, public schools may promote equality of the sexes, and the curriculum may reflect the norm of sexual equality, for example in matters of employment, the workplace, and the family (in the form, say, of the two-career family). Burtt claims that, for most parents, such discussions carry "innocuous messages or positive moral lessons. They support these textbooks because the books' messages echo or at least do not disturb their own convictions. Those who see the specter of secular humanism in stories of . . . gender equality cannot be equally sanguine (ibid.)." Again, Burtt is insensible to the connection between the political egalitarianism that construes the sexes as intellectually, politically, and morally equal, on the one hand and, on the other hand, the political egalitarianism that neither champions nor discriminates against any particular faith. But she does articulate the anxiety plausibly felt by parents whose investment in the otherworldly claims of religion is challenged by a secular political and intellectual culture whose claims are solidly anchored in this world.

The challenge is real. Public institutions such as courts of law, schools, and the Internal Revenue Service rarely advert to what some persons of religious faith regard as "transcendent truths" as criteria for making decisions about citizens, for drawing distinctions among them, for adjudicating disputes between them. Research in sociology, political science, economics, psychology—and the perspectives of most political parties, for that matter—approach social problems, public policy, and moral dilemmas in secular, not religious, ways. Some persons of faith may feel left out of such approaches and the worldviews that inform them. More important, some persons may fear that their public school children are being led astray from what they, the parents, consider to be the best approach to such issues. Fundamentalists of this kind feel threatened by the secular world.

For its part, public education could serve the child both as member of society as a whole (as citizen) as well as a unique individual with particular gifts and needs and goals. Some communities (some religious fundamentalists, for example) might reject a curriculum that would facilitate the child's ultimate participation in the political life of his or her community and society and in making decisions about the best way to organize political life and approach its manifold problems. A society of political liberalism rejects any particular community that discourages its children from thinking about and discussing freely competing conceptions of life, and from choosing freely according to preference.[16]

Consider now the issue of immigration. Boundaries are closed by delimited territory and by membership defined in these geographic terms: persons outside those boundaries are not members. They are closed where states regulate the citizens' behavior through administrative and bureaucratic institutions, as in the modern welfare state: those institutions affect only members of that state, not citizens of other states. They are closed where states are governed by democratic means, where membership is a form of political entitlement: nonmembers are not entitled. They are closed where states secure civil rights for their citizens: nonmembers may enjoy certain rights but fewer rights than those enjoyed by members. Unrestricted immigration threatens each of these state-supported arrangements; it threatens citizenship, including the citizenship sought by immigrants. Democratic arrangements and citizenship are secured in part through closed boundaries. According to Rainer Bauböck, a "comprehensive concept of citizenship which contains individual as well as collective rights, civil and political as well as social rights can only be institutionalized within communities bounded both territorially and in terms of membership. In this way democratic citizenship reinforces the territorial segmentation of the global political system" (1994:19). A democratic community may aspire to public deliberation in which citizens participate in their legal self-determination: in the selection of representatives who legislate laws binding on all members of the community. But even here, citizenship is always "segmented": Citizenship in one place is distinct from citizenship in another, just as membership in one community hardly implies or entails membership in others. Neither democratic legitimation nor justice requires homogeneity among communities or among laws that apply in the same way to all communities.

Segmentation writ large describes the international political boundaries of nation-states. Within any nation-state, segmentation may describe boundaries less exclusive, where any given person's memberships are multiple. A citizen is a member simultaneously of a local community, a state or region or province, and a country, as well—but also of an occupational group, a political party, an ethnicity, a religious faith, and so on. Immigration concerns both types of segmentation. Overlapping memberships exist within the state, but a public policy of enlightened localism urges that some forms of membership be allowed to overlap state-based boundaries as well because some communities of rights (from private contracts to criminal sanctions for murder to international treaties among states) traverse such boundaries. In an increasingly global world, state-based membership could become a web of overlapping memberships as the space occupied by the public sphere expands beyond national boundaries and forms of democratic citizenship expand correspondingly. One example is dual citizenship; another is poly-citizenship; a third example is citizenship in supranational organizations, such as a European Union that became the primary locus of the individual's citizenship rather than his or her country; a fourth example is membership in the European Union simultaneously with membership in states beyond Europe, such as Israel or Canada.

Membership is nationally bounded where the needs of the resident population trump those of would-be residents—wherever the latter would impact, negatively, the conditions of life for current residents and citizens, for example by overburdening a community's resources in jobs, education, and medical care. Membership is not bounded nationally where citizenship exceeds state-based boundaries, although not necessarily all the way to "global citizenship as the political counterpart of the world economy" (Turner 1990:213). In a public policy of enlightened localism, membership is no longer bounded nationally when a country's welfare requires it to address some of the reasons for flight in the communities of departure, such as unemployment and poverty, epidemic illness, political repression, or religious persecution. Membership is not bounded nationally where the potential host bears some responsibility for the causes of immigration, or where potential immigrants have preexisting personal or collective ties to the target state (such as persons joining a close member of the family, say, a spouse or children, or those bound by ethnic, linguistic, religious, or other deep-seated identities). On humanitarian grounds, one could argue that membership may not be bounded nationally where the target state is better situated than other potential hosts to accept political refugees (if not limited numbers of persons seeking better economic opportunities). In these ways the indeterminate rules of membership can be made determinate.

One might argue that material value—money, goods, or services—offers an instrumental end to some means but not an end with a moral status in and of itself (unlike human beings, for example). In that case arguments for the unbounded flow of material value across national borders cannot be analogized to arguments for the free flow of humans. Immigrants would not be seen (at least not by liberal democratic states) merely as economic agents but rather as potential citizens, with potential rights and obligations of citizens, including the political, social, and economic benefits of citizenship. This design does not configure citizenship, potential citizenship, and immigrants primarily in terms of the receiving country's economic welfare.

NORMATIVE BOUNDARIES THAT ARE OPEN

Boundaries may also define, or demarcate, in ways that enlarge rather than restrict membership or inclusion of possible members. Citizenship can be as bounded as social and other forms of identity and it can be as broadening as public education, where education is understood as expanding the intellectual and other horizons of students by exposing them to viewpoints beyond those of the home, perhaps in ways ultimately enhancing the person's opportunities in life.[17] Bounded citizenship can be as broadening as education also in the sense of electoral representation where citizenship offers the enfranchised some measure of pursuing or realizing some of their social and political convictions and aspirations (even if only through elected representatives), a topic I explored in chapter 2 and to which I will return in chapter 6.

Wider rather than narrower horizons of citizenship hold out the promise (as does compulsory education) of a social order in which the arbitrary facts of familial or national origin are somewhat neutralized: in the sense of limiting the individual less than would otherwise be the case. Citizenship can equip citizens with enhanced political opportunities and legal resources to realize rights, pursue goals, satisfy needs, and transcend the social conditions of their birth. This possibility need not deny the cultural and other boundedness I spoke of earlier. Wherever possible, an enlightened localist policy would support broadened horizons for persons locally situated. Educational policy that endorses compulsory education is liberalizing in a way analogous to immigration policy that supports the movement of peoples from less liberal to more liberal forms of citizenship. A multiplicity of locally autonomous groups are more likely, the more liberal the polity, for example, in curricular choices made locally or where immigrants and the host community alike preserve aspects of their respective ways of life even as they accommodate some of the diverse ways of life around them. Local autonomy is less likely in the illiberal polity—in the sense, for example, that hierarchy, centralization, or traditionalism are not liberal ways of organizing a polity, and certainly not ways disposed to local forms of control and responsibility.

Social and political spheres of life imply each other. They even interpenetrate where, for instance, a community's political self-understanding impacts the social identity of individual citizens. Thus a secular democratic community might be more concerned with strictly legal equality than a religious community that, even if democratic, might seek theological or doctrinal rather than popular guidance on some issues of communal concern to both types of community, such as the teaching of religion in schools or the appropriate level of tolerance for religious dissenters or nonconformists or other "outsiders." To be sure, some types of public policy facilitate such interpenetration. Thus color-conscious public policy in, say, affirmative action in university admissions or the distribution of governmental contracts, understands itself as antiracist and would be so understood in whatever community that embraced it. There it would impact the social identity of both recipients (the social identity of persons previously discriminated against would now be enhanced) and observers, whose support for such a policy might affirm their solidarity with persons previously discriminated against.

Of course the political and normative identity of a liberal constitution will shift as the polity itself changes; as society organizes itself in new ways, it will render the indeterminate rules of the Constitution determinate in new ways. Many factors induce change in the polity, including the various consequences of immigration and naturalization (as well as developments in compulsory education). Spatial allegiances—allegiances that particularize individuals in territorial terms—are central to citizenship yet, by themselves, are inadequate for political life. Education can expand the intellectual horizons of students, just as immigration can expand the territorial horizons of citizenship (and quality of life). Both can expand a person's horizons beyond the contingencies of his or her birth. Immigration can expand the horizons of both immigrants and populations already resident: expansion in the sense not of extending the rights of citizenship across state boundaries, toward ending all domestic control of immigration, but of offering to immigrants a citizenship that is more than merely membership defined topographically. Expanded horizons of citizenship might mean sharing a common commitment to particular political structures, such as legal equality among citizens and significant local control over many communal affairs (as well as sharing, for example, the common language or languages in which political and social affairs are conducted and which facilitate popular participation). For native or nonnative residents, expanded horizons of citizenship might refer to ways in which their own citizenship could be enriched by immigrants—economically, culturally, or otherwise. One thinks of the vitality contributed by immigrant French Huguenots to Prussia, or to various African countries by immigrant Indians, or to various Southeast Asian countries by immigrant Chinese, or to various European and other countries by Jews. Political justice may obligate the host to naturalize at least some of those immigrants who enrich their adopted communities with their labor and knowledge, and perhaps sometimes even with their new perspectives on old communities.

Note that the abstract principle of autonomy, the indeterminate rule about autonomy, implies no consensus on the content of an educational minimum, or a specific curriculum that might be in the child's best interests, nor even agreement on clear and definite goals in literacy, numeracy, or basic information about the child's community and society. Nonlocal levels of public policy will leave many aspects of education (above a certain minimum) to the accident of a pupil's geographical location; to contingencies of local demographics (racially, culturally, ethnically); to local size (of living in a village rather than a metropolis, for instance); and to the chances of local wealth and the patterns of its distribution.

In public policy guided by enlightened localism, the relationship between local and nonlocal levels of authority might take the form of contract rather than regulation. A contract can realize a "horizontal" relationship (an association of equality) between local and nonlocal levels of authority. It provides an alternative to a "vertical" or hierarchical (or otherwise unequal) relationship. One or the other nonlocal level (say, state or federal) might award grants to a particular local level on a competitive basis for the best local proposal to address local goals (by the school board, for example, or by a group of parents or students, or some combination thereof). A contractual relationship between local and nonlocal levels and nonlocal grants to the local level and, in general, different agreements for different localities might encourage consent between local and nonlocal levels. It might encourage consent where "best" is defined through discussion between the levels rather than decisions simply imposed, hierarchically, by one level on the other. (The provision of social welfare might be constructed similarly along lines more contractual than hierarchical, but development of this idea would take us beyond the program of the present chapter.)

Let us extend this line of thought to our other example: privileges of the nonlocal community, in other words, where privileges of society as a whole accrue only to members of local or particular communities. On this account, persons who are not members of a society (tourists, transients, and others) should not receive membership in a state. Persons who could never be considered integratable members of a society should not be granted the right to freely enter the state that organizes and governs that society, nor should they be granted the right to reside in it permanently, free of ever being subject to expulsion. Rights of permanent residence and family reunification should extend only to those who are already members. These boundaries need not be rigid; indeed, the rapid expansion of communication and the concomitant expansion of public spheres, as well as a "growing interdependency within a global system due to an exponential increase of externalities of policies implemented at any level below the global one" (Bauböck 1994:16), call for more flexible boundaries, certainly with respect to immigration and emigration. And some outsiders should be allowed to become insiders. Some outsiders will be able to claim priority in access (alien spouses of insiders, for example), and those who cannot should be guaranteed fair procedures for competing for the limited number of entrances. Determining the size of that number should "address the root causes of poverty, unemployment, ecological disaster, mass disease, war and repression in sending states," as well as "co-ordinate a gradual extension of receiving capacities among target states" (ibid.:330). Any state that provides a right of exit creates potential burdens on at least one member of the community of nations, namely, whichever country becomes the host. For enlightened localist policy, any state's right of exit entails that the same state is obligated to allow entry to at least some persons or persons (especially, but not only, refugees) whose national membership places them at significant social or political risk. If the community of states allows a general right of exit, then it should take upon itself a general responsibility for refugees. More specific responsibility should be borne by states for a variety of reasons: those who are, in part, responsible for generating some of the reasons people seek to leave their country, such as war; those who are, in part, historically responsible for having created a colonial relationship, thereby having created a special relationship with the country of flight; those states with which the refugees have other kinds of special relationships, such as the presence of relatives who arrived before them.

THE INDETERMINATE DIMENSION OF CITIZENSHIP

The issues of compulsory education and immigration are related in their acute concern with citizenship: Immigration is a matter of becoming a citizen and, in a different sense, so is schooling. But a public policy of enlightened localism (one that copes with indeterminacy in rules of both citizenship and immigration) reveals dimensions beyond the previous rubric's question concerning opened or closed normative boundaries. Let us first consider citizenship as a function of education. Schooling may induct the young into a political culture. Immigration may induct outsiders into a new political culture—at best, in the same sense in which good schooling (at least in liberal democratic states) introduces students, critically, into democratic political culture. Preservation of a given political culture depends on inserting each new generation into that culture, even as it changes, and even in its multiple, contested interpretations. Its enhancement depends also on that induction—as well as on the further dimensions of admitting some outsiders to membership status.

Although individual motives will not necessarily find more respect in smaller rather than in larger democratic collectives, smaller collectivities may be better situated to recognize and respond to the unique voices and preferences of its constituents. For similar reasons, smaller collectivities may be more interested in meeting those preferences. This likelihood increases the more the local community is self-chosen and when decisions by any one member affect others. Such lights guide enlightened localist policy.

Citizenship in modern states contains within it a combination of agreement and disagreement among citizens and between citizens and other members of the polity. Not all forms of disagreement are socially deleterious; some may have socially positive consequences. A public policy of enlightened localism embraces forms of diversity and disagreement because it recognizes the advantages of always questioning the values and perspectives held by the majority (or otherwise defining for the status quo). Not only is consensus often empirically unlikely, it is not always desirable.

Diversity in norms and convictions is relevant to the question of which home environments best serve the child's interests, and which of those interests diverge from some of the cultural or normative links with the home. In the likely case that not all families share many of the perspectives of their community's majority, dissenting families will not freely embrace the majority's preferences. Overlapping educational cultures, goals, and understandings between the child's home and school can hardly be mandated by a majority. Majoritarianism is not a viable alternative to consensus.

Perhaps more than any other society-wide institution, schools offer venues for critically examining beliefs, values, and commitments. At more elementary levels of schooling, the potential for developing the student's critical cognitive capacity are smaller, but in any case the potential should increase significantly as the child progresses through subsequent levels of schooling. A strong notion of democratic (rather than, say, authoritarian) citizenship finds this desirable, not threatening. Enlightened localist policy advocates a citizenship that contributes to the goal of a child's increasing, and increasingly critical, autonomy. It opposes, then, Burtt's argument that "critical rationality can seem to some parents an education that might undermine their child's growth in grace. Parents would not want their child exposed to materials that offend their religious beliefs not because of some reflexive intolerance to the presentation of other views, but because they do not want their child corrupted by a premature or improperly mediated introduction to 'other forms of religion and to the feelings, attitudes and values of other students'" (1994:64). With this line of thought Burtt assumes the existence of different kinds of rationalities. And she assumes that the rationality of religions (whatever that might be) is less critical than secular rationality (whatever that might be). Enlightened localism takes a different approach, arguing that society at large should support rational political deliberation, if necessary against parochial communities.[18] Thus the state should support rational political deliberation (against parents, if necessary), including deliberation on competing ideas about how best to organize society and conduct one's life (even if deliberation includes discussion of perspectives that offend against those of the parents). And while enlightened localism supports homeschooling as a matter of deferring to local interests, it would require governmental oversight precisely to ensure that the parent-cum-teachers provided their children-cum-students perspectives beyond (and sometimes contrary to) those held by the parents. While the goal of having pupils consider new perspectives is more easily accomplished in public schools, it could also be pursued by means of professional oversight over homeschoolers.

Let us turn now to our other issue: the relationship between citizenship and immigration. Citizenship is a social good when it confers political and legal rights not available to noncitizens. On a global scale, citizenship in a constitutional democratic state is a very scarce good because only democratic states begin to provide and protect robust civil and other rights. Only here is something like equal citizenship possible, in the sense of equality before the law: ideally regardless of economic or social inequalities or racial or ethnic differences.

Restrictions on mobility would then seem tantamount to unequal citizenship. If freedom of movement within a state's boundaries creates a certain kind of equality among citizens, then freedom of movement between state boundaries might create a certain kind of equality among citizens of different countries. The distinction between citizen and alien then becomes somewhat less rigid because equality among citizens of different nations entails less inequality of citizen and alien. This line of thought makes the most sense at the level of legal equality. But material inequality among nations cannot be overcome simply through legal equality (indeed, some degree of economic wealth might constitute one condition for realizing legal equality). Citizens of poor countries constitute one kind of alien, and citizens of rich countries constitute another; the latter is socially and economically privileged, even as an alien, and quite unlike the former, hence Rainer Bauböck's suspicion that "immigration control seems to confirm that citizenship in liberal democracy is . . . a protection of relative privilege rather than a bundle of rights that appeal to universalistic values" (1994:330). In that case the liberal state, with its mostly closed boundaries, is basically a private club, in which case no one enjoys a prima facie right of immigration.[19] Citizens and aliens then are not equal, and some aliens are more privileged than others. Freedom of movement between state boundaries does not entail equal access of citizen and alien alike to domestic labor markets, and therefore it entails no redistribution of wealth among the various nations and regions of the world. Not until some supranational entity (or entities) regulates domestic labor markets instead of national states (one model is suggested by the goals, not yet realized, of the European Union) will substantive—and not only formal or legal—equality among citizens of different nations become possible.

As a condition for the naturalization of immigrants in a liberal democratic state, the host community following a public policy of enlightened localism may expect would-be citizens to consent to existing practices in political culture, and to constitutional principles as well. It may expect citizens to recognize and respect existing boundaries, which also means that it may expect most immigrants to commit to naturalization. Of course immigrants are likely to be more committed to their host country the more their legal rights and status approach those enjoyed by citizens.

But a public policy of enlightened localism will not demand acculturation to the point of identity with native citizens. To be sure, consent to constitutional principles nonetheless implies aspects of identity. Indeed, it implies cultural identity in the sense of political culture. For immigrants it implies some degree of political and cultural resocialization if the immigrants come from lands that do not share the host community's constitutional principles and political-cultural practices.

THE INDETERMINATE DIMENSION OF RIGHTS

Of course public policy always implies one or another rule or norm of citizenship, and specific rules of citizenship entail certain rights, including rights both individual and collective: the right of collectivities to regulate entrance, the right of individuals to exit collectivities, and, more problematical, the right of some outsiders to enter, as well as for some entrants to become citizens. Public policy confronts three different sets of indeterminate norms: rights among equals, rights among unequals, and equality among communities.

Rights Among Equals

Enlightened localism offers itself as a critical alternative to parochial localism. Parochial localism in political contexts is characterized by the individual's uncritical, perhaps unthinking, sharing of the sympathies and antipathies of a particular locale, whether physical and concrete (a country, for example) or symbolic and abstract (say, adherence to a particular religious faith). Enlightened localism is also a theory of boundedness with respect to the civil rights of citizenship. It is a conception of access to participation in the political process, as well as a notion of protection from the arbitrary or unlawful exercise of governmental power. Integrating new citizens into the polity means integrating them into these rights, rights that entail that qualified candidates for political participation be provided opportunities to satisfy the requirements for participation, for example through naturalization. Such rights of citizenship are rights among equals, or plausibly among those who might be allowed to become legal equals.

Rights among equals figure in our other issue as well. Public policies of enlightened localism might deliberate the issue of compulsory schooling through a combination of coercion and cooperation between local and nonlocal levels of public policy. They would invoke nonlocal authority (always a potential source of coercion) when local behavior, policies, or remedies violate the Constitution. Only in such cases would nonlocal policy regularly trump local policy. Such an arrangement of jurisdiction is analogous to the doctrine of constitutionalism, which places certain rights beyond local and majoritarian adjudication. This arrangement also provides one aspect of a certain check and balance between local and nonlocal levels of public authority. Here, again, the nonlocal trumps the local.

We observe an additional aspect of check and balance when the local trumps the nonlocal. A common problem of indeterminacy arises from interpretive differences over what rules mean in the area of dispute and how properly to apply them there. An ever-present question is, Which level of legal interpretation should decide: the local or the nonlocal? Except in cases involving civil rights (but also, as I argued under the preceding rubric, where society at large must support rational political deliberation when necessary against parochial communities), a public policy of enlightened localism would grant policy makers at the local level the privilege of enforcing their interpretation over that of nonlocal policy makers. Nonlocal legal and political pressure would still be needed to correct educational systems operated in a manner violative of civil rights, or that stymied rational political deliberation. Absent such violations, local policy makers would not apply nonlocal judgments or perspectives to the local community. Policy makers would engage only local answers to determine the best options for any given pupil.

RIGHTS AMONG UNEQUALS

Local and nonlocal levels of public policy are never equal, although a public policy of enlightened localism allows each under different circumstances to be stronger than the other. In the relationship between local and nonlocal levels, the enforcement of rights by nonlocal policy entails not flexibility but rigidity (at least for the moment, or at least in this particular connection). Here the nonlocal compels the local to conform to the nonlocal. Nonlocal intervention at local levels of education is more likely to concern provisions for equal citizenship than the development or implementation of new programs, or higher standards in existing programs.

Some issues of civil rights may require nonlocal pressure to be applied at the local level of public policy to encourage local levels to behave in ways they may resist. Some behavior may never be changed except through coercion. (The fight against racism in the United States, the struggle to interpret the indeterminate rule of formal equality in ways that further substantive equality, was aided effectively by the intervention of the Supreme Court, which prohibited racial segregation in pubic schools[20] even as a majority of Americans supported such segregation at the time, yet two decades later came to support racial integration.) Here nonlocal levels of public policy could play a special and irreplaceable role in bringing about remedial changes in political community.

Both education and immigration reveal a disjointed citizenship or unequal forms of citizenship among groups that are hardly outsiders. In the case of education, minors are excluded from some forms of political participation, such as voting or determining the curriculum of their compulsory education, even as they are accorded (and, with time, increasingly accorded) individual rights in other areas. In the case of immigration, some immigrants might be considered "citizens" in a sense social but not legal or political. Immigrants of this sort may include resident aliens who are part of the local labor force, pay local taxes, send their children to local schools, and patronize local merchants. In enlightened localist policy, a resident alien's communal membership might be extended to citizenship, not only in the sense of rights of family reunification or permanent residence but also in the sense of rights of citizenship.

Equality Among Communities

Perhaps only wealthy states, and in particular wealthy liberal states, can afford (and might even be inclined) to provide the resources and opportunities of such citizenship. Such states constitute a small minority of the world's sovereign countries. Rights of citizenship could neutralize the accidents of birth and offer the individual citizen opportunities and resources to better his or her social position. Such rights are the strongest, and the most meaningful, within democratic institutions, which provide for "citizenship" quite beyond simple membership in a nation–state, for example, citizenship as membership in a self-determining community of legal equals. But democratic institutions do not exist on a global scale; indeed, they are bounded in part precisely to protect them from an undemocratic and economically impoverished environment. Some people in the latter environment will be potential immigrants, their numbers likely always to exceed the potential hosts' capacities and readiness to receive and accept. The nationally bounded regulation of labor markets and the regulation of conditions of employment imply significant and enduring restrictions on immigration. Completely open access could endanger both the political and the economic integrity of the potential host.

Here the boundedness of citizenship protects relative privilege vis-à-vis the international environment: "Just as the 'haves' within a nation tend to resist when the 'have nots' make their claims to equal citizenship, so the sharp division of rich nations and poor nations bodes ill for the evolution of a sense of global public interest as a foundation for a 'federation' of Open Republics. Full membership in the community of States is like full citizenship within a nation: no dependent State can hope to be a full member" (Karst 1994:70). Of course in a liberal democracy the protection of such privilege for some, and the exclusion of others from privilege, stands in tension with democratic norms of equality at the level of the individual nation, or at the rare level of regional alliances among relatively similar nations, most notably today the European Union. The imperatives of the world economy may be global, but those of political and social privilege tend to be more local.[21] And democratic states in particular, above all the Western industrialized states facing large-scale immigration,

> cannot ignore the concerns of the electorate. Since they are complex bureaucracies, they cannot ignore the concerns of civil servants or organized pressure groups either. . . . No state can afford to pursue a policy that does not promise clear benefits to enough of its constituents, if not immediately, then in the near future. Doing good for the world at large . . . must be associated with the probability of the people at home doing

well—or at least doing better than otherwise would be likely." (Scanlan 1994:107)

With the ever-increasing mobility of populations, a policy of enlightened localism in liberal polities must address ways in which bounded citizenship might be extended, yet without damaging the sustainability of current benefits of citizenship. Material inequalities among countries, as well as the fact that some are more closed culturally (Russia and Japan, for example) than others (such as the United States or Canada), limit—but do not preclude—the effectiveness of enlightened localism.

PUBLIC POLICY AND THE INDETERMINATE RULE OF LEGAL EQUALITY

To return from the sphere of international relations to the abiding domestic example of this book, the pursuit of racial justice in a racist society, and the relative merits of color blindness and color consciousness to that end: What might public policy in the spirit of enlightened localism entail? Consider racially preferential treatment in hiring or firing faculty at a public high school (which, in comparison with affirmative action, involves special, temporary, and nongeneralizable measures necessary to prevent discrimination against disadvantaged or underrepresented groups). Could one qualification among others for a position legitimately include race, such that in a tie between a black and a white person (who are equally qualified by all other criteria), black would break the tie in hiring or firing?

Reflect again on the three questions asked of an enlightened localist approach in the previous chapter. First: What need or interest is to be satisfied? The answer is fairness, specifically fairness in a society of institutionalized unfairness, and in this case as nondiscrimination in hiring or firing. Nondiscrimination gives equal consideration to all qualified candidates, so that the person hired is the most qualified. Some qualifications for some positions may legitimately include social purposes. Given the goal of racial justice in a society still racist, one social purpose is changing society in the direction of equality of opportunity regardless of ascriptive characteristics such as race. Toward creating the basic conditions for such a society, preference might be given to qualified African American candidates over better qualified nonblack candidates (in a school or department in which there would otherwise be no black teachers). For color itself can be one qualification (but only one among many) for a teaching position at a public school if the teacher's being black can facilitate the purpose of the teaching position, where that purpose (according to the local school board) includes breaking down racial stereotypes, specifically where black teachers can serve as role models for black children (teaching them what they can aspire to) as well as to white children (demonstrating one important way in which black citizens are valuable contributors to society).

Second: What would be a decentered standpoint distinct from particular perspectives or self-seeking urges? The localist nature of the answer lies in its contextual character: It cannot be generalized for all groups, at all times. Its advisability would depend on specific cases, for example only as a tiebreaker between two equally qualified candidates. Its legitimacy would derive from the manner of determining the set of qualifications for hiring; for example as the result of open, transparent, ongoing democratic deliberation by persons authorized to make the decision (such as a school board). The policy would be temporary and always reviewable, to be abandoned when social conditions had been created in which race would be irrelevant in best providing for disadvantaged students of any color. It would be tailored to discriminate against relatively advantaged persons and rejected if it discriminated against individuals who were relatively disadvantaged. And it would compensate those individuals disproportionately burdened by the social purpose of creating a society of equality of opportunity regardless of race.

Third: What relations of reciprocity already exist among contending parties or viewpoints? On the one hand, proponents of color blindness as well as proponents of color consciousness support the notion of social justice as social fairness; both oppose discrimination, if in different ways. On the other hand, advocates and critics of preferential hiring practices alike reject the notion of hiring unqualified candidates, even as they disagree on what is to be included or excluded from the set of qualifications.

Disagreement among people who nonetheless stand in some degree of reciprocity follows in part from different moral understandings and in part from different understandings of the proper relationship, in a secularized society, between law and morality in the public sphere. The next chapter continues this book's general quest for an enlightened localist response to indeterminate norms. The peculiar contribution of the following chapter will be to address the relationship between law and morality, finding parallels between that relationship and the connection between social structure and human agency, as well as between color consciousness and color blindness in public policy. By doing so, it will complete the task I set for myself of displaying in this book at least three (of many possible) venues for practical applications of coping in politics with indeterminate norms.

CHAPTER 6
Enlightened Localism in Law and Morality

This book has repeatedly taken up the example of disadvantages that flow from membership in a multiply disfavored race. This chapter sustains that focus by picking up the theme of chapter 2, not so much with respect to proceduralism (which chapter 2 developed as a major feature of coping in politics with indeterminate norms) as with regard to a color-conscious public policy. Chapter 2 argued for a color-conscious approach to designing electoral districts in response to racial injustice in a political system that concentrates the benefits of elections in white majorities. This chapter develops this idea further by showing that, ultimately, color consciousness and color blindness are complementary in ways that social structure and human agency, as well as law and morality, are also complementary. Each of these three combinations—and this chapter will show that these three pairs are analogous to each other and therefore comparable—allow for an enlightened localist approach to political action under circumstances of normative indeterminacy. In this sense Niklas Luhmann locates political modernity in a society's "capacity for 'action' [that can] only be sustained through politics. One or a few must act for all, and they must be obliged and bound (how else?) through morality and law. Thus, down through the modern period, the peculiar amalgam of morality, law and politics remained the dominant focus for reflection on society" (1982:337).

In chapter 2 I argued that color-blind configurations of electoral districts can realize equal voting power in one form only: where each citizen casts an equally weighted vote. But in liberal constitutional states today politics is effective less in the form of the individual enfranchised citizen than in the form of group politics. With respect to the latter form of politics, color-conscious districting aims both at increasing the number of African American legislators (or, more precisely, by making it more possible for those who wish to elect African American representatives to have a viable opportunity to do so), and at composing legislatures favorable to the interests of the black community, particularly efforts against racial injustice in legislative priorities. Where black Americans have a better chance at electoral success—through color-conscious districting— representation of blacks in the legislature will increase and so, too, will representation of a political commitment to using legislative means to overcome racial injustice, a goal that black citizens can further also by electing nonblack candidates who share this commitment. (Thus the goal of color-conscious districting is not the simple numerical one of electing blacks to Congress in numbers proportionate to their presence among all enfranchised citizens.) Even though racial injustice is not an issue that belongs to any particular racial group, racial minorities that have suffered most from such injustice surely are among those sectors of society most concerned with the issue. In a society where race impacts powerfully many aspects of the individual's experiences and opportunities, initial positions in life (such as parents' level of education and socioeconomic status), as well as her or his chances over the entire course of a lifetime, color consciousness is directly relevant to the politics of justice, as I shall show.

The politics of justice is normative in the multiple ways I will explore in this chapter. It is also indeterminate, in part because the social phenomenon of race is itself indeterminate in the following sense: Race "exists," but that existence is variable, interpretive, and multi-edged; thus race is at once an instrument of oppression and an instrument of solidarity that can be mobilized against oppression. To advocate color-conscious electoral districting, then, is to invoke race in two senses each opposed to the other—as the problem (race qua racism) but also as the solution (a solution mediate if not ultimate)—where members of oppressed groups self-identify as a racial group, where they themselves determine that identity in positive ways, generating solidarity within the group (and potentially with other, like-minded groups) toward political action as a group, in electoral and legislative efforts against negative stereotypes and other forms of racism. A racist society imposes the strategic necessity of "racing justice," that is, of pursuing ultimately color-blind justice by color conscious means (as I shall argue at the end of this chapter). Under these circumstances, color-neutral public policy can only perpetuate a racist form of color consciousness.

An enlightened localist approach treats the normative indeterminacy of race, and the moral indeterminacy of color consciousness, first by treating race and race consciousness differently in different circumstances. It does so by creating positive racial identities and by rendering political participation in elections a viable means for the victims of racism themselves to pursue justice and equality in legislation for all citizens. In this spirit Amy Gutmann cogently argues that "when race consciousness flows from the experience of identification as a member of an oppressed group, it also serves to unite members of the group to struggle against their oppression," such that "race consciousness among oppressed peoples often leads to the creation of vibrant and valuable cultures (importantly plural, not singular), as it has in American history. These cultures, while associated with the experience of oppression, take on a highly valued life of their own, primarily but not only for the descendants of the people whose oppression first and foremost informed the culture" (1996:166–167). But she is quite mistaken when she would somehow "decouple racial identity from the color consciousness that is necessary for unity in the struggle against racial oppression" (ibid.:167).

Color consciousness can only be a matter of racial identity because the object of racism is never "color" as such, but always this or that specific conventional "color." Even then it is not the actual color that counts—Homer Adolphe

Plessy of the landmark case *Plessy v. Ferguson*[1] was white in color—but the race. Thus in 1896 the Supreme Court of the United States was satisfied that "legal equality"—understood in the parochially localist sense of the unexamined customs, mores, and usages of a population that clearly benefited white people and clearly degraded and disadvantaged black citizens—required the chromatically white Mr. Plessy of the Negro race to find accommodation solely in those public carriages intended by management for members of the black race—whatever the range of pigmentation among individual members of that race.

LAW AND MORALITY AS TRANSFORMERS OF STRUCTURE AS CONFINING, INTO STRUCTURE AS ENABLING

In this context an enlightened localist approach to coping with indeterminacy proceeds along three parallel tracks (each comprising one section of this chapter). As we shall see, these tracks display the complementarity of social structure and human agency, of law and morality, and of color consciousness and color blindness.

Structure/agency, law/morality, and color consciousness/color blindness are three major forces of macrosocial integration today (three among many). They are related to each other as organizing features of society. Each is one such feature; each is related to the others in a continuum of ways of composing society, from levels more general to ones more specific. Structure and agency are the most general of the three features; law and morality are less general; and color consciousness and color blindness are less general still.

Structure and agency come always paired: the individual experiences both noncontingency, in her or his social environment, as well as contingency, in his or her competent behavior in that environment. Law and morality also always come paired: legal norms need morality for ultimate grounding, whereas law enforces norm-conformative behavior where moral norms are not adequately anchored in citizens' hearts and minds. Color blindness and color consciousness always come paired as well. From the standpoint of racial equality, where color consciousness imposes a hierarchy of chromatic value, color blindness recommends itself; and where color blindness does not allow for self-identifying racial groups to construct solidarities both to create positive self-images and to advocate for legitimate group interests, there color consciousness recommends itself. The fact that each of these three organizing features of society always come paired means that coping in politics with indeterminate norms does not assume the simplistic form of an either/or choice: either structure as oppressive (where ascription to a collective identity denies individual autonomy) or structure as enabling (where collective identity is a means to realizing individual rights and liberties); either law as the a-moral liberalism of a primarily economic community or law as the deeply moral republicanism of a primarily ethical community; either color consciousness as racism or color consciousness as affirmative self-determination.

Of these three pairs of organizing features, I shall emphasize law and morality because law and morality provide the medium through which structure as confining can be transformed into structure as enabling, which means: through which color consciousness as facilitative of racism can be transformed into color consciousness as facilitative of racial equality. The translation of structure into enablement, and of racial consciousness into consciousness of racial equality, generates empowerment within an enlightened localist approach to coping in politics with indeterminate norms—not in the form of an either/or choice, but in the form of a both/and approach—because social structure like individual agency and because color consciousness like color-blindness carries more than one valence simultaneously. Here enlightened localism approaches law and morality as a "translator": between structure and agency and between color blindness and color consciousness. A democratically self-determining society can make normative choices among options by drawing on this transformative power of law and morality: in what instances to prefer structure over agency (for example, when to prefer the principle of constitutionalism over the principle of democratic theory) or when to prefer color consciousness over color blindness (for example, when messages from a racially oppressed group would fall on deaf legislative ears if phrased in color-blind terms). In coping with indeterminate norms, normative choices among structural and agential options—normative choices between the citizen's social identity constructed in terms of one set of collective identities rather than another (for example, race constructed in *this* way rather than *that*)—can only be written in the language of law and morality.

I shall begin with the complementarity of structure and agency as a roundabout approach to a second complementarity, that of law and morality, which in turn can be applied to choosing between color-conscious and color-blind approaches to public policy.

STRUCTURE AND AGENCY

I begin by drawing on Anthony Giddens's concept of the "duality of structure," showing how structure is at once both constraining and enabling. By this means I shall argue that color consciousness is constraining or oppressive as well as enabling and a means to racial justice. By "structure" I refer to rules and resources "organized as properties of social systems" (Giddens 1994:66). Structure often mightily inclines the individual agent and his or her social environment simultaneously (although in neither case exhaustively, given for example the unintended consequences of action). A duality of structure lies in the "essential recursiveness of social life, as constituted in social practices: structure is both medium and outcome of the reproduction of practices. Structure enters simultaneously into the constitution of the agent and social practices, and 'exists' in the generating moments of this constitution" (ibid.:4–5). The duality of structure captures the mutual dependence of structure and agency, the fact that structure is both enabling and constraining. Duality explains how it is that the individual experiences both noncontingency in his or her social environment as well as contingency in his or her competent behavior in that environment. When, for example, we learn a language, we experience a language's systematic, noncontingent, social character (either we understand and use shared understandings of grammar and syntax, or we don't). But when we use language to express our own meanings, intentions, and ideas, we experience language's specific, contingent, and individual character (for example the poetic license of e.e. cummings proceeds on the basis of a good grasp of standard grammar and syntax). As competent speakers we experience the "'rule-governed creativity' of sentence formation in the day-to-day use of language" (ibid.:17).

In somewhat similar fashion, race as a social phenomenon is normatively indeterminate because it is ambivalent, possessed of two mutually exclusive values: as something oppressive as well as something that can facilitate individual autonomy in a political sense. Race can be and has been socially oppressive, even as it entails nothing relevant in political liberalism to the distribution of basic liberties or opportunities; even as it entails no natural differences and no differences that imply either moral attributes or moral deficiencies; even as it entails no genetic differences that justify the kinds of classifications we in the United States are long familiar with (for example, in the choices offered us by the government to describe ourselves on the national census as black, white, American Indian or Alaskan native, Asian or Pacific Islander). Racial identity can be oppressive for all members of a racial group even though it does not suggest that all members have the same political preferences, commitments, or beliefs, or that all members would support the same candidates for public office, or that only legislators who come from that group can serve its interests. In these ways individual members of a disfavored racial group experience their racial identity as an oppressive structure, for which they are not responsible, yet which they cannot control.

Against this oppressive structure in the form of collective identities, political liberalism constructs politics first and foremost as a politics of individualism—associating the state directly with the individual rather than with any of the groups of which the individual is a member (just as it constructs private economic relations among citizens as relations among freely contracting individuals). To be sure, politically liberal states also allow for distinctions among groups. Thus in the United States only citizens can vote, women are not subject to a military draft, felons lose the right to vote, and Native Americans have a direct relationship to the federal government, unmediated by any of the several states. Against oppressive structure in the form of collective identities, political liberalism allows each individual considerable latitude for self-definition in his or her worldview, political orientation, occupation, consumption preferences, place of residence, religious faith, intimate associations, and whether to have children, but in principle also:

whether one views oneself as, say, a "generic American" or instead as a member of a particular ethnic or cultural or some other group (as a Korean immigrant, say, or as a Evangelical Christian, or as a self-identified Creole). Defining oneself in terms of individual identity entails a distinction between an "authentic" self—who one really is (here we have structure that enables)—and an "inauthentic" self—an identity one rejects for oneself (here we have structure that oppresses). A politically conservative homosexual may reject for himself or herself the cultural understanding of homosexuals displayed by radical gay rights organizations (the same collective identity can be oppressive for one member, emancipatory for another). A gay person may reject the insistence of her or his environment (in the workplace, the military, as a member of the clergy) that she or he deny or submerge that identity, unlike heterosexuals who are free to publicly acknowledge their sexual orientation (thus the individual is oppressed when he or she is denied a desired collective identity). A Hispanic person with no interest in his or her Hispanic ascription prefers to be perceived in ethnically "neutral" terms (thus one might reject a collective identity even though one does not feel oppressed by it), whereas another might wish to emphasize that identity. The politics of authenticity are the politics of self-identification: structure as enabling not confining. Self-identification involves a politics of recognition, of public acknowledgment of one's choice, the choice of one's authentic identity.

Whether oppressive or enabling, there is no alternative to structure: In one way or another the individual's self, authentic or otherwise, is embedded always in this or that collective identity, and more likely in several collective identities: from ethnicity to race to socioeconomic status and religious belief to occupational group and political leaning. Anthony Appiah writes

> It is, among other things, my being, say, an African-American that shapes the authentic self that I seek to express. And it is, in part, because I seek to express my self that I seek recognition of an African-American identity. . . .[R]ecognition as an African-American means social acknowledgment of that collective identity [indeed] not just recognizing its existence but . . . demonstrating respect for it. If . . . I see myself as resisting white norms, mainstream American conventions, the racism (and, perhaps, the materialism or the individualism) of "white culture," why should I . . . seek recognition from these white others? (1996:94)

Here we can identify structure as something emancipatory only by defining it in opposition to structure as something oppressive. We then define authenticity as that which rejects social convention. To recognize structure in the one sense is to reject structure in the other sense.

Hence the legal recognition of a group identity—in the sense of color-conscious public policy—can oppress the individual member, or it can enable him or her to resist oppression. Race is an oppressive structure in which the ascription of a group identity imposes on the individual member certain normative and descriptive expectations in terms of which people treat the individual despite, and contrary to, his or her self-understanding. Ascription generates a kind of "cultural geneticism," free riding on the basis of structure: "[Y]ou earn rights to culture that is marked with the mark of your race or your nation—simply by having a racial identity" (ibid.:90), as though every Greek (which is not a racial group, of course) the tourist meets in Athens today personally built the Parthenon; as though all Asian American students excelled in math; as though all young African American men were the kinds of violent predators one reads about in the daily newspaper.

Individual identity in one sense refers to morally significant features in terms of which only individuals, never groups, might be identified: in terms of intelligence or stupidity or sympathetic traits such as kindness, humility, and patience (or unsympathetic ones such as greed, cruelty, indifference, selfishness, and arrogance). None of these qualities serves as the basis for collective identities; none characterizes a recognizable social group in the sense that would allow us to advocate, in a culturally plausible sense: Affirmative action for the gullible. A public march affirming the witty as deserving of respect. Civil recognition of the domestic unions of charming people. Visitation rights for the spouses of avaricious persons. Concentrated electoral districts for the morally insightful, if not for the emotionally obtuse. If treated as ascriptive characteristics of identifiable groups, such features would be experienced as either oppressive or simply bizarre.

By contrast, *collective identity* can refer to "culture" in the sense that every person is a kind of cultural "artifact," is cultured just as he or she is also "sexed," "raced," and "classed." Collective identity then appears as this or that shared culture: martial arts, say, as culturally Asian American; jazz as culturally African American; Constitution-drafting as culturally European American. Structure is not oppressive when race-based cultural identity is a source of individual and collective flourishing, of diversity, of enrichment, of meaning for members and nonmembers (if cognoscente) alike. Race-based collective identity of this kind is a social good, hence its elision through cultural homogenization impoverishes society as a whole. Here governmental recognition and support through public policy would be akin to funding by the National Endowment for the Humanities for art or literature or essays of a racially self-identifying but nonracist nature, or the promotion of national identity (Billie Holiday as cultural ambassador to American allies), or to the formation of youth through school curricula (inclusion of Toni Morrison's novels in high school English courses). On the other hand, structure is oppressive when race-based cultural identity reduces individual identity to collective culture, in the sense of stereotyping or "scripting" the individual according to expectations deriving not from a particular individual identity but solely from membership in a particular group, community, or culture.

Of course different members of the same group may well be differently related to, or have different relationships with, the culture ascribed to them collectively. Those relationships may shift over time. And of course individuals are creatures and creations and consumers of multiple cultures simultaneously. One need not be Chinese American to enjoy Sichuan cuisine, or a black American to play the blues, or Native American to be guided by forms of spirituality practiced by peoples indigenous to the United States.[2]

Structure and agency mutually condition each other when identity requires both a "sender" (the carrier of the identity) and a "receiver" (someone who recognizes the identity in some fashion not wholly different from the carrier's self-understanding). For example, structure in the form of a collective identity involves "white society's" recognition of a black identity in the sense that black identity is "centrally shaped by American society and institutions: it cannot be seen as constructed solely within African-American communities. African-American culture, if this means shared beliefs, values, practices, does not exist: what exists are African-American cultures, and though these are created and sustained in large measure by African-Americans, they cannot be understood without reference to the bearers of other American racial identities" (Appiah 1996:95-96).

Structure is oppressive when collective identities subsume the individual in large categories, that is, when the individual loses his or her uniqueness, only finding recognition in terms of being an exponent or exemplar of some group: as if this banker were first and foremost a woman (because she happens to be female) or that lawyer were above all African American (because he happens to be black) or that writer were most significantly homosexual (because she happens to be a lesbian) or that politician above all were an Arab American (because he happens to be the son of immigrants from Egypt). Here the categories "female," "black," "homosexual," and "Arab American" are structures that defeat the individualist cast of the "authentic self."

Structure can also be oppressive when self-identification as a member of a group is not in fact voluntary, when ascription to a collective identity denies individual autonomy: "By the time the vast majority of Americans fill out the census forms, enrollment forms for schools, application forms for jobs, and governmental mortgage, scholarship, and loan forms asking what race we and our children are, we have been told the answer by the way we have been treated ever since we were too young to choose for ourselves" (Gutmann 1996:116). But even when oppressive, group identification may not be entirely so; it can be oppressive in part, but it can also be enabling in part; in fact, structure and agency are always intertwined. Many collectivities—certainly racial groups—share no specific set of beliefs or values, commitments or knowledge, even as society often perceives each group as having some common culture, carried by each of its individual members. On the other hand, group identities sometimes make a good deal of sense, and when they do, it is because they are acquired socially, not genetically, when group identity for the individual member is both structure and agency, that is, has both oppressive and enabling properties simultaneously. Identity can be structural in some ways: For example, no one chooses his or her skin color, and no one chooses the social significance or cultural valence of his or her skin color.

In a larger sense still, no one in society is free to completely invent him- or herself. Structure is present when the ingredients of any self we might want to construct for ourselves are mined from stores already provided by the society and culture of which we already are a part, in which we are competent, through which we have whatever knowledge we have. Our agency lies in our capacity to make choices; structure lies in the boundedness of those choices, in the fact that although we choose among options, we do not choose the set of options in terms of which we choose: we paint only with a pre-given palette of colors. The group creates the individual, or rather the individual is generated "dialogically" not "monologically"; agency derives from structure, in the sense that the individual's capacity to choose and self-determine is only possible against the background of structure, the background of group-identity: "[I]t is in dialogue with other people's understandings of who I am that I develop a conception of my own identity"; "my identity is crucially constituted through concepts (and practices) made available to me by religion, society, school, and state, and mediated to varying degrees by the family," such that "dialogue shapes the identity I develop as I grow up: but the very material out of which I form it is provided, in part, by my society," by "its language in 'a broad sense'" (Appiah 1996:95).[3]

We once again observe that structure and agency always come paired. We know structure where we are no more free to make ourselves up than we are able to control the meanings that other people attach to our features, our characteristics, our choices. We are limited, as agents, by structure: We may well reject a particular characteristic beyond our control, and by which we are identified by others; we may wish ourselves more intelligent or physically attractive; we may wish (like Nietzsche) that our native tongue were some other.[4] But amid this structure we may still exercise agency, at least when we can reject the meaning or significance that others attach to that characteristic (such as the racist's attribution of moral and cultural inferiority to a particular race or skin color). Precisely because structure and agency are paired, color consciousness (as an element in public policy) is double-edged: It imposes some degree of structure on us even as it still provides us some degree of agency.

Race in a "raced" world is so much a part of our everyday experience that we cannot ignore race, or racial meanings; and race consciousness inevitably imposes certain "scripts" or expectations on us that we are bound to recognize and to be recognized by. In light of historical experience, then, we do not expect Asian Americans to be members of the Ku Klux Klan, just as we don't expect klansmen to be Mexican immigrants, just as we don't expect Mexican immigrants to be at the forefront of the Gay Rights movement. At the same time, color consciousness affords significant degrees of freedom in how we work with that structure, in how we interpret individual autonomy with respect to race, in the messages we send, particularly as a group. As mediated by agency, structure is fluid not static, and thus color consciousness can be both oppressive and enabling. We Americans redefine the image of African Americans when we elect blacks to Congress, in this way identifying blacks with the American government rather than only in marginalized opposition to it. Color consciousness can imply a hierarchy of chromatic value or moral capacity, but it need not. Color consciousness can be defined in terms of division, inequality, and tyranny but equally in terms of social justice, legal equality, and civic fairness.

The fact that structure and agency always come paired means that we never confront the simple bivalent choice: either color consciousness as racism (and nothing else) or color consciousness as affirmative self-determination (and nothing else). Color consciousness carries more than one valence simultaneously, for example in the claim that "black citizens—although as varied in political views and interests as whites—tend to support programs that improve opportunities in education, employment, health care, housing, and child care for individuals in need far more than do whites. Black citizens also distrust government more than do white citizens, perceiving it to be 'white-run' in a way that neglects their basic interests" (Gutmann 1996:155). And color consciousness sends more than one message in the question, When we "advocate that government should take one stance toward race and individuals another . . . what message is conveyed to individuals about their own identities when government distributes benefits and burdens on the basis of race? Or . . . what are the implications for concerted political action by oppressed minorities when we downplay the role of race in individual identity?" (Wilkins 1966:15). We can capture this ambivalent quality of color consciousness (itself a kind of indeterminacy) by analyzing it in the distinctly normative terms of law and morality.

LAW AND MORALITY

The tension between structure and agency, between the constraints that color consciousness places on all who invoke it, on the one hand, and the significant degrees of agential freedom we have in our use of color consciousness, on the other hand, demonstrates that agents not only passively internalize social norms but also actively manipulate them. Individuals can assume a calculative attitude toward norms: "[A]n actor may 'calculate the risks' involved in . . . a given form of social conduct," for example the "likelihood of the sanctions involved being . . . applied, and [the actor] may be prepared to submit to them as a price to be paid for achieving a particular end" (Giddens 1994:87). A social norm, then, is not legitimate in any robust sense if based on a value consensus that the individual only passively (and perhaps unconsciously) accepts because he or she has simply (and likely unconsciously) internalized it. Social norms—such as the legal and political meaning of race and color—can be negotiated, or rather have a negotiated character: The normative order is produced in the same sense that social meanings are produced, indeed the normative order is produced through meanings, that is, the social structures that set parameters on individual agency are themselves the congealed products of agency. In this sense Giddens claims that "actors who either conform or transgress normative prescriptions may negotiate in some degree what conformity or transgression *are* in the context of their conduct, by means of that conduct, thereby . . . affecting the sanctions to which it is subject" (ibid.:87). In this way, among others, the individual reflexively monitors his or her conduct as a feature of social life, such that "reasons and intentions are not definite 'presences' which lurk behind human social activity, but are routinely and chronically . . . instantiated in that activity. The intentional character of human actions" is not an "articulation of discrete and separate 'intentions,' but a continuous flow of intentionality in time," and not some "set of conscious states that in some way 'accompany' action" (ibid.:39–40).

To say that social life is not played out by human puppets pulled on the strings of norms that the individual internalized in the course of his or her socialization, but rather that social life is consciously "enacted,"[5] is to say that structure does not simply impose itself on individual agency, but rather that agency in part uses structure to articulate itself. In this sense we communicate linguistically by following the fixed, given rules of grammar, but this linguistic structure is also the very medium in which we create, in which we generate new sentences, new meanings, new ideas, and the medium in which we analyze the very linguistic structure that provides the medium for creative analysis in the first place. Here our creativity is governed by rules, in the sense that we reproduce those rules each time we employ them. But even as they limit our creativity in some ways (even the poet is bound by some rules of grammar), they immediately facilitate our creativity in other ways (the rules of grammar do not hobble the flights of poetic imagination but rather are the very means thereto). Indeed, we sometimes modify those rules and use those rules as the very basis on which we modify them; thus sometimes to use a rule is to change it.

In the political terms of color consciousness as a guide to public policy, the individual bearer of rights and beneficiary of liberties is not simply a creature of unyielding social structure, a puppet of fixed, given social norms. He or she is an agent with some degree of freedom to articulate him- or herself "creatively" within that normative structure, or in terms of that normative structure. Common life in liberal democratic societies need not be structured in terms of the a-normativity of an economic liberalism that conceives of politics mainly as the guarantor of the economic liberty of private contracting parties, no more than it need be structured in terms of the deep normativity of republicanism, which understands politics as morals by other means, and the polity as a primarily ethical community led by a state devoted to citizens' moral improvement.

An enlightened localist approach to the participatory proceduralism of deliberative democracy provides an alternative: a radically democratic purchase on the rule of law, in which rationally capable subjects give themselves the reasonable political structure in terms of which they shape and regulate a common life. In this context, color-conscious public policy emerges as a resource in efforts aimed at racial justice, efforts that use social structure as an enabling device for individual agency, drawing creatively on the similarities and differences between law and morality, each of which embodies the tension between structure and agency. In some respects law and morality each provides a structure within which the other articulates itself. Thus legal legitimacy cannot contradict morality, that is, a legal order is legitimate if it does not contradict the social order's basic moral principles. In this sense positive law is related to morality internally. But this internal relation in no way implies a hierarchy of norms; it in no way entails the superiority of morality over law.[6] Positive law can accord with moral insights when law and morality, like structure and agency, stand in complementary relationship, when they equally express an intersubjectively shared way of life. Both law and morality concern the organization of human behavior, the ordering of particular relationships among people. Both seek the general recognition of those norms. Both would resolve conflicts consensually, against the background of such norms.

Private legal subjects (here we have normative agency) enjoy equal individual rights and liberties (here we have normative structure) that enable individuals to participate in their community's self-organization, where structure and agency, and law and morality, come together. Participation then means that citizens themselves decide, in the mutual exercise of their political autonomy, what their interests and priorities, what their values and standards of justification are. This discursive mode of sociation among agents rests on structures in multiple ways: as a self-organizing legal community (one structure) that employs a procedural concept of democracy (another structure) to implement its will through the medium of law (yet a third structure). These are normative structures when they provide for the robust participation of free and equal consociates, in public discussions oriented to generating understandings of issues and policies that lie in the interest of all members of a voluntary association. After all, democratic political participation facilitates a certain institutional normativity: the proceduralism of legislation and a common political language that reinforces the solidarity of a populace that actively steers legislation in the normative directions it chooses for itself.

On the one hand, law institutionalizes the conditions for the discursive exercise of morality, for example in the form of legal rights to political liberties. On the other hand, such law has an internal normativity in the self-referential sense of constitutionalism: the idea of a people binding itself by rules specifying the sources of political power and by rules specifying how citizens can acquire and use that power. This is the secular normativity of positive law, and of secularized politics, based on democratic procedure rather than higher law of some sort. Through the procedures provided by constitutional norms and through the principles of democracy more generally, citizens debate, seek clarity, and construct their normative commitments themselves. Constitutional norms do not thereby become imitations of moral norms, nor do principles of democracy thereby become moral. Of course democratic institutions of self-determination are guided not only by moral arguments but also by prudential arguments brought to bear in the legislative procedure. Legal discourses cannot operate in a completely self-referential fashion, like some monad that provides all of its own inputs, and where all inputs are already existing norms internal to that discourse. On the contrary, legal discourse constantly requires external inputs, such as nonlegal norms that can serve as the grounds for specific legal norms. And legal discourse must always be open to arguments from extra-legal sources, including prudential ones.[7]

Moral reasons impose a structure on political agency different from that imposed by legal reasons. A morality that assumes universal validity presupposes all of humanity as its addressee; by contrast, a legal system can address itself only to *this* political community, as distinct from all other political communities. Moral propositions measure themselves against a virtual "republic of world citizens" (in distinction to international law, which neither imagines nor recognizes any such republic), whereas legal propositions measure themselves against the collective self-understandings of a concrete way of life. Moral propositions are valid if acceptable to everyone; by contrast, legal propositions are valid if acceptable to all members of the relevant concrete community. In this way moral norms make claims on persons quite beyond their formal incorporation into a legal community—indeed, sometimes contrary to that community, such as a critique of slavery in a slave society, or civil disobedience in a redeemable social order, or revolutionary overthrow in one utterly irredeemable.

On the other hand, legal norms stabilize behavioral expectations more effectively than moral norms. Here the relevant difference between legal and moral norms is the difference in the ways in which each is indeterminate, which I shall specify. As I have argued throughout this book, more than a few social norms are often, if not typically, indeterminate. This thesis applies to legal and moral norms alike; neither escapes indeterminacy. To that argument I now append the claim that indeterminacy marks moral norms even more deeply than it does legal norms. Consequently, law is better placed than morality to resolve indeterminacy, even as it can do so only on a case-by-case basis, and only in ways that, in some measure, are ad hoc. Thus moral norms can never possess a functional equivalent of legal norms' stabilizing capacity.

Indeterminacy marks moral norms more deeply than legal norms because moral norms lack certain formal properties: (1) immediate technical usefulness, (2) concreteness, (3) specificity, (4) "constructedness," and (5) a rational basis of validity. After analytically separating law and morality in these five ways, I shall identify another five ways in which they are also complementary, and how each actually requires the other. In this logic lies the enlightened localist approach to color consciousness as public policy.

1. Legal norms must presuppose the possibility of valid judgments, whereas moral norms are ever in search of grounds for making valid judgments. Thus moral norms must be internalized in the individual's personality to be effective in guiding behavior, which means that moral norms can ground themselves (as one method among others) by making themselves already always presupposed: what the individual internalizes, he or she usually simply presupposes. By contrast, legal norms to some extent contain within themselves, interwoven, both value orientations and effective motivation. To that extent, laws, unlike moral norms, need not be internalized by the individual to be effective guides to behavior.

Further, legal norms are useful in a way more immediate than moral norms because the criteria for judging between lawful and unlawful are given in determinately binding ways by socially recognized institutions, whereas in framing and forming moral judgments individuals today often are left to their own devices. To be sure, some persons may follow the moral dictates of institutions such as a particular religion or other worldview. But even here, those persons are free to decide whether and when to follow those dictates, and no such institution can lay claim to, or insist on, the allegiance of all members of society. By contrast, legal institutions, such as legislatures, courts, and governmental bureaucracies, make and enforce precisely that claim.

Legal norms are enforced by the violence of the state, or often simply the threat of state violence, and laws that are not enforced cease to be laws in any meaningful sense. Moral norms may be enforced, but if so, not directly or unambiguously; they may become effective beyond the personal level only when translated into the legal code, with its power to coerce wherever morality remains impotent. A moral norm that no one observes is of questionable validity.

2. Legal norms are clearly generated in legislation, in judicial interpretation, and in doctrinal jurisprudence; moral norms have no agreed-upon and universally recognized mode of generation. The meaning of legal validity is circumscribed by legislatures, by judicial holdings, and by doctrinal jurisprudence. These institutions and practices define rules precisely, in part by systematizing decisions from the bench. On the other hand, the meaning of moral validity is not circumscribed by any generally recognized institution. And moral validity has no set of authoritative interpreters and adjudicators—certainly not for a modern, liberal, secular, democratic society.

3. Legal norms regulate particular legal communities—their validity and application are sharply and precisely limited to this or that community—whereas moral norms often claim validity beyond any particular community. Legal norms express

the wills of particular legislators, of the particular citizens who elected them, and of the particular judges and other government officials who interpret those norms. Moral norms, by contrast, claim validity beyond the convictions of any social institution, set of officials, or community of citizens. They regard themselves as valid even for persons not party to their selection or interpretation. Indeed, persons who might reject those norms can do so with impunity in part because of their legal right to freedom of conscience and to freedom of religious belief and practice.

Further, the application of legal norms is specified narrowly, within spheres of interaction mediated by specific social institutions (from private contracts to marriage laws to statutes regarding primary and secondary education to the regulation of donations to political campaigns). By contrast, the authority of moral norms extends across boundaries between the public and private spheres of life: It pertains to social relationships for which a group or community, or even an entire society, is responsible (as in the claim that society as a whole has a moral responsibility to avoid racially unjust results in legislation). And the authority of moral norms, but not of legal norms, extends to relationships for which one is personally responsible.

4. Both legal and moral norms are constructed by human beings. Exactly how norms are constructed, by whom, when, and where, is always much clearer with legal norms than with moral norms. Some people maintain that some moral norms are "discovered" not created (for example, in natural law as understood by some Catholics). But in complex modern societies, in terms of which I have developed the theory of enlightened localism, social integration no longer entails what Émile Durkheim (1984) describes as the absorption of the individual personality into a "collective personality." Social integration takes place increasingly through conscious decisions on the individual's part, through choices she or he makes among alternatives, rather than through unexamined communal belief. Thus social solidarity is no longer already given, for example through religious consensus (as Durkheim thinks it was for most communities in the European Middle Ages). Rather it must first be achieved, by the participants themselves, through democratic procedure (as I argued in chapter 2). Even human rights, which might be thought the most viable form of natural law today, if conceived (as today they often are conceived, by organizations such as the United Nations) in terms of citizens' practice of democratic self-determination, are then conceived solely in legal terms, without reference to their undeniable moral content.

5. Finally, the validity of positive law has a rational basis. A modern legal system can stabilize behavioral expectations only when it can maintain, from generation to generation, its claim on the citizenry's free and willing compliance. It can redeem that claim only as long as the citizenry as a whole can regard the law as legitimate. Legality is then universal within society, as an aspect of equal citizenship, granting

rights and imposing burdens more or less equally on society's members, and doing so as a condition of membership. In other words, legal regulations can be legitimate only insofar as they are addressed to all members of a legal community and only insofar as they are in the interest of all members. And only legitimate legal regulations can ground the obligatory character of, say, a contract between autonomous legal persons.

To be sure, the rational basis of positive law's validity has a moral component but a strictly secular one; thus not "moral agreement grounded in the sacred" but "moral agreement that expresses in rational form what was always intended in the symbolism of the holy: the generality of the underlying interest"; not a "sacred foundation of legitimation" but a "foundation on a common will, communicatively shaped and discursively clarified in the political public sphere" (Habermas 1987:81). The law's capacity to change hearts and minds (with respect to race, for example) is then in part its moral force:

> The popularity of programs that are perceived to help blacks is highly volatile, shifting with citizens' perception of the state of the law and the moral commitments of political leadership. When white citizens are asked for their views on a set-aside program for minorities—"a law to ensure that a certain number of federal contracts go to minority contractors," 43 percent say they favor it. But when they are told that the set-aside program for minorities is a law passed by both houses of Congress, the support significantly increases to 57 percent." (Gutmann 1996:150)

In these five ways, then, legal and moral norms differ from each other. In part they perform different social functions, in a kind of normative division of labor. But law and morality also stand in a mutually reinforcing relationship to each other, to the point that each often requires the other (in just the way structure and agency each requires the other). Morality supplements law in three ways: First, because legal rules cannot ground themselves ultimately, a regime of legal rules (in other words, the rule of law) needs extra-legal norms, indeed an entire background culture that is moral rather than legal in nature. A regime of legal rules must have recourse to background norms on which to ground these rules. For that reason the judicial interpretation of indeterminate legal rules must go beyond the text of the statute, or beyond the four corners of the constitutional document, to provide itself an external justification, one that may well be moral. Second, democratic institutions cannot perpetuate themselves without the cultural "oxygen" of an engaged public habituated and attuned to legal liberty. Yet law cannot compel this constant input of citizens' initiatives, spontaneity, passions, and concerns. Here morality supplements law by providing that oxygen, the behavioral expectations of a liberal political culture, out of which popular interest and participation regenerates itself from generation to generation. Third, political rights in a liberal democracy are based on the logic of citizens seeking mutual understanding about their respective normative commitments, about the problems of the day, and about mutually satisfactory ways of dealing with those problems. But the law can hardly compel citizens to follow this logic; it can hardly require them to engage their individual rights in ways that will facilitate their coming to an understanding on issues in the public sphere, matters of public policy, questions for deliberative politics. Here morality supplements law by obligating citizens to the public use of their individual rights in just these ways.[8]

For its part, law supplements morality in three ways: First, when moral cognition is not anchored in citizens' personality structures, in their motivations and mind-sets, sufficiently to secure behavior that conforms to the relevant moral norms, there law supplements morality by enforcing norm-conformative behavior while still leaving space for some degree of individual autonomy. Positive law is the sole medium capable of establishing mutually respectful relationships, even among strangers, where that respect derives from a moral responsibility. Second, when expectations of moral behavior are inadequate to secure moral behavior, law can superimpose threats of sanctions on those expectations, coercing the desired behavior (or coercively prescribing the undesired behavior) by threatening sanctions for noncompliance. Third, the law may sometimes take the lead in creating popular acceptance for new moral obligations. Thus President Harry Truman's desegregation of the American armed forces following the Second World War contributed, as did the Supreme Court's unanimous decision in *Brown v. Board of Education* in 1955,[9] to persuading the vast majority of American citizens that the norm "separate but equal" perpetuates racial inequality, and that racial integration is a moral affirmation of legal equality, as the equality of morally equal citizens.

COLOR CONSCIOUSNESS AND COLOR BLINDNESS

From the complementarity of structure and agency, as well as of law and morality, we gain insight into the similar complementarity of color consciousness and color blindness. Consider structure in the law. Legal structure is enabling in a political sense when it allows citizens to realize such moral goals as racial justice. It can do so in at least three ways.

First, the single most effective response to the racial injustice suffered by black Americans is to make their votes more effective by creating majority black districts in areas where black residents now are defeated, again and again, by racial-bloc voting, in their attempts to influence electoral outcomes. The legislature is key to progress on some of the most important issues within the black community today, including poverty and unemployment, poor schools and poor health care, and inadequate housing. The legislature defines, decides, and funds the government's role in policies of social welfare, workfare, and child care. These goals are directly supported by overcoming racial injustice in legislation by creating electoral districts in which the majority of voters are black and in which nonblack residents enjoy a legal standing strictly equal to that of their black coresidents. The overarching goal is not racial segregation (which prevents people of different races from interacting with each other as they wish), rather, it is the harnessing of democratic proceduralism to overcome racial injustice by concentrating in a few districts the electoral strength of black residents, rendering that strength effective at the voting booth and in the halls of Congress.

Second, electoral reform as the reshaping of districts seeks to render more effective the votes of the least advantaged. It can do so even as it preserves all citizens' equality of voting power, even as it sustains the liberty of any individual to cast a vote weighted equal to that of any other citizen, and even as it maintains the standing of any one citizen equal to the standing of any other. Concentrating the electoral strength of a disadvantaged group in a few districts does not violate the legal equality of residents who are not members of that group, nor does it deny to residents of other districts the Fourteenth Amendment guarantees of due process and equal protection of the laws.[10]

Third, we may ask, Does enhanced representation of the least advantaged racial groups lead to better legislation? The answer revolves around the definition of "racially unjust outcomes in legislation." Definition cannot be neutral, for reasons I explained in chapter 2, where I advocate proceduralism not as some neutral method of politics but, in terms of enlightened localism, as a method of progressive politics. But even as a matter of partisan perspectives, of disagreements, and of political commitments, definition here would not preclude, in Iris Young's words, procedural "mechanisms for the effective recognition and representation of the distinct voices and perspectives of those of its constituent groups that are oppressed or disadvantaged" (1990:184). To be sure, such mechanisms cannot guarantee just outcomes in legislation. And they will still protect incumbents, thus unfortunately not threatening some existing power constellations. And, as designed primarily for African American voters, such mechanisms are not immediately generalizable to other disadvantaged groups; rather, the voting strengths and electoral prospects of each group must be assessed separately, in light of the contingencies and peculiarities of each. Every one of the other disadvantaged groups and ascriptive communities must ask whether it is worse off because of such mechanisms designed for and deployed on behalf of black citizens. In fact the African American community's experience with such mechanisms may well generate strategies that could be adapted to the interests of other groups in overcoming unjust legislative outcomes. In this sense, enhanced representation of society's least advantaged racial groups may indeed lead to better legislation, at least for some disadvantaged groups.

But color-conscious legal structure must never be allowed to undermine mutual moral identification among individual human beings as equals and as equally worthy of respect and dignity. Electoral redistricting that serves solely or primarily to encourage citizens to identify only with others of the same race may undermine this moral insight. The goal of color-conscious politics must then be to relate color consciousness to color blindness in the way structure and agency, or law and morality, are best interrelated: as complementary. An enlightened localist approach can distinguish among different contexts, to determine when the one or the other is best advised. Thus the government needs to be color conscious if it is to recognize the ways in which race continues to influence the rights, prospects, and opportunities of individual citizens. On the other hand, citizens should refrain from tightly scripting their fellow citizens in terms of racial group identity; here color blindness is necessary, as a kind of regulative principle, an ultimate goal, as the goal of becoming a society no longer racist. Yet a third mode is warranted in yet another context: The construction of multicolor, cross-racial political coalitions, in electoral districts and legislatures alike, where black residents might have a viable chance to swing close elections, would bring together color consciousness and color blindness, structure and agency, law and morality, in a deliberative democracy coping with normative indeterminacy through enlightened localism.

CODA

Social Cooperation in the Absence of Political Unity

In this book I have sought to address the question: Taking into account, in current social life, the practical limits of persuasion and conviction-guided action, but at the same time seizing available techniques, how should a society cope in politics with indeterminate norms? I responded with a theory of enlightened localism, derived equally from proceduralism (chapter 2) and pragmatism (chapter 3) and broadly applicable across normative spheres of daily life, including social critique (chapter 4), public policy (chapter 5), and law and morality (chapter 6). The theory begins as a sort of sociology of moral knowledge, with the given norms of actual communities, and then seeks prescriptively to enhance the mundane perspective of groups and individuals: to progress from unexamined or parochial forms of localism to enlightened forms. When norms are indeterminate, I have argued, politics needs to span the tension between the more limited conditions of a local standpoint and the less limited conditions of a perspective beyond. An enlightened localist approach begins with cognitive and normative standards immanent to a society's cultures, understandings, and practices but then transcends them. Transcending a local standpoint need not take us all the way to a universal one; less-than-universal validity lies across disputes or among communities within society. Enlightened localism spans this tension without breaking on it by resisting appeals to universal criteria no longer available in our modern, "disenchanted" world of multiple competing worldviews, each appealing to sources of justification not equally plausible to many of the heterogeneous groups comprising contemporary liberal democratic societies.

Nearly half a century ago Shelden Wolin, at the end of a magisterial review of the entire history of Western political thought, identified this absence of political unity, and this lack of normative claims of universal validity, as the major political problem of our time. In his account, we in the West today are caught between two equally unacceptable options: either democracy under liberal and tolerant conditions of fragmentation or unity but only under a totalitarian order, such as the former Soviet Union and its satellite states so recently unbound by the events of 1989. In Wolin's account, attempts to understand human society in terms of class orientation, group orientations, or occupational orientation are fragmenting:

> But man as member of a general political society is scarcely considered a proper subject for theoretical inquiry, because it is assumed that "local

citizenship"—man as trade-unionist, bureaucrat, Rotarian, occupant of a certain income-tax bracket—is the primary or determinant influence on how man will behave as a political citizen. The same procedure is followed in dealing with beliefs. The individual is viewed as a shopper carrying several distinct parcels, one containing his "vocational" ideology, another his "class" ideology, a third his "minority" attitudes, and perhaps, a fourth and more discreet one holds his "religious ideology." (1960:430)

In this way social and political theory splinters a coherent normative unity animated by normative universals. Individuals appear but only in fragments, and, in fact, in just the sort of fragments that interests a theory of enlightened localism. Up to a point I accept Wolin's description of the current landscape in political society. But where Wolin sees desperately discouraging obstacles, I see overlooked opportunities.

By Wolin's lights, if political fragmentation is acceptable at all, then only because fragmentation is the "necessary price for achieving some measure of individual self-determination and participation in the modern world" (1960:433). For the "alternative of reviving the political dimension of existence seems an invitation to totalitarianism," and in the twentieth century "totalitarian systems have re-asserted the political with a vengeance," destroying the "autonomy of groups and replac[ing] it with a highly coordinated general policy," orienting "every major human activity toward political goals," through "propaganda and controlled education that have instilled among the citizens a strong sense of the political order and a firm belief in the exalted status of political membership" (ibid.:433-434). But localism only as the lesser of two evils is more resignation than recommendation. Wolin's account of localism hardly inspires the adjective *enlightened*, which my theory favors. But Wolin fails to see how nonauthoritarian politics is possible under the fragmented conditions of normative and epistemic indeterminacy: how social equity, political fairness, and legal justice are possible even when aspects of the social, political, and legal order appear to be arbitrary, inconsistent, or subjective.

By contrast, I have argued that fragmented, localized persons can indeed come to see themselves as members of a political unity—just not one outfitted with universalistic features. For that reason, a society splintered into a multiplicity of groups entails no special form of political responsibility owed to society as a whole. If locally valid norms could somehow be transformed into universally valid ones, they would be like a caterpillar once fattened up and then formed into a chrysalis, out of which it soon crawls, and then soars on multicolored wings, transformed into a dazzling butterfly. By some similarly spectacular transformation, but this time of consciousnesses, citizens would acquire attachments: not the striking wings of a swallowtail but the cognitive and affective attachments to a political unity brought forth entirely in the imaginations of the people. Locally valid norms would then find agreeable form and pleasing appearance in universalism "in drag."

To be sure, political unity, bound by norms of universal validity, might well be imagined out of particularity, in the willed merger of different localisms. Thus in medieval Europe an "overwhelmingly visual and aural Christendom assumed its universal form through a myriad of specificities and particularities: this relief, that window, this sermon, that tale, this morality play, that relic" (Anderson 1994:23). But then, in a movement that reverberates down to our day, the rationalist secularism of the European Enlightenment led to the disintegration of religious universalism. Perhaps any universalism possible thereafter—perhaps any universalism possible today—is possible only as an imagined unity, as a secular transformation of social fragmentation into political unity, of moral pluralism into determinate norms.

In just this sense Benedict Anderson analyzes the emergence of nationalism as an "imagined community" in the Western hemisphere between 1776 and 1838, beginning with the Declaration of Independence of George III's thirteen North American colonies, and including Toussaint L'Ouverture's rebellion in 1791 which, by 1806, led to the New World's second independent republic, this time guided not by cousins of London's privileged classes but by former slaves forcibly removed from their African homelands. And then it

> remained for Mark Twain to create in 1881, well after the "Civil War" and Lincoln's Emancipation Proclamation, the first indelible image of black and white as American "brothers": Jim and Huck companionably adrift on the wide Mississippi. But the setting is a remembered/forgotten antebellum in which the black is still a slave. These striking nineteenth-century imaginings of fraternity, emerging "naturally" in a society fractured by the most violent racial, class and regional antagonisms, show as clearly as anything else that nationalism . . . represented a new form of consciousness. (Anderson 1994:203)

Political unity with universalistic features (of which nationalism is but one species) can be imagined by means of a narrative of identity, deriving perhaps from something common (language, religion, culture) but descending more likely from History (with a capital H) emplotted in ways to allow citizens to read unity "genealogically." Unity so read expresses a coherent, integrating continuity over time, by reshaping the citizen's heart and mind, beliefs and identity, in part through state control over public education, in part through the various bureaucracies: Breathing social life into an imagined political unity by creating shared beliefs and behaviors out of the intergenerational flow of citizens through a battery of institutions educational, legal, medical, and cultural. But, I would argue, such unity is spurious: Even if sometimes in some ways effective, it is delusory nonetheless.

HARMONY NOT UNITY

Uniformity is the peculiar geography of imagined political and normative unity. Uniformity fears topographical anomalies, regions of moral heterogeneity and boroughs of normative indeterminacy from which localisms might one day sally forth to challenge universalism. Pluralism is a problem for unity, and unity reacts by imagining the particular as somehow representative of a series. And if by some kind of virtual miscegenation an imagined political unity transformed disparate individuals into a culturally unified people, how many of those individuals would recognize themselves so categorized? Even if quite a lot, might at some point their irremediable localness spill out into politically and culturally "transvestite" identities, uncontainable by imagined identities complete and unambiguous? Such eruptions of indeterminacy and localism could be expected, for example, when an imagined unity confronted natural barriers, when for example it could not assimilate sex, parentage, social class, alienage, or—as we saw repeatedly in chapters 1, 2, and 6—race. Such eruptions could be expected whenever an imagined political unity confronted preexisting, deep-seated identities that did not fit the imagined grid, such as identities based in religious faith.

Enlightened localism, by contrast, seeks harmony or cooperation among the diverse normative commitments of a complex modern society, and among the fragmented identities of a cosmopolitan population. It resists Wolin's claim that the "specialized roles assigned the individual, or adopted by him, are not a full substitute for citizenship because citizenship provides what the other roles cannot, namely an integrative experience which brings together the multiple role-activities of the contemporary person and demands that the separate roles be surveyed from a more general point of view" (1960:434).[1] A "general point of view" that would unify the individual might reduce difference to identity, as though democratic politics required of all citizens, with all their differences, some kind of politically unifying serial number.

Wolin's counterargument contends that localism is politically disintegrative, rendering society a "series of tight little islands, each evolving towards political self-sufficiency, each striving to absorb the individual members, each without any natural affiliations with a more comprehensive unity" (ibid.:431). Localism, it would seem, chops up the individual as a political agent and precludes a general life expressible in political forms.

My reply: The meaning and application of social norms often need not (indeed, often cannot) be consistent over time or between cases. The validity of any given interpretation or application can be relative only to the particular community of interpreters. Moral validity then is relative not absolute, and cultural meanings are local not universal. Here enlightened localism seeks harmony among the shards of modern life, harmony, for example, in the sense of a mobile, such as those constructed by Alexander Calder in which the parts are not seamlessly integrated but nonetheless hold together in their differences. Here pluralism is possible without an imagined unity among all the parts.

CRITICAL CAPACITY OF LOCALISM

This analogy between art and politics is suggestive. Both the pragmatism and the postmodernism I discussed in chapter 3 display a peculiarly aesthetic element; for both, the aesthetic has distinct consequences for the social critique I discussed in chapter 4. As for postmodernism: Gilles Deleuze and Félix Guattari (1972), the early Jean-François Lyotard (1974), and the early Michel Foucault (Megill 1985) aestheticize away any notion of meaningful political activity. They contend that rationality itself has been colonized and infected by modernity (and by the modern capitalist order in particular), so much so that the oppressed individual's only defense is to abandon rational, public political action for a heightened subjectivism, for a preoccupation with the individual's precious interiority (contributing then to the very political fragmentation deprecated by Wolin). On this account, spiritual and psychological interiority is supposed somehow to counter the repressive features of the modern age. Accordingly art and libidinal desire (reflecting the peculiar individuality of author or artist, reflecting something both private and non-rational) become the topics, indeed the instruments of a defensive "politics"—the passive defense of the cultural refugee.

Enlightened localism derives in part from one of the alternatives to postmodernism: from pragmatism. The "classical" pragmatism of John Dewey has an aesthetic impulse that, like postmodernism, stresses the imagination.[2] Yet it does so in critical counterpoint to established social norms: "[I]magination is the chief instrument of the good . . . [hence] art is more moral than moralities. For the latter either are, or tend to become, consecrations of the status quo. . . . The moral prophets of humanity have always been poets even though they spoke in free verse or by parable" (1958:348). In Richard Rorty's work (which at turns is both postmodern and pragmatist) the aesthetic impulse (like everything else in the new pragmatism) takes a linguistic turn, on whose analysis truth is contingent and historically situated: "[S]ince truth is a property of sentences, since sentences are dependent for their existence upon vocabularies, and since vocabularies are made by human beings, so are truths" (1989:20). Hence, "what matters in the end are changes in the vocabulary rather than changes in belief, changes in truth-value candidates rather than assignments of truth-value" (ibid.:47–48). This aesthetic sense animates a linguistically inspired form of political action: "[P]rogress, for the community as for the individual, is a matter of using new words as well as of arguing from premises phrased in old words" (ibid.). Social progress, through the medium of new vocabularies, means political engagement in an aesthetically constructive sense, one that conveys the political implication of Rorty's (ibid.:13) wide understanding of the term *poet*, namely "one who makes things new."

As we saw in chapter 3, the rule-skepticism characteristic of pragmatist jurisprudence does not dismiss the potential value and use of rules. Rule skepticism can allow, without contradiction, for a notion of "coherence-through-rules." The aesthetic constructivism of such pragmatism lies in its flexibility to define its positions as necessary to solve given problems. This is also Dewey's understanding: "[R]ules of law should form as coherent generalized logical systems as possible. But these logical systemizations of law in any field . . . are clearly . . . subservient to the economical and effective reaching of decisions in particular cases" (1931:12).

Further, whereas postmodern aestheticism is personalized and subjectivized to an extent that debilitates political interests and action, aestheticism in a pragmatist mode is fully compatible with a focus on, say, legal rights and social justice. Like postmodern aestheticism, some pragmatist versions would resist societal repression through art and imagination. Unlike most postmodernism, however, a pragmatist aestheticism does not thereby forsake this world for another; indeed it instrumentalizes the aesthetic toward addressing social and political issues and problems. By contrast, the otherworldly ethic of most postmodern aestheticism simply expresses the alienation experienced by various of its authors (no doubt shared by some of their readers). But as nothing more than a mere reflection of that alienation, such an ethic cannot engage, critically, the problem and its sources. Pragmatist instrumentalism alone, as a rational, this-worldly ethic, can redeem its claims to offer practical guidance to real people in concrete situations. The politicized interiority of postmodern aestheticism provides no such guidance.[3] A politics of interiority is incapable of discursive persuasion; postmodernism is irrational when it rejects rational critique. It is insensitive to issues of normative indeterminacy when, amid political fragmentation, it provides no language with which to articulate the practical, down-to-earth, vernacular political needs for legal rights, social justice, and personal autonomy. And its hyperindividualism—for example, in its stress on desire and satisfaction—easily precludes the sort of intersubjective agreement that alone could render an assertion warrantable (or otherwise rationally persuasive) to the community confronted with a problem requiring a choice among alternatives, choice as a precondition of necessary or desired action.

This incapacity for rational, political persuasion surfaces even in the true pragmatist among the postmoderns, Richard Rorty, who articulates an ethics of taste in the form of a "private morality" (1986:10-11). Such an aesthetic is privatistic and individualist, without social compass; it is oriented toward gratifying the self, oblivious to concerns with the welfare of others. Rorty's

> idea that everyone can be a unique individual simply by fashioning oneself through the free and personal choice of life-styles cannot hide the fact that not only the range of viable life-style options but the individual's

very awareness and choice are severely constrained and relentlessly programmed by societal forces or sanctions far beyond his power to resist, let alone control. This late-capitalist paradox of the privatized quest for self-fulfillment issuing in the loss of real autonomy and integrity of self is perfectly reflected in Rorty's deep contradiction of exhorting self-enrichment while denying the very existence of a self that could be enriched. (Shusterman 1988:352)

A pragmatist aestheticism, by contrast, resonates with an enlightened localism that would construct noncoerced agreement within a community in the absence of universally valid norms. The notion of finding common ground among contending perspectives finds clear expression in no less a paragon of Enlightenment modernism than Immanuel Kant (1724-1804), for whom aesthetic judgment is not determinative

because it does not subsume the particular under the general. Rather, it judges particulars without presupposing universal rules or a priori principles, relying instead on the ability to convince others of the rightness of the evaluation. When, for example, I call a painting beautiful, I assume my taste is more than a personal quirk, but somehow expresses a judgment warranting universal assent. I imaginatively assume the point of view of the others, who would presumably share my evaluation. Aesthetic judgment . . . cannot be legitimated by being brought under a concept or derived from a universal imperative; it requires . . . a kind of uncoerced consensus building that implies a communicative model of rationality as warranted assertability. (Jay 1993:80)[4]

Quite beyond pragmatist aesthetics, indeed beyond analogy between art and politics, unity is not necessary for the possibility of social critique (as we saw in chapter 4). Rational critique is possible without trying to stretch the tight skin of universally valid norms over the unwieldy body of normatively fragmented populations. It is possible when the critic appreciates his or her standpoint as only one among many, and not necessarily or always the best, but one ever open to challenge and defense. Enlightened localism allows for rational critique in the absence of political unity and without normative claims of universal validity.

HORIZONTALITY NOT VERTICALITY

Against Wolin, I would argue that a liberal democracy should not attempt to "restore the political art as that art which strives for an integrative form of direction, one that is broader than that supplied by any group or organization" (1960:434). My alternative—political localism—allows citizens to achieve solidarity, through language, by building particular solidarities. After all, a particular language is open to anyone who learns it; in principle it is open to anyone and thus can serve as an organ of popular inclusion.[5] It belongs to its competent users, and it belongs to them equally, in a fraternity (unintentionally and for the most part unconsciously) created daily by the users themselves.

Under the previous rubric we saw how modern art provides an analogy for enlightened localist politics when it allows for coherent interaction among diverse parts without requiring some all-embracing unity or universally valid norms. Similarly, language provides an analogy for democracy in a localist sense because it operates on the principle of "horizontality": Linguistically competent citizens are equal to each other, with no one above the laws of grammar and syntax, for example. Language does not operate on the principle of "verticality" when, in political terms, dynastic marriages, for example, "unite" disparate peoples under a royal apex, as in the "belief that society was naturally organized around and under high centers—monarchs who were persons apart from other human beings and who ruled by some form of cosmological (divine) dispensation. Human loyalties were necessarily hierarchical and centripetal because the ruler, like the sacred script, was a node of access to being and inherent in it" (Anderson 1994:36). Consider the contrast between a sacred script (part of an imagined political unity, and often a purveyor of universally valid norms) and ordinary everyday language. Enlightened localism roots political life firmly in the participation of all persons affected and concerned. Even in rapidly growing numbers, these persons relate themselves to each other communicatively, despite differences and fragmentations and plural normative commitments, without requiring political unity or normative universalism.

This is the robustly democratic perspective on political participation I spoke of in the introduction. It does not require the kind of normative and political unity Wolin imagines. Three-quarters of a century before Wolin published his book, Ferdinand Tönnies (1855-1936) argued for a notion of community based on relationships of mutual affirmation, relationships of solidarity: "Every such relationship represents unity in plurality or plurality in unity. It consists of assistance, relief services, which are transmitted back and forth from one party to another and are to be considered as expressions of wills and their forces" (1957:33). Here I would appropriate Tönnies selectively, indeed against the grain because I have argued for relationships of mutual affirmation but not as *Gemeinschaft* (in which understanding is always already given by a homogeneous culture and shared traditions), but rather as *Gesellschaft* (in which relations among citizens are rather transitory and superficial and in which understanding must be actively achieved by its disparate and heterogeneous participants who need not resort to some imagined unity and universalism).[6]

Progressive politics in a secularized age is to be had only in a radically democratic sense but also in the sense of ordinary language, which can provide for communal understanding even though it has never been agreed upon (or imagined) as a means of achieving understanding. And "just as language cannot be made by agreement," so "real concord cannot be artificially produced. That is not to say, however, that many kinds of agreement are not arrived at artificially. Understanding and concord grow and blossom forth from existing buds if the conditions are favorable" (Tönnies 1957:49). Normative indeterminacy need not defeat those conditions; and enlightened localism can cope with the politics they make possible.

Notes

INTRODUCTION

1. 347 U.S. 483.

2. A "separate Negro school, where children are treated like human beings, trained by teachers of their own race, who know what it means to be black in the year of salvation 1935, is infinitely better than making our boys and girls doormats to be spit and trampled upon and lied to by ignorant social climbers, whose sole claim to superiority is ability to kick 'niggers' when they are down. I say, too, that certain studies and discipline necessary to Negroes can seldom be found in white schools" (Du Bois 1935:335).

CHAPTER 1
INDETERMINACY IN SOCIAL AND POLITICAL NORMS

1. I analyze legal indeterminacy specifically as a matter of political judgment in Gregg (2003a: ch. 5).

2. *Plessy v. Ferguson*, 163 U.S. 537.

3. *Brown v. Board of Education*, 347 U.S. 483.

4. Benjamin Gregg (1992).

5. Additional theses may well apply. My concern is not to develop an exhaustive list but rather to show that theses of this type apply.

6. Therefore we have no a priori grounds to reduce legal discourse to some unitary feature, such as the self-determination of the legal subject (as in liberalism); or a *Grundnorm* as the principle of origin and criterion of validity for legal norms (as in legal positivism) (Kelsen 1970); or quasi-natural features (as in logical positivism); or ethical essences (as in some views of natural law or natural right); or to ideological constructs (as in Marxist or Freudian theory). Nor have we reason to assume that law is based on some common ground of rational agreement. If law has neither unitary feature nor general foundation, its application and meaning may be expected to be contingent.

7. As Harold Garfinkel (1967:104–115) shows for example with respect to rules by which jurors decide what the legally enforceable situation is.

8. Benedict Anderson suggests that one

> aristocratic or pseudo-aristocratic derivation of colonial racism was the typical "solidarity among whites," which linked colonial rulers from different national metropoles, whatever their internal rivalries and conflicts. This solidarity, in its

curious trans-state character, reminds one instantly of the class solidarity of Europe's nineteenth-century aristocracies, mediated through each other's hunting-lodges, spas, and ballrooms; and of that brotherhood of "officers and gentlemen," which in the Geneva convention guaranteeing privileged treatment to captured enemy officers, as opposed to partisans or civilians, has an agreeably twentieth-century expression. (1994:152–153)

9. Richard Posner (1990b:1658) notes that an essay by Max Radin (1930:884) "clarifies and in so doing emphasizes the parity of statutes and the common law. Judges, it is true, are not free to revise a statute, as they are free to do with a common law doctrine. But interpretation is a creative rather than contemplative task—indeed judges have as much freedom in deciding difficult statutory (and of course constitutional) cases as they have in deciding difficult common law cases."

10. Correspondingly, for legal formalism justice consists in the impartial application of norms deriving their legitimacy from the prior consent of those subject to the norms. In a purely formal process the judge derives and applies norms established by the legislature (in a substantive process). The legislature determines the content of the norm, while the judge merely applies or enforces (without contributing to or modifying) that content.

11. 497 U.S. 547 (1990).

12. Compare Karl Llewellyn's (1960:521–535) "thrust and parry" list of canons of statutory construction in American law.

13. In Du Bois's words, "As long as the Negro student wishes to graduate from Columbia, not because Columbia is an institution of learning, but because it is attended by white students; as long as a Negro student is ashamed to attend Fisk or Howard because those institutions are largely run by black folk, just so long the main problem of Negro education will not be segregation but self-knowledge and self-respect" (1935:331).

14. This is not Bell's position; he says that this premise "fails to encompass the complexity of achieving equal educational opportunity for children to whom it so long has been denied" (1995b:7).

15. 418 U.S. 717 (1974).

16. 433 U.S. 406 (1977).

17. *Dayton Board of Education v. Brinkman*, 433 U.S. 406, 410 (1977).

18. *Milliken v. Bradley*, 418 U.S. 717, 741 (1974).

19. In this sense Bell argues that "Many white parents recognize a value in integrated schooling for their children, but they quite properly view integration as merely one component of an effective education"; and "successful magnet schools may provide a lesson that effective schools for blacks must be a primary goal rather than a secondary result of integration" (1995a:26).

CHAPTER 2
COPING WITH INDETERMINACY THROUGH PROCEDURALISM

1. As a mundane example of equality through proceduralism, consider the "physical proceduralism" in the corporeal arrangement of a meeting such that equal numbers of all

parties to a dispute are present and seated in a way that, symbolically or otherwise, privileges no party. The interesting examples are all much more complex.

2. As Pierre Bourdieu points out so cogently: "If faut répudier les vestiges de moralisme, religieux ou politique, qui inspirent souterrainement nombre d'interrogations d'apparence épistémologique. Dans l'order de la pensée, il n'y a pas, comme le rappelait Nietzsche, d'immaculée conception; mais il n'y a pas davantage de péché originel. Et ce n'est pas parce que l'on pourrait découvrir que celui qui a découvert la vérité avait intérêt à le faire que cette découverte s'en trouverait tant soit peu diminuée. Ceux qui aiment croire au miracle de la pensée 'pure' doivent se résigner à admettre que l'amour de la vérité ou de la vertu, comme toute autre espèce de disposition, doit nécessairement quelque chose aux conditions dans lesquelles il s'est formé, c'est-à-dire à une position et à une trajectoire sociales" (1997:11–12).

3. As delineated, for example, by Nagel 1986.

4. It matters a great deal what those irrational biases are, of course. Fair treatment might well follow the elimination of some irrational biases.

5. "The right of citizens of the United States to vote shall not be denied or abridged by the United States or by any State on account of sex."

6. I do not argue in Iris Young's sense that the "impartiality and rationality of the state depend on containing need and desire in the private realm of the family. The public realm of citizens achieves unity and universality only by defining the civil individual in opposition to the disorder of womanly nature, which embraces feeling, sexuality, birth and death, the attributes that concretely distinguish persons from one another. The universal citizen is disembodied, dispassionate (male) reason" (1990:110). In fact civil society is not particularly orderly, and "feeling, sexuality, birth and death, [and] the attributes that concretely distinguish persons from one another" might display significant order. Civil society is certainly full of affect. Political campaigns, for example, all too often instrumentalize the voter's emotional sensibilities to ignore or downplay or even camouflage the candidate's substantive stance.

7. On the one hand, impartiality as a quality of truth refers to independence from particular perspectives within the populace; impartiality refers to the exclusion of particularity from claims to validity. On the other hand, truth is impartial when it embraces the whole of reality rather than merely this or that particular aspect: Impartiality captures the ensemble of particular aspects rather than their exclusion. One can bring these two hands together only in the Zenlike assertion that impartiality means to take account of all particularity, but also to exclude it.

8. The horizons of plausible interpretation at any given time stand in a fruitfully dynamic, rather than barren or static, relationship with the past whenever the interpreter *critically* reconsiders the ways in which current interpretations may be derived from, and perhaps continue to be influenced by, past ones, in a sense nicely captured by Hans Georg Gadamer: "In Wahrheit ist der Horizont der Gegenwart in steter Bildung begriffen, sofern wir alle unsere Vorurteile ständig erproben müssen. Zu solcher Erprobung gehört nicht zuletzt die Begegnung mit der Vergangenheit und das Verstehen der Überlieferung, aus der wir kommen. Der Horizont der Geganwart bildet sich also gar nicht ohne die Vergangenheit. Es gibt so wenig einen Gegenwartshorizont für sich, wie es historische Horizonte gibt, die man zu gewinnen hätte. *Vielmehr ist Verstehen immer der Vorgang der Verschmelzung solcher vermeintlich für sich seiender Horizonte*" (1972:289).

9. According to Clifford Geertz,

Confronting our own version of the council-man mind with other sorts of local knowledge should not only make that mind more aware of forms of legal sensibility other than its own, but make it more aware also of the exact quality of its own. This is, of course, the sort of relativization for which anthropology is notorious. . . . But it is one that neither argues for nihilism, eclecticism, and anything goes. . . . It is, rather, one that welds the processes of self-knowledge, self-perception, self-understanding to those of other-knowledge, other-perception, other-understanding; that identifies, or very nearly, sorting out who we are and sorting out whom we are among. And as such, it can help both to free us from misleading representations of our own way of rendering matters judiciable (the radical dissociation of fact and law, for example) and to force into our reluctant consciousness disaccordant views of how this is to be done (those of the Balinese, for example) which, if no less dogmatical than ours, are no less logical either. (1983:181–182)

10. Whereby for Émile Durkheim "punishment is above all intended to have its effect upon honest people. Since it serves to heal the wounds inflicted upon the collective sentiments, it can only fulfill this role where such sentiments exist, and insofar as they are active. Undoubtedly, by forestalling in minds already distressed any further weakening of the collective psyche, punishment can indeed prevent such attacks from multiplying" (1984:63).

11. In the spirit of George Herbert Mead,

[O]nly in so far as he takes the attitudes of the organized social group to which he belongs toward the organized, co-operative social activity or set of such activities in which that group as such is engaged, does [the individual] . . . develop a complete self or possess the sort of complete self he has developed. (1967:155)

In politics, for example, the individual identifies himself with an entire political party and takes the organized attitudes of that entire party toward the rest of the given social community and toward the problems which confront the party within the given social situation; and he consequently reacts or responds in terms of the organized attitudes of the party as a whole. He thus enters into a special set of social relations with all the other individuals who belong to that political party; and in the same way he enters into various other special sets of social relations, with various other classes of individuals respectively, the individuals of each of these classes being the other members of some one of the particular organized subgroups (determined in socially functional terms) of which he himself is a member within the entire given society or social community. (ibid.:156–157)

12. In this sense Benedict Anderson argues that

all communities larger than primordial villages of face-to-face contact (and perhaps even these) are imagined. Communities are to be distinguished, not by their falsity/genuineness, but by the style in which they are imagined. Javanese villagers have always known that they are connected to people they have never seen, but these ties were once imagined particularistically—as indefinitely stretchable nets of kinship and clientship. Until quite recently, the Javanese language had no word meaning the abstraction "society." We may today think of the French aristocracy of the *ancien régime* as a class; but surely it was imagined this way only very late. (1994:6-7)

13. In Gregg (2003), ch. 2, I address this issue within a broader analysis of how notions of equality often are configured in terms of the advantaged group's model of relations between the sexes, as well as in terms of native-born, middle-class white feminists, on the one hand, and immigrant women and women of color on the other hand.

14. National Crime Victim Survey, Bureau of Justice Statistics, U.S. Department of Justice, 2000.

15. The recognition of difference does not require the citizen, especially in the pubic sphere, to abandon all of his or her group affiliations, particular beliefs, or commitments.

16. The notions of 'being-in-itself' and 'being-for-itself' come from G. W. F. Hegel (1770-1831), who captures the speculative, metaphysical splendor of what interests me solely as a post-metaphysical, expressly political phenomenon: "[W]ir sagen, daß etwas für sich ist, insofern als es das Anderssein, seine Beziehung und Gemeinschaft mit Anderem aufhebt, sie zurückstoßen, davon abstrahiert hat. Das Andere ist in ihm nur *als* ein Aufgehobenes, als *sein Moment*; das Fürsichsein besteht darin, über die Schranke, über sein Anderssein so hinausgegangen zu sein, daß es als diese Negation die unendliche *Rückkehr* in sich ist" (Hegel 1974:175).

17. "The right of citizens of the United States to vote shall not be denied or abridged by the United States or by any State on account of race, color, or previous condition of servitude."

18. 42 U.S.C. §§ 1973 to 1973bb-1 (1982 and Supp. IV 1986).

19. Civic inclusion also refers to the proportion of elected officials from the relevant minority, as well as to the relative responsiveness of the political system to minoritarian concerns and interests.

20. Karlan determines dilution by comparing the "likely electoral success of the minority group under a plan using single-member districts with that group's observed success under at-large elections: if the minority would have a greater ability to elect its preferred candidates from geographically defined districts than it enjoys under at-large elections, dilution has occurred" (1989:177).

21. 377 U.S. 533.

22. 377 U.S. 555.

23. 393 U.S. 544.

24. Guinier advocates a solution to racial discrimination and polarization in the political process different from mine, but her solution makes my point in the extreme case. She advocates a system of cumulative voting, whereby the "share-holders of a corporation . . . multiply the number of votes they are entitled to cast by the number of directors on the ballot and then distribute these votes however they wish. For example, a shareholder could cast all of her votes for only one director in one race and forego voting in the other elections" (Guinier 1995:233, n. 91). Here "each voter is given the same number of votes as open seats, and the voter may plump or cumulate her votes to reflect the intensity of her preferences. Depending on the exclusion threshold"—the minimum number of minority

group members required to guarantee representation in this system—"politically cohesive minority groups are assured representation if they vote strategically. Similarly, *all* voters have the potential to form voluntary constituencies based on their own assessment of their interests. As a consequence, semiproportional systems such as cumulative voting give more voters, not just racial minorities, the opportunity to vote for a winning candidate" (ibid.:222-223). She would not employ cumulative voting "in the absence of evidence that existing electoral arrangements are operating unfairly," nor would she impose it on "nonconsenting jurisdictions nationwide" (ibid.:233, n. 91).

CHAPTER 3
COPING WITH INDETERMINACY THROUGH PRAGMATISM

1. Cf. Frankenberg (1985).

2. Cf. John Dewey (1924:19, 27).

3. We can distinguish between two kinds of universalism: an extra-social or nonsocial kind and a social kind. Nonsocial are universalist assertions that otherworldly forces, or this-worldly forces of nonhuman nature, or even the biological nature of humans, determine the political and social constitution of human societies. Thus the need for food and shelter is universal but implies no particular political, economic, or cultural arrangement toward the satisfaction of those needs. Social are universalist claims that all human societies display certain features (such as a division of labor, or an incest taboo). Pragmatism rejects the first kind of universalism, not the second.

4. William James, however, articulates a correspondence theory within pragmatism: "Ordinary epistemology contents itself with the vague statement that the ideas must 'correspond' or 'agree'; the pragmatist insists on being more concrete, and asks what such 'agreement' may mean in detail. He finds first that the ideas must point to or lead towards *that* reality and no other, and then that the pointings and leadings must yield satisfaction as their result" (1975:104).

5. The "power to act" refers to the consequences of belief. Of course, types of consequences will differ.

6. Cf. Rorty 1990:1818.

7. Even if one regards Ronald Dworkin's notion of law as integrity as problematic,

> the immediately pertinent point is that if his argument is sound, there is no obvious reason why a legal pragmatist (in Dworkin's sense of the term) could not embrace it and still maintain [his or] her pragmatic belief that we should respect the past only insofar as it is useful for promoting future good. The reason we should try to treat law as the expression of a single, coherent set of principles, the pragmatist would argue, is that by doing so we promote the best kind of community. Thus, rather than standing *in opposition to* pragmatism, law as integrity could be subsumed *within* pragmatism. (Smith 1990:418)

8. As James points out in reply to one of the more obvious objections to coupling truth with satisfaction:

But here I think I hear some critic retort as follows: "If satisfactions are all that is needed to make truth, how about the notorious fact that errors are so often satisfactory? And how about the equally notorious fact that certain true beliefs may cause the bitterest dissatisfaction? Isn't it clear that not the satisfaction which it gives, but the relation of the belief *to the reality* is all that makes it true?" . . . It is the *inherent relation to reality* of a belief that gives us that specific truth-satisfaction. . . . The satisfaction of *knowing truly* is thus the only one which the pragmatist ought to have considered. . . . What *constitutes* truth is not the sentiment, but the purely logical or objective function of rightly cognizing the reality, and the pragmatist's failure to reduce this function to lower values is patent. (1975:105–106)

9. 381 U.S. 479.

10. Although we might find it difficult, rationally, to reject an inference that violated a principle we nonetheless were unwilling to amend.

11. 514 U.S. 549.

12. Art. 1, sec. 8 of the Constitution provides, in part, that "Congress shall have Power . . . to regulate Commerce . . . among the several States."

13. *U.S. Code*, vol. 18, sec. 922(q).

14. Cf. Williams 1987:495.

15. A shared way of life may allow pragmatism to treat normative conflicts as spheres in which we advance hypotheses, debate methods, and (when we arrive at conclusions) agree that all conclusions are tentative. Ideally, the "we" who participate are not some elite but rather as many cooperative participants from the relevant community as possible. Of course to distinguish among competing preferences, in such a way as to win the assent of participants, presupposes a shared metric in terms of which they can draw distinctions and order their preferences accordingly: the metric of a shared way of life. Such a metric, of course, is always open to interpretation and subject to revision. Dewey advocates a politically dynamic way of life, a type of communal experimentalism, a joint inquiry into social ends, as open and participatory as possible within the constraints of the state: The "ends of liberalism are liberty and the opportunity of individuals to secure full realization of their potentialities" (1935:56–57) Further, the "crisis in liberalism is connected with failure to develop and lay hold of an adequate conception of intelligence integrated with social movements and a factor in giving them direction. . . . It is the tragedy of earlier liberalism that just at the time when the problem of social organization was most urgent, liberals could bring to its solution nothing but the conception that intelligence is an individual possession" (ibid.:44–45).

16. Concurring opinion in *Brown v. Allen* (344 U.S. 443, 540 [1953]). Of course, these opinions may not be final in the long run, for example when they are overturned by subsequent opinions of the Supreme Court, or significantly reinterpreted, or ignored in practice or negated by new legislation.

17. Belief is akin to habit, the "establishment of a habit" or of a "rule of action" (Peirce 1992b:129), while doubt is "not a habit, but the privation of a habit" (Peirce 1905:168). Belief is socially and personally stabilizing in several ways, for example as a "habit of mind essentially enduring for some time, and mostly . . . unconscious; and like other habits, it

is ... perfectly self-satisfied" (ibid.). But self-satisfaction need not be self-debilitating or intellectually stultifying. Solutions to the myriad problems, big and small, that confront groups and individuals every day "are not stored by the actors in their consciousness but employed for new actions, which, being routine in character, run their course outside the actors' consciousness. It is only the new ... problem that renders the routines and 'habits' ineffectual and requires new learning" (Joas 1993:22), for "we cling tenaciously, not merely to believing, but to believing just what we do believe" (Peirce 1992a:114).

18. Peirce even claims that the "irritation of doubt causes a struggle to attain a state of belief" (1992a:114).

19. Hence a "habit is good or otherwise, according as it produces true conclusions from true premises or not; and an inference is regarded as valid or not, without reference to the truth or falsity of its conclusion specially, but according as the habit which determines it is such as to produce true conclusions or not" (Peirce 1992a:112). Even the "[v]alidity of the principles is determined by the coherency of the consequences produced by the habits they articulate" (Dewey 1938:13).

20. See *Church of Lukumi Babalu v. Hialeah* (508 U.S. 520 [1993]).

21. This arrangement was in fact briefly practiced in Beijing during the "Great Proletarian Cultural Revolution" (which altogether lasted from 1966 to 1976) when the color red was thought by some self-appointed ideologues to be more "revolutionary" than any competitor on the chromatic spectrum, a color then that could only signal political advance, never stasis—even for presumably politically indifferent trucks and bicycles.

22. Cf. one salutary alternative: Braybrooke (2001).

23. One leading postmodern author, Jacques Derrida speaks of "the play of relative indetermination" (1988:144), yet dismisses talk of "some vague 'indeterminacy'" in favor of "undecidability" (ibid.:148.). In fact the "undecidable" is so precisely because it is itself indeterminate or is subject to factors that render it such.

24. Similarly Lyotard urges a notion of justice "not linked to that of consensus," recognizing the "heteromorphous nature of language games" and the "principle that any consensus on the rules defining a game and the 'moves' playable within it *must* be local" (1984:xxiv). Accordingly, postmodern society is characterized by "institutions in patches."

25. I term such a localism "enlightened" to distinguish it also from Rorty's self-proclaimed "frank ethnocentrism" in the face of relativism, "letting our philosophical view dictate terms in which to describe the dead"—reasons such as regarding past generations in terms of their "benighted times" and "outdated language," and for purposes "for which it is useful to know how people talked who did not know as much as we do" (1984:50)

26. For their part, if Nicholson and Fraser are to realize an antifoundationalist form of feminism, they must "develop a method for discussing gender relations as oppressive without invoking universal principles of justice or human nature" and will "have to show how they can talk about women as a group without falling back on universal claims about a woman's identity" (Smiley 1991:1580–1581). Iris Young characterizes the dilemma of postmodern normative theory as a contradiction between norms based on "certain values derived from a conception of the good human life," that is, a "conception of human nature"—and the antifoundationalist consequence of rejecting the "very idea of a human nature as misleading or oppressive" (1990:36).

27. The postmodern standpoint is distinguished from a purely epistemological position like skepticism (which is why the ancient Greek skeptics were not postmodern). The postmodern version constitutes a form of "openness" at the level of practice, not only at the level of consciousness. Gilles Deleuze offers a vivid account of this openness in depicting Foucault's notion of power: Social "institutions are not sources or essences, and have neither essence nor interiority. They are . . . mechanisms which do not explain power, since they presuppose its relations. . . . There is no State, only state control, and the same holds for all other cases" including "the Family, Religion, Production, the Marketplace, Art [and] Morality" (1988:5). Winter contends that the postmodern perspective is one not of *radical*, but of *alternative*, skepticism: It radicalizes not skepticism but "our concept of constraints" qua contingency (1994:241). It doesn't undermine values but emphasizes that they are "profoundly human products made real by human action" (ibid.:235).

28. This point emerges from even the briefest glance at several of Foucault's major works. In *Archéologie du Savoir* (1969) he argues that discourse is both an act and a product of domination: Statements are independent of all intentional meanings, yet discourse is generated by society's control over natural and social processes. *L'Ordre du Discours* (1971) analyzes knowledge as power: Power itself (embedded in institutions such as the school, prison, and factory) actually generates social integration without recourse to human action. *Surveiller et Punir* (1975) denies all viable influence of social groups: Social processes are nothing but the systemic increase of power, and all human behavior is but the raw material for peculiarly subjectless power strategies. The later Foucault might be interpreted to have modified his stance somewhat, suggesting that the individual is constituted "not just in the play of symbols . . . [but also] in real practices—historically analyzable practices" (1983:250). If "the play of symbols" refers to knowledge, and if "historically analyzable practices" are not only matters of power, then Foucault might be interpreted as no longer equating knowledge with power—hence, no longer as reducing all human behavior to mere fodder for subjectless stratagems of power.

29. Winter concludes that the "unity of a community . . . sliver[s] and fragment[s] into a thousand components and competing perspectives. . . . [A]ny discourse of 'community' is suspect as a discourse of oppression" (1992:794-795). From a non-postmodern starting point, Margaret Jane Radin and Frank Michelman reach a similar conclusion: Where Foucauldian postmodernism obtains, we cannot "possibly hope to find the unprescribed yet predialogic 'community' required for undominated dialogue" (1991:1041-1042).

30. The pragmatist Underhill Moore captures this aspect in his description of a legal institution as the "happening over and over again of the same kind of behavior" (1923:609).

31. Similarly Richard Posner (a pragmatist without being postmodern) argues that most judges believe without evidence (indeed in the face of contrary evidence) that the judiciary's effectiveness depends on a belief by the public that judges passively interpret unambiguous texts, that judges find law and do not make it. Yet the lack of independent evidence for this belief poses no problem for law's practical functioning or normative validity: Legal institution and public each believe in the other's belief about itself, creating "a world in which expectations and a sense of mutual responsibility confirm one another without any external support" (1990a:190).

32. I find support for this argument in Martha Nussbaum, who criticizes the "skeptical maneuver [that claims]: once we recognize that the values involved in our moral debates

are human and historical, all then seem to have equal weight" (1994:217). That they do not all have equal weight is the point of singular justice: The absence of universal moral criteria need not entail the incapacity to evaluate values, to embrace some and reject others, or to order them in different respects. If the absence of universal moral criteria does not entail absolute moral relativism, then the distinction between just and unjust is still coherent: Justice in that sense is "singular" not "plural."

33. J. M. Balkin similarly claims that the postmodern notion of 'deconstruction' doubts the very "boundaries that determine who is a proper subject of justice—that is, to whom justice is owed" (1994:1137). Indeed, deconstruction entails "a responsibility without limits" (Derrida 1990:953). Of course boundaries and limits are standards distinguishing, for example, just from unjust, knowable from unknowable, responsibility from nonresponsibility. Derrida readily acknowledges as much, indeed in the context of postmodernism: A "deconstructionist approach to the boundaries that institute the human subject . . . as the measure of the just and the unjust, does not necessarily lead to . . . the effacement of an opposition between just and unjust but [rather] . . . to a reinterpretation of . . . boundaries" (ibid.:953). But a standard that sets boundaries and limits—a standard that sets other standards—is a transcendental standard. By relying implicitly on the transcendental, Derrida confounds the very antifoundationalism he professes. Because his notion of 'justice'— addressed to events and persons in all their singularity—is a transcendentalism, it constitutes the very foundationalism postmodernism rejects. The notion collapses in on itself.

34. In Gregg (2002) I further analyze political conflict resolution under conditions of moral pluralism involving Muslim immigrant communities from North Africa, the Indian subcontinent, and Turkey and their relationship to state and society in France, Germany, and England today. There I consider the procedural possibilities for resolution, as I do in chapter 2 of this book with respect to equality in electoral participation for black Americans in the United States today.

35. Lyotard, by contrast, embraces localism but nonetheless rules out, as oppressive in the extreme, any strong form of agreement (1984:81).

CHAPTER 4
ENLIGHTENED LOCALISM IN SOCIAL CRITIQUE

1. And if not always persuasive to all citizens equally, then at least persuasive enough to politically activate groups beyond the usual elites, including otherwise skeptical groups whose skepticism feeds off poverty, discrimination, and other forms of social marginalization: persuasive, for example, in Antonio Gramsci's spiritually uplifting, utopian Marxist sense of an "ideologia politica che si presenta non come fredda utopia né come dottrinario raziocinio, ma come 'fantasia' concreta operante su un popolo disperso e polverizzato per suscitarne e organizzarne la volontà collettiva" (1975:951).

2. Jürgen Habermas (1984:115), identifies several of these universalist procedures and standards: the meaning of an utterance consists in the reasons that can be offered for it; to understand the meaning of an utterance is to know the conditions of its validity. Here epistemic or normative "truth" is identified not through intuition or tests of consistency but solely through discussion, specifically through discussion oriented toward reaching

understanding among individuals or groups. A normative discussion of this type presupposes an impartial point of view. The very act of engaging in dialogue assumes a belief in the possibility of consensus, which in turn assumes that people engage in discussion under conditions that neutralize all motives except that of cooperatively seeking truth. Of course, from the outside observer's perspective (but not from the participant's), these universalist presuppositions can lead to "bad" morals as well as to "good" ones.

3. Of course not all conventional norms are based on arbitrarily privileged conditions and perspectives. Norms such as standardized units of measurement, industrial-safety standards, or certification standards for health-care workers potentially benefit everyone in the community. See Smith (1988:181).

4. *Pace* Foucault (1980:112–113, 131, 133).

5. Some localist propositions make good sense. Debates between rival ethical principles, says Alisdair MacIntyre (1981:273), can only be settled where they arise: in history. And ethical confidence, says Bernard Williams (1985:170), is "basically a social phenomenon" and requires confirmation by others and depends in various ways on institutions and public discourse. Other localist propositions are questionable. If the good for human beings can be elaborated and possessed only within an ongoing social tradition, as Geoffrey Galt Harpham (1992:50) asserts, then the critic could hardly extricate himself or herself from those aspects of social practices contaminated by power, because the critic could not draw on any standpoint external to that of the participants. Stuart Hampshire (1989:91) rightly claims that we cannot evaluate a statement if we remove it from any presupposed type of discourse and suspend all presuppositions of the background knowledge appropriate to this type. But we need no presupposed background of known constancies because of what Hampshire calls the "infinite complexity of features which could be quoted, however unreasonably, as possibly relevant to the truth of the judgment, which is always an abstraction from all these complicating possibilities" (ibid.). A "background of known constancies" probably does not exist for everyone, rather, at most, only for some groups and only some of the time. Hence it could ill serve as the broad, normative foundation for claims to truth that Hampshire has in mind.

6. Contrary to what advocates of plurality might think, plurality of social narratives implies neither an expansion of the number of participants in any given dispute or disagreement (but merely an increased number of disputes), nor equality among participants.

7. A localist standpoint cannot distinguish them when these two categories of statements differ; in some cases they may coincide. In some cases both types of statements may be appropriate in the same circumstances (in different ways, but together as an expression of morally justified self-interest), as when an African-American says, "In light of racial inequality, black citizens should receive special consideration in the distribution of such social goods as admission to universities or professional schools, or in the distribution of governmental contracts."

8. Rorty (1984:50) advocates "frank ethnocentrism" as an alternative to relativism, a position I developed in chapter 3. Understanding alternatives is a prerequisite for mutual understanding, maybe even for moral responsibility (insofar as dialogue with others may promote critical self-reflection), and certainly for the epistemic goal of correctness. Hampshire even deduces a "universal necessity of respect for . . . fairness" from the empirically observable "diversity of conceptions of the good": fairness in negotiations and concessions

form the sine qua non of a shared morality "independent of specific conceptions of the good" (1989:118-119).

9. See Feyerabend (1988).

10. See Alexander (1988).

11. As are those of natural scientists; see Zuckerman (1988:547).

12. A question for natural scientists as well; see Gilbert and Mulkay (1984:13-14). Both science (making causal judgments and singular counterfactual conditional judgments) and social critique (making normative judgments) presume background knowledge of at least temporarily unquestioned constancies.

13. As in the case of natural scientists; see Zuckerman (1988:548).

14. As must natural scientists; see Collins (1983:272).

15. According to Giddens, the unintended consequences of action are "systematically incorporated within the process of reproduction of institutions" (1994:59).

16. Hobbes imagines a polity based on the proceduralism "that a man be willing, when others are so too, as far forth as for peace and defense of himself he shall think it necessary, to lay down this right to all things, and be contented with so much liberty against other men as he would allow other men against himself" (1985: ch. 14). Three centuries later John Rawls (1971:13) likewise imagines a just polity in terms of a "voluntary scheme" in which members recognize obligations as "self-imposed." In Hobbes's procedural polity, one person's concern with another is a concern with that person's power, not his interests, for the "value or worth of a man is, as of all other things, his price—that is to say, so much as would be given for the use of his power—and therefore is not absolute but a thing dependent on the need and judgment of another" (1985:ch. 10). Similarly in Rawls's procedural polity, members are "mutually disinterested," "not taking an interest in one another's interests" (1971:13). Hobbes, according to David Gauthier, "shows us that moral and social relationships are possible among persons in contexts in which they take no interest in one another's interests" (1979:559). On the enlightened localist alternative, people would be less concerned with each other's identities and more concerned with each other's interests. Here cooperation is possible despite normative difference.

17. See *Church of Lukumi Babalu v. Hialeah*, 508 U.S. 520 (1993).

18. 163 U.S. 537.

19. See Quine (1963). Consciousness is fundamentally linguistic, according to Sellars (1956). Most knowledge begins with the capacity to use words; knowledge of particulars or of concepts is an abstraction from knowledge of propositions, not something temporally prior to it. If knowledge is a relation to propositions rather than a privileged relation to the objects propositions aim at, then justification of belief is a public and intersubjective matter, not private, not objective.

20. See Giddens and Turner (1987).

21. For example, Kuhn (1970:199-200).

22. I paraphrase Wilfred Sellars's assertion that "empirical knowledge, like its sophisticated extension, science, is rational, not because it has a foundation but because it is a self-correcting enterprise which can put any claim in jeopardy, though not all at once" (1956:300).

23. Harpham makes a similar point: Ethical discourse "operates through a calculation of 'distance': too great a distance between a principle and interest produces stilted maxims; too little produces apologias, bad faith, and false consciousness" (1992:45).

24. Cf. Bohman (1991:222).

CHAPTER 5
ENLIGHTENED LOCALISM IN PUBLIC POLICY

1. Pierre Bourdieu limns the contours of an indeterminate political community at the international level, an ambiguity at the very heart of the Western political community today with respect to the single most important "bilateral" relationship in the contemporary world, that between Western Europe and the United States: a sovereign Europe as a major player on the world stage and, at the same time, a heteronomous Europe being hollowed out economically and culturally by the hegemonic power of America: "L'Europe est foncièrement amgiguë, d'une ambiguïté qui tend à se dissiper lorsqu'on la considère dans une perspective dynamique: il y a d'une part une Europe autonome à l'égard des puissances économiques et politiques dominantés et capable, à ce titre, de jouer un rôle politique à l'échelle mondiale; il y a d'autre part l'Europe liée par une sorte d'union douanière avec les États-Unis et vouée, de ce fait, à un destin analogue à celui du Canada, c'est-à-dire à être progressivement dépossédée de toute indépendance économique et culturelle à l'égard de la puissance dominante. En fait, l'Europe vraiment européenne fonctionne comme un *leurre* dissimulant l'Europe euro-américaine qui se profile et qu'elle facilite en obtenant l'adhésion de ceux qui en attendent l'inverse exact de ce qu'elle fait et de ce qu'elle est en train de devenir" (2001:68).

2. Philip Selznick, for instance, finds that "participation in communities is mediated by participation in families, localities, personal networks, and institutions. This 'core' participation *preserves the identity . . . of the participants*" (1989:507). According to Amitai Etzioni, "commitment to discharge one's responsibilities is acquired, first of all, in the family," while schools form the "second line of defense. . . . Finally, neighborhoods have a role in shoring up responsibilities" (1992:110).

3. John Goldberg (1990:1335), discussing the views of Justice Benjamin Cardozo.

4. *Prince v. Massachusetts*, 321 U.S. 158 (1944).

5. *People v. Benn*, 87 Misc. 2d 139, 385 N.Y.S. 2d 222 (Crim. Ct. 1976).

6. *People v. Pointer*, 151 Cal.App. 3d 1128, 199 Cal.Rptr. 357 (1984).

7. Regarding abortion: *Bellotti v. Baid*, 443 U.S. 622, 634 (1979); regarding contraception: *Carey v. Population Services International*, 431 U.S. 678 (1977).

8. *Pierce v. Society of Sisters*, 268 U.S. 510 (1925).

9. Burtt suggests that, for most fundamentalist parents, the question is not so much a "political difference over citizenship goals . . . [as it is] a cultural clash centered on differing judgments of what values and dispositions best equip children to deal with the modern world" (1994:62). But any notion of 'citizenship' in a democratic society makes value judgments about how best to "deal with the modern world"; any notion of citizenship entails normative commitments. In other words, the question of what content a society has its children learn in school is also a question what kind of citizens a society wants its youth to

become. Burtt's distinction between the "content-oriented question of *what children will learn*" and the "process-oriented one of who decides how these lessons will be conveyed" (ibid.) is spurious.

10. *Plyler v. Doe*, 457 U.S. 202 (1982).
11. 406 U.S. 205 (1972).
12. Ibid., pp. 222–226.
13. When parents and their children disagree, generally children are not accorded a right to the free exercise of religion that trumps that of their parents; the law is parent centered. From the perspective of enlightened localism, children in this context should enjoy certain constitutional rights. The question of whether children should be subject to the state's curricular choices, where these offend the parents' religious convictions, is more decisive for the child than for its parents. Accordingly, the question appropriately takes account of the child's judgment and wishes, rather than simply ignoring them, as in parent-centered law.
14. Disagreement might follow from claims to moral obligation of insiders to outsiders, ranging from no obligation ever to some obligation sometimes to significant obligation in many instances. Then agreement on the first issue would occur in a broader context of disagreement. We then observe how agreement on general principles can be undone by disagreement on concrete particulars.
15. Parents who understandably want the best for their children define "best" in terms of their own worldview, including political and religious convictions and other views shaped in part by the peculiarities of their respective biographies. An overly ambitious parent might disregard the child's ability-appropriate preference for less demanding curricular or extracurricular commitments. A parent less gifted or more gifted than his or her child might discourage its preference for forms or levels of achievement that do not resonate with the parent. The Amish parent may not want his or her child to continue in school after the eighth grade, or many parents (for a variety of reasons) may object to their children receiving sex education in school (while not providing any at home)—although in both cases the child might well choose differently, and perhaps better, than the parent. Noncoincidence of interest between parents and child is acute with respect to the developmental needs of the child's mind and character—the very heart of the issue in the debate over compulsory education.
16. Society as a whole would therefore reject Burtt's apologia for a particular community treating female children as inferior on the basis of the community's religious or customary convictions:

> A principal can and should defend a curriculum which seeks to awaken professional aspirations in girls as well as boys, but parents who want their children excused from the relevant classes because their religion specifies certain role-bound duties for the sexes must have their wishes respected. Girls raised in this way will make decent, law-abiding citizens, even if, from the standpoint of liberal democratic ideals, they have not been treated entirely justly. (1994:69)

Burtt regards any practice not expressly unconstitutional as therefore permissible within whatever particular community inclined to that practice. But constitutions, like any complex regime of rules, are indeterminate with respect to what some legal rules mean and how judges and others should apply them. Where law is indeterminate, no theory, rule, or principle constrains a judge to interpret or apply a law in a particular way. Consequently a case could have several different answers, yet all of them equally valid. Burtt's reliance on the Constitution as a criterion of acceptability founders on the rocks of indeterminacy.

17. Could such a policy actually deny certain choices to children of religiously fundamentalist parents? Burtt mistakenly argues that sometimes an autonomous choice for one's parents' lifestyle or worldview may require that the individual, as a child, not be exposed to alternatives: "[C]ertain of these lives may depend for their possibility on not being exposed too early or too insistently to secular alternatives" (1994:66). This is choice by default: choosing X in part because of never having been exposed to alternatives Y or Z, or not having been exposed to them before ways have become settled.

18. In Gregg (2003) I develop a complete theory about how society at large (which I conceive of as a kind of "generalized community" guided by "thin" norms) might best relate to particular communities of deep normative commitments (which I describe as "normatively thick").

19. Cf., in agreement: Walzer (1983:40–41); in disagreement: Ackerman (1980:8).

20. *Brown v. Board of Education of Topeka*, 347 U.S. 483 (1954).

21. Although, as Pierre Bourdieu points out at that rare level of regional alliances, the imperatives of political and social privilege can be transnational as well, and the solution then can only be that of taking transnational political control over the transnational economy: "Si l'on peut lutter contre l'État national, il faut défendre les fonctions 'universelles' qu'il remplit et qui peuvent être remplies aussi bien, sinon mieux, par un État supranational. Si l'on ne veut pas que ce soit la Bundesbank qui, à travers les taux d'intérêt, gouverne les politiques financières des différents États, est-ce qu'il ne faut pas lutter pour la construction d'un État supranational, relativement autonome par rapport aux forces économiques internationales et aux forces politiques nationales et capable de développer la dimension sociale des institutions européennes? Par example, les mesures visant à assurer la réduction du temps de travail ne prendraient tout leur sens que si elles étaient prises par une instance européenne et applicables à l'ensemble des nations européennes" (1998:47).

CHAPTER 6
ENLIGHTENED LOCALISM IN LAW AND MORALITY

1. 163 U.S. 537 (1896).

2. Strikingly, even "cultural values that have been tied to the history of racial oppression are potentially open to all individuals, regardless of their color" (Gutmann 1996:167).

3. George Herbert Mead supports this claim at the level of social psychology:

The individual experiences himself as such, not directly, but only indirectly, from the particular standpoints of other individual members of the same social group, or from the generalized standpoint of the social group as a whole to which he belongs. For he enters his own experience as a self or individual, not directly or immediately, not by becoming a subject to himself, but only in so far as he first becomes an object to himself just as other individuals are objects to him or in his experience; and he becomes an object to himself only by taking the attitudes of other individuals toward himself within a social environment or context of experience and behavior in which both he and they are involved. (1967:138)

4. "Ein Buch zum Denken, nichts weiter: es gehört Denen, welchen Denken *Vergnügen* macht, nichts weiter . . . Daß es deutsch geschrieben ist, ist zum Mindesten unzeitgemäß: ich wünschte es französisch geschrieben zu haben, damit es nicht als Befürwortung irgend welcher reichsdeutschen Aspirationen erscheint" (Nietzsche 1970:114).

5. In a sense systematically analyzed in ethnomethodological studies, beginning with Harold Garfinkel (1967).

6. But neither are law and morality simply equally plausible alternatives to each other. In the functional organization of modern societies, law can better accomplish what in earlier societies was the task mainly of morality: the norming of communal members' behavior. Law can do so, among other reasons, because it does not require the kind of normative homogeneity that a functionally viable morality requires, and that in complex modern societies is empirically unlikely, increasingly so in a globalizing world. But even then, law preserves some aspects of morality, and remains in relationship to morality; a purely positive legal regime, à la Hans Kelsen, is socially and politically unworkable. Norberto Bobbio delineates the analogous relationship between the rule of law (in the sense uniquely captured by the word *Rechtsstaat*) and the democratic state: "Uno dei maggiori problemi di ogni convivenza civile é quello di creare delle istituzioni che permettano di risolvere i conflitti, se non tutti i conflitti che possono sorgere in una società almeno la maggior parte, senza che sia necesario ricorrere alla forza, se pure alla forza legittima, perché esercitata dal sovrano, e legale, perché esercitata nell'ambito delle leggi che la regolano. L'insieme delle istituzioni che rendono possibile la soluzione di conflitti senza il ricorso alla forza costituiscono, oltre lo stato di diritto, lo stato democratico, vale a dire lo stato in cui vige la regola fondamentale che in ogni conflitto vincitore è non già colui che ha piú forza fisica ma colui che ha piú forz persuasiva, cioè colui che con la forza della persuasione . . . è riuscito a conquistare la maggioranza dei voti. In linguaggio funzionalistico si può dire che il metodo democratico è il surrogato funzionale all'uso della forza per la soluzione dei conflitti sociali. Un surrogato non esculsivo ma del quale non si può disconoscere l'enorme importanza per ridurre l'ambito del puro dominio: il dibattito al posto dello scontro fisico, e dopo il dibattito il voto al posto dell'eliminazione fisica dell'avversario. Mentre la istituzione dello stato di diritto influisce sull'uso della forza regolandola, l'istituzione dello stato democratico vi influisce riducendone lo spazio di applicazione" (1985:17-18).

7. I take issue then with Niklas Luhmann's claim that in a functionally differentiated legal system,

> all regulation must be self-regulation. There may be political control of legislation, but only the law can change the law. Only within the legal system can the change of legal norms be perceived as change of the law. This is not a question of power or influence, and this is not to deny that the environment and particularly the political system has an impact on the legal system. But the legal system reproduces itself by legal events and only by legal events. Political events (e.g., elections) may be legal events at the same time, but with different connections,

linkages, and exclusions for each system. Only legal events (e.g., legal decisions but also events like elections insofar as they are communicated as legal events) warrant the continuity of the law and only deviant reproduction . . . can change the law. (1990:229)

8. Cf., in this spirit, JürgenHabermas (1996).

9. 347 U.S. 483.

10. "No State shall make or enforce any law which shall abridge the privileges or immunities of citizens of the United States; nor shall any State deprive any person of life, liberty, or property, without due process of law; nor deny to any person within its jurisdiction the equal protection of the laws."

CODA
SOCIAL COOPERATION IN THE ABSENCE OF POLITICAL UNITY

1. Wolin claims that localism is antipolitical: "Long ago Aristotle had insisted that the political association, by virtue of its superior comprehensiveness and purpose, had a stronger claim on men's loyalties than any lesser association and that political membership was therefore superior to other forms of membership" (1960:433). He claims that political responsibility can be meaningful "only in terms of a general constituency," such that "no multiplication of fragmentary constituencies will provide a substitute" (ibid.:433). In this way he makes unity more or less indivisible from political consciousness. Enlightened localism, by contrast, offers political consciousness without requiring unity in a strong, universalist sense.

2. For another aesthetic perspective also derived from "classical" pragmatism (this time concerning judicial activity), see Karl Llewellyn (1942).

3. To be sure, the later Lyotard contends that the critical potential of postmodern art lies in a heightening of the critical potential of modern art. This argument starts from the traditional notion that "aesthetics sometimes functions as an unpleasant mirror" to reveal alienation or injustice (Jameson 1984:xix). According to Lyotard, modern aesthetics in its "form, because of its recognizable consistency, continues to offer to the reader or viewer matter for solace and pleasure," whereas postmodern aesthetics "denies itself the solace of good forms, the consensus of a taste which would make it possible to share collectively the nostalgia for the unattainable" (1984:81). But Lyotard here is atypical of those postmodern authors whose aesthetics as a form of subjectivism hardly seems critical, as in the assertion: "Legality does not belong to the moral but to the aesthetic order. There is a validity to aesthetic judgments, but it is founded upon feeling not . . . concepts. . . . [T]he legality of the felt . . . puts into play a subjective attachment to a particular order and organization of experience. . . . [A]s an art . . . law can account for common experience, for 'legality without concepts,' for a conformity to law without law" (Goodrich, Douzinas, and Hachamovitch 1994:26).

4. I adopt Kant somewhat against the grain. Given his belief in universal standards of aesthetic judgment, Kant does not regard modern Western art as expressive of social and cultural pluralism; he does not think an artwork draws coherence from some kind of communion among artist and consumers and critics and meanings widely shared within a

community or society. But he does regard aesthetic judgment as a kind of subjectivity whose coherence resonates with other subjectivities, and here he reinforces my project. The individual's aesthetic judgment begins with the immediate, particular, socially embedded experience of reacting to a particular artwork; it does not begin with any kind of universality. My aesthetic pleasure is always particular, but for Kant it can be universally valid nonetheless. Thus when I perceive with pleasure an artwork and judge it accordingly, my pleasure is subjective and yet is equally valid for all other persons, inasmuch as the noncognitive conditions of any one human subject's aesthetic judgment are the same for all other human subjects: "Mit einer Wahrnehmung kann aber auch unmittelbar ein Gefühl der Lust (oder Unlust) und Wohlgefallen verbunden werden, welches die Vorstellung des Objekts begleitet und derselben statt Prädikats dient, und so ein ästhetisches Urteil, welches kein Erkenntnisurteil ist, entspringen. Einem solchen, wenn es nicht bloßes Empfingungs-, sondern ein formales Reflexionsurteil ist, welches dieses Wohlgefallen jedermann als notwendig ansinnt, muß etwas als Prinzip a priori zum Grunde liegen, welches allenfalls ein bloß subjektives sein mag . . . , wie ein ästhetisches Urteil auf Notwendigkeit Auspruch machen könne. Hierauf gründet sich nun die Aufgabe, mit der wir uns jetzt beschäftigen: wie sind Geschmacksurteile möglich? welche Aufgabe also die Prinzipien a pirori der reinen Urteilskraft in *ästhetischen Urteilen* betrifft, d.i. in solchen, wo sie nicht (wie in den theoretischen) unter objective Verstandesbegriffe bloß zu subsumieren hat und unter einem Gesetze steht, sondern wo sie sich selbst, subjektiv, Gegenstand sowohl als Gesetz ist" (1974:138).

5. Even as language also sometimes divides people, sometimes even despite itself. Anderson, for example, notes the "paradoxical concept *négritude*—essence of African-ness expressible only in French" (1994:123).

6. Whereas Tönnies conceives of the "relationship itself, and also the resulting association, . . . either as real and organic life—this is the essential characteristic of the *Gemeinschaft* (community); or as imaginary and mechanical structure—this is the concept of *Gesellschaft* (society)" (1957:33).

Bibliography

Ackerman, Bruce. 1980. *Social Justice in the Liberal State.* New Haven: Yale University Press.
Adams, John. 1851. *Works,* vol. 4: Little, Brown.
Alexander, Jeffrey. 1988. "The New Theoretical Movement," in *Handbook of Sociology,* ed. Neil Smelser, 77-101. Newbury Park, Calif.; Sage.
Anderson, Benedict. 1994. *Imagined Communities: Reflections on the Origin and Spread of Nationalism.* London: Verso.
Anderson, Charles. 1990. *Pragmatic Liberalism.* Chicago: University of Chicago Press.
Appiah, K. Anthony. 1996. "Culture, Identity: Misunderstood Connections." In *Color Conscious: The Political Morality of Race,* ed. K. Anthony Appiah and Amy Gutmann, 30-105. Princeton: Princeton University Press.
Balkin, J. M. 1994. "Transcendental Deconstruction, Transcendent Justice." *Michigan Law Review* 92:1131-1186.
Bauböck, Rainer. 1994. *Transnational Citizenship: Membership and Rights in International Migration.* Aldershot, U.K.: Edward Elgar.
Bell, Derrick. 1995a. "*Brown v. Board of Education* and the Interest Convergence Dilemma." In *Critical Race Theory,* ed. Kimberlé Crenshaw, Neil Gotanda, Gary Peller, and Kendals Thomas, 20-29. New York: New Press.
———. 1995b. "Serving Two Masters: Integration Ideals and Client Interests in School Desegregation Litigation." In *Critical Race Theory,* ed. Kimberlé Crenshaw, Neil Gotanda, Gary Peller, and Kendall Thomas, 5-19. New York: New Press.
Benhabib, Seyla. 1986. *Critique, Norm, and Utopia.* New York: Columbia University Press.
Benjamin, Martin. 1990. *Splitting the Difference: Compromise and Integrity in Ethics and Politics.* Lawrence: University Press of Kansas.
Bobbio, Norberto. 1985. "La crisi della democrazia e la lezione dei classici," in *Crisi della Democrazia e Neocontrattualismo,* ed. Norberto Bobbio, Giuliano Pontara, and Salvatore Veca, 9-33. Rome: Editori Riuniti.
Bohman, James. 1991. *New Philosophy of Social Science: Problems of Indeterminacy.* Cambridge: MIT Press.
Bourdieu, Pierre. 1997. *Méditations pascaliennes.* Paris: Seuil.
———. 1998. "Le mythe de la 'mondialisation' et l'État social européen," in *Contre-feux. Propos pour servir à la résistance contre l'invasion néo-libérale,* 34-50. Paris: Éditions Raison d'Agir.
———. 2001. "Contre la politique de dépolitisation," in *Contre-feux 2. Pour un mouvement social européen,* 57-72. Paris: Éditions Raison d'Agir.
Braybrooke, David. 2001. *Natural Law Modernized.* Toronto: University of Toronto Press.

Burtt, Shelley. 1994. "Religious Parents, Secular Schools: A Liberal Defense of an Illiberal Education." *Review of Politics* 56:51-71.
Cardozo, Benjamin. 1921. *The Nature of the Judicial Process*. New Haven: Yale University Press.
Carmichael, Stokely. 1971. *Stokely Speaks: Black Power Back to Pan-Africanism*. New York: Random House.
Carmichael, Stokely, and Charles Hamilton. 1967. *Black Power: The Politics of Liberation in America*. New York: Random House.
Cohen, Felix. 1933. *Ethical Systems and Legal Ideals*. New York: Falcon.
Collins, Harry. 1983. "The Sociology of Scientific Knowledge: Studies of Contemporary Science." in *Annual Review of Sociology*, ed. Ralph Turner and James Scott, 9:265-285. Palo Alto, Calif.: Annual Reviews.
Connolly, William. 1991. *Identity/Difference*. Ithaca: Cornell University Press.
Crenshaw, Kimberlé. 1995a. "Introduction." In *Critical Race Theory*, ed. Kimberlé Crenshaw, Neil Gotanda, Gary Peller, and Kendall Thomas, xiii-xxxii. New York: New Press.
———. 1995b. "Mapping the Margins: Intersectionality, Identity Politics, and Violence against Women of Color." In *Critical Race Theory*, ed. Kimberlé Crenshaw, Neil Gotanda, Gary Peller, and Kendall Thomas, 357-383. New York: New Press.
Deleuze, Gilles. 1988. *Foucault*. Minneapolis: University of Minnesota Press.
Deleuze, Gilles and Félix Guattari. 1972. *L'anti-Oedipe*, vol. 1 of *Capitalisme et schizophrénie*. Paris: Les Editions de Minuit.
Derrida, Jacques. 1988. *Limited Inc*. Evanston: Northwestern University Press.
———. 1990. "Force of Law: 'The Mystical Foundation of Authority.'" *Cardozo Law Review* 11:920-1045.
Dewey, John. 1922. "Valuation and Experimental Knowledge." *Philosophical Review* 31:325-351.
———. 1924. "Logical Method and Law." *Cornell Law Quarterly* 10:17-27.
———. 1931. *Philosophy and Civilization*. New York: Minton, Balch.
———. 1935. *Liberalism and Social Action*. New York: G. P. Putnam's Sons.
———. 1938. *Logic: The Theory of Inquiry*. New York: Henry Holt.
———. 1941. "My Philosophy of Law." In *My Philosophy of Law: Credos of Sixteen American Scholars*, 73-85. Boston: Boston Law Book.
———. 1958. *Art as Experience*. New York: Capricorn Books.
———. 1968. *Philosophy and Civilization*. Gloucester, Mass.: Peter Smith.
Du Bois, W. E. B. [1903] 1996. "The Souls of Black Folk," in *Writings*, 357-547. New York: Library of America.
———. 1935. "Does the Negro Need Separate Schools?" *Journal of Negro Education* 4, no. 3: 328-335.
Durkheim, Émile. [1893] 1984. *The Division of Labor in Society*, trans. W. D. Halls. New York: Free Press.
———. [1912] 1995. *The Elementary Forms of Religious Life*, trans. Karen Fields. New York: Free Press.
Dworkin, Ronald. 1977. *Taking Rights Seriously*. Cambridge: Harvard University Press.
———. 1986. *Law's Empire*. Cambridge: Harvard University Press.
Ehrenreich, Nancy. 1990. "Pluralist Myths and Powerless Men: The Ideology of Reasonableness in Sexual Harassment Law." *Yale Law Journal* 99:1177-1234.

Ely, John Hart. 1980. *Democracy and Distrust.* Cambridge: Harvard University Press.
Etzioni, Amitai. 1992. "The Other Side of the Rights Coin." *ABA Journal* 78:110.
Feldman, Stephen M. 1993. "The Persistence of Power and the Struggle for Dialogic Standards in Postmodern Constitutional Jurisprudence: Michelman, Habermas, and Civic Republicanism." *Georgetown Law Journal* 81:2243-2290.
Feyerabend, Paul. 1988. *Against Method,* rev. ed. London: Verso.
Fish, Stanley. 1990. "Almost Pragmatism: Richard Posner's Jurisprudence." *University of Chicago Law Review* 57:1447-1475.
―――. 1994. "Play of Surfaces: Theory and the Law." In *There's No Such Thing as Free Speech,* 180-199. New York: Oxford University Press.
Fisher, William, Morton Horwitz, and Thomas Reed, eds. 1993. *American Legal Realism.* New York: Oxford University Press.
Foucault, Michel. 1969. *Archéologie du Savoir.* Paris: Editions Gallimard.
―――. 1971. *L'Ordre du Discours.* Paris: Editions Gallimard.
―――. 1975. *Surveiller et Punir.* Paris: Editions Gallimard.
―――. 1978. *The History of Sexuality.* New York: Pantheon Books.
―――. 1980. *Power/Knowledge: Selected Interviews and Other Writings 1972-77,* ed. C. Gordon. New York: Pantheon Books.
―――. 1983. "On the Genealogy of Ethics: An Overview of a Work in Progress." In *Michel Foucault: Beyond Structuralism and Hermeneutics,* 2nd ed., ed. Hubert L. Dreyfus and Paul Rabinow, 229-252. Chicago: University of Chicago Press.
―――. 1988. "The Ethic of Care for the Self as a Practice of Freedom: An Interview with Michel Foucault," in *The Final Foucault,* ed. James Bernauer and David Rasmussen, 1-20. Cambridge: MIT Press.
Frankenberg, Günther. 1985. "Critical Comparisons: Re-Thinking Comparative Law." *Harvard International Law Journal* 26:411-455.
Gadamer, Hans Georg. 1972. *Wahrheit und Methode. Grundzüge einer philosophischen Hermeneutik.* 3rd edition. Tübingen: Mohr.
Galston, William A. 1987. "False Universality: Infinite Personality and Finite Existence in Unger's *Politics.*" *Northwestern Law Review* 81:751-765.
Garfinkel, Harold. 1967. *Studies in Ethnomethodology.* Englewood Cliffs, N.J.: Prentice-Hall.
Gates, Henry Louis Jr. 1992. *Loose Canons: Notes on the Culture Wars.* New York: Oxford University Press.
Gauthier, David. 1979. "Thomas Hobbes: Moral Theorist." *Journal of Philosophy* 76:547-559.
Geertz, Clifford. 1983. "Local Knowledge: Fact and Law in Comparative Perspective." In *Local Knowledge: Further Essays in Interpretive Anthropology,* 167-234. New York: Basic Books.
―――. 1986. "The Uses of Diversity." *Michigan Quarterly Review* 23:105-123.
Gellner, Ernest. 1970. "Concepts and Society." In *Ratiionality,* ed. Bryan R. Wilson, 18-49. Evanston and New York: Harper and Row.
Giddens, Anthony. 1984. *The Constitution of Society: Introduction to the Theory of Structuration.* Berkeley and Los Angeles: University of California Press.
―――. 1994. *Central Problems in Social Theory: Action, Structure, and Contradiction in Social Analysis.* Berkeley and Los Angeles: University of California Press.

Giddens, Anthony, and Jonathan Turner, eds. 1987. *Social Theory Today*. Cambridge: Polity.
Gilbert, G. Nigel, and Michael Mulkay. 1984. *Opening Pandora's Box: A Sociological Analysis of Scientists' Discourse*. Cambridge: Cambridge University Press.
Goldberg, John C. P. 1990. "Community and the Common Law Judge: Reconstructing Cardozo's Theoretical Writings." *New York University Law Review* 65:1324-1372.
Goodman, Nelson. 1983. *Fact, Fiction, and Forecast*. Cambridge: Harvard University Press.
Goodrich, Peter, Costas Douzinas, and Yifat Hachamovitch. 1994. "Introduction: Politics, Ethics, and the Legality of the Contingent." In *Politics, Postmodernity and Critical Legal Studies*, ed. Peter Goodrich, Costas Douzinas and Yifat Hachamovitch, 1-31. London: Routledge.
Gotanda, Neil. 1995. "A Critique of 'Our Constitution is Color-Blind.'" In *Critical Race Theory*, ed. Kimberlé Crenshaw, Neil Gotanda, Gary Peller, and Kendall Thomas, 257-275. New York: New Press.
Gramsci, Antonio. [1948-51] 1975. *Quaderni del Carcere*, v. 2. Torino: Giulio Einaudi.
Gregg, Benjamin. 1992. "The Parameters of Possible Constitutional Interpretation." In *Vocabularies of Public Life: Empirical Essays in Symbolic Structure*, ed. Robert Wuthnow, 207-233. London: Routledge.
———. 2002. "Proceduralism Reconceived: Political Conflict Resolution under Conditions of Moral Pluralism." *Theory and Society* 31:741-776.
———. 2003. *Thick Morality, Thin Politics: Social Integration Across Communities of Belief*. Durham: Duke University Press.
Guinier, Lani. 1995. "Groups, Representation, and Race-Conscious Districting: A Case of the Emperor's Clothes." In *Critical Race Theory*, ed. Kimberlé Crenshaw, Neil Gotanda, Gary Peller, and Kendall Thomas, 205-235. New York: New Press.
Gutmann, Amy. 1996. "Responding to Racial Injustice." In *Color Conscious. The Political Morality of Race*, ed. K. Anthony Appiah and Amy Gutmann, 106-178. Princeton: Princeton University Press.
Habermas, Jürgen. 1984. *The Theory of Communicative Action*. Vol. 1, *Reason and the Rationalization of Society*, trans. Thomas McCarthy. Boston: Beacon.
———. 1987. *The Theory of Communicative Action*. Vol. 2, *Lifeworld and System: A Critique of Functionalist Reason*, trans. Thomas McCarthy. Boston: Beacon.
———. 1996. *Between Facts and Norms: Contributions to a Discourse Theory of Law and Democracy*, trans. William Rehg. Cambridge: MIT Press.
Hampshire, Stuart. 1989. *Innocence and Experience*. Cambridge: Harvard University Press.
———. 1993. "Political Liberalism." *New York Review of Books*, 12 August, 43-47.
Harpham, Geoffrey Galt. 1992. *Getting It Right: Language, Literature, and Ethics*. Chicago: University of Chicago Press.
Hart, H. L. A. 1961. *The Concept of Law*. Oxford: Oxford University Press.
Hegel, Georg Wilhelm Friedrich. [1831] 1974. "*Wissenschaft der Logik, Erster Teil, Erstes Buch: Die objective Logik*." In Hegel, *Werke in zwanzig Bänden*, v. 5. Frankfurt am Main: Suhrkamp.
Hesse, Mary. 1980. *Revolutions and Reconstructions in the Philosophy of Science*. Bloomington: Indiana University Press.
Hirschman, Albert. 1970. *Exit, Voice, and Loyalty: Responses to Decline in Firms, Organizations, and States*. Cambridge: Harvard University Press.
Hobbes, Thomas. [1651] 1985. *Leviathan*. London: Penguin Books.

Holmes, Oliver Wendell. 1961. *Holmes–Pollock Letters*, ed. Mark Howe. Cambridge: Harvard University Press.
James, William. [1909] 1975. *The Meaning of Truth*. Cambridge: Harvard University Press.
Jameson, Fredric. 1984. Foreword to *The Postmodern Condition*, by Jean-François Lyotard. Minneapolis: University of Minnesota Press.
Jay, Martin. 1993. *Force Fields: Between Intellectual History and Cultural Critique*. London: Routledge.
Joas, Hans. 1993. *Pragmatism and Social Theory*. Chicago: University of Chicago Press.
Kant, Immanuel. [1785] 1991. *Metaphysics of Morals*, trans. Mary Gregor. Cambridge: Cambridge University Press.
———. [1790]. 1974. *Kritik der Urteilskraft*. Hamburg: Felix Meiner.
Karlan, Pamela. 1989. "Maps and Misreadings: The Role of Geographic Compactness in Racial Vote Dilution Litigation." *Harvard Civil Rights–Civil Liberties Law Review* 24: 173-248.
Karst, Kenneth. 1994. "Out of Many, One?" *Indiana Journal of Global Legal Studies* 2:65-70.
Kelsen, Hans. 1970. *The Pure Theory of Law*. Berkeley and Los Angeles: University of California Press.
Kuhn, Thomas. 1970. *The Structure of Scientific Revolutions*. Chicago: University of Chicago Press.
Landers, Scott. 1990. "Wittgenstein, Realism, and CLS-Undermining Rule Skepticism." *Law and Philosophy* 9:177-203.
Llewellyn, Karl. 1941-1942. "On the Good, the True, the Beautiful, in Law." *University of Chicago Law Review* 9:224-265.
———. 1960. *The Common Law Tradition*. Boston: Little, Brown.
Lovibond, Sabina. 1989. "Feminism and Postmodernism." *New Left Review* 178:5-28.
Luhmann, Niklas. 1982. *The Differentiation of Society*. New York: Columbia University Press.
———. 1989. "Law as a Social System." *Northwestern Law Review* 83:136-150.
———. 1990. *Essays on Self-Reference*. New York: Columbia University Press.
Lyotard, Jean-François. 1974. *Economie Libidinale*. Paris: Editions de Minuit.
———. 1984. *The Postmodern Condition: A Report on Knowledge*. Minneapolis: University of Minnesota Press.
Lyotard, Jean-François, and Jean-Loup Thebaud. 1985. *Just Gaming*. Minneapolis: University of Minnesota Press.
Machiavelli, Niccolò. [1519] 1975. *The Discourses on the First Decad of Titus Livy*. London: Routledge and Kegan Paul.
———. [1525] 1878. *The History of Florence*. London: George Bell and Sons.
MacIntyre, Alasdair. 1981. *After Virtue*. Notre Dame: University of Notre Dame Press.
Malcolm X. 1970. *By Any Means Necessary: Speeches, Interviews, and a Letter by Malcolm X*, ed. by George Breitman. New York: Pathfinder.
Margolis, Joseph. 1986. *Pragmatism without Foundations*. Oxford: Basil Blackwell.
Mead, George Herbert. [1934] 1967. *Mind, Self, and Society*. Chicago: University of Chicago Press.
Megill, Allan. 1985. *Prophets of Extremity*. Berkeley and Los Angeles: University of California Press.
Moore, Underhill. 1923. "Rational Basis of Social Institutions." *Columbia Law Review* 23:609-617.

Nagel, Thomas. 1986. *The View from Nowhere*. New York: Oxford University Press.
Nicholson, Linda, and Nancy Fraser, eds. 1988. *Feminism/Postmodernism*. New York: Routledge.
Nietzsche, Friedrich. 1970. *Nachgelassene Fragmente, Herbst 1887 bis März 1888*, in *Nietzsche Werke Kritische Gesamtausgabe*, part 8, vol. 2. Berlin: Walter de Gruyter.
Nussbaum, Martha C. 1994. "Valuing Values: A Case for Reasoned Commitment." *Yale Journal of Law and the Humanities* 6:197-217.
Peirce, Charles Sanders. [1877] 1992a. "The Fixation of Belief." In *The Essential Peirce*, vol. 1, ed. Nathan Houser and Christian Kloesel, 109-123. Bloomington: Indiana University Press.
———. [1878] 1992b. "How to Make Our Ideas Clear." In *The Essential Peirce*, vol. 1, ed. Nathan Houser and Christian Kloesel, 124-141. Bloomington: Indiana University Press.
———. 1905. "What Pragmatism Is." *The Monist* 15:161-181.
Peller, Gary. 1995. "Race Consciousness." In *Critical Race Theory*, ed. Kimberlé Crenshaw, Neil Gotanda, Gary Peller, and Kendall Thomas, 127-158. New York: New Press.
Pitkin, Hanna. 1967. *The Concept of Representation*. Berkeley and Los Angeles: University of California Press.
Plato. [c. 366-362 B.C.E.] 1952. *Statesman*, trans. J. B. Skemp. London: Routledge and Kegan Paul.
Posner, Richard. 1990a. *The Problems of Jurisprudence*. Cambridge: Harvard University Press.
———. 1990b. "What Has Pragmatism to Offer Law?" *Southern California Law Review* 63:1653-1670.
Prado, C. C. 1987. *The Limits of Pragmatism*. Atlantic Highlands, N.J.: Humanities Press International.
Quine, Willard V. O. 1963. "Two Dogmas of Empiricism." In *From a Logical Point of View*. New York: Harper and Row.
Radin, Margaret Jane, and Frank Michelman. 1991. "Pragmatist and Poststructuralist Critical Legal Practice." *University of Pennsylvania Law Review* 139:1019-1058.
Radin, Max. 1930. "Statutory Interpretation." *Harvard Law Review* 43:863-885.
Rawls, John. 1971. *A Theory of Justice*. Cambridge: Harvard University Press.
———. 1981. "The Idea of an Overlapping Consensus." *Oxford Journal of Legal Studies* 7:1-25.
Raz, Joseph. 1998. "Multiculturalism." *Ratio Juris* 11:193-205.
Rhoads, John. 1991. *Critical Issues in Social Theory*. University Park: Pennsylvania State University Press.
Rorty, Richard. 1979. *Philosophy and the Mirror of Nature*. Princeton: Princeton University Press.
———. 1982. *Consequences of Pragmatism*. Minneapolis: University of Minnesota Press.
———. 1984. "The Historiography of Philosophy: Four Genres," in *Philosophy in History: Essays on the Historiography of Philosophy*, ed. Richard Rorty, J. B. Schneewind, and Quentin Skinner, 49-75. Cambridge: Cambridge University Press.
———. 1986. "Freud and Moral Reflection." In *Pragmatism's Freud: The Moral Disposition of Psychoanalysis*, ed. Joseph Smith and William Kerrigan, 1-27. Baltimore: Johns Hopkins University Press.

———. 1989. *Contingency, Irony, and Solidarity*. Cambridge: Cambridge University Press.
———. 1990. "The Banality of Pragmatism and the Poetry of Justice." *Southern California Law Review* 63:1811-1819.
Scanlan, John. 1989. "A View from the United States: Social, Economic, and Legal Change, the Persistence of the State, and Immigration Policy in the Coming Century." *Indiana Journal of Global Legal Studies* 2:79-141.
Schlag, Pierre. 1989. "Missing Pieces: A Cognitive Approach to Law." *Texas Law Review* 67:1195-1250.
Sellars, Wilfred. 1956. "Empiricism and the Philosophy of Mind," in *Minnesota Studies in the Philosophy of Science*, eds. Herbert Feigl and Michael Scriven, vol. 1: *The Foundations of Science and the Concepts of Psychology and Psychoanalysis*, 253-329. Minneapolis: University of Minnesota Press.
Selznick, Philip. 1989. "Dworkin's Unfinished Task." *California Law Review* 77:505-513.
Shklar, Judith. 1964. *Legalism*. Cambridge: Harvard University Press.
Shusterman, Richard. 1988. "Postmodernist Aestheticism: A New Moral Philosophy?" *Theory, Culture, and Society* 5:337-355.
Smiley, Marion. 1991. "Gender Justice without Foundations." *Michigan Law Review* 89:1574-1590.
Smith, Adam. [1759] 2000. *The Theory of Moral Sentiments*. Amherst, N.Y.: Prometheus.
Smith, Barbara Herrnstein. 1988. *Contingencies of Value: Alternative Perspectives for Critical Theory*. Cambridge: Harvard University Press.
Smith, Steven D. 1990. "The Pursuit of Pragmatism." *Yale Law Journal* 100:409-449.
Sunstein, Cass. 1991. "Preferences and Politics." *Philosophy and Public Affairs* 20:3-34.
Tönnies, Ferdinand. [1887] 1957. *Community and Society*, trans. C. P. Loomis. East Lansing: Michigan State University Press.
Tribe, Laurence. 1988. *American Constitutional Law*, 2nd ed. Mineola, N.Y.: Foundation Press.
Turner, Bryan. 1990. "Outline of a Theory of Citizenship." *Sociology* 24:189-217.
Wallace, Anthony. 1970. *Culture and Personality*. 2nd ed. New York: Random House.
Walzer, Michael. 1983. *Spheres of Justice: A Defense of Pluralism and Equality*. New York: Basic Books.
———. 1987. *Interpretation and Social Criticism*. Cambridge: Harvard University Press.
———. 1988. *The Company of Critics: Social Criticism and Political Commitment in the Twentieth Century*. New York: Basic Books.
Weber, Samuel. 1985. "Afterword" to *Just Gaming*, by Jean-François Lyotard and Jean-Loup Thebaud. Minneapolis: University of Minnesota Press.
Wilkins, David. 1996. "Introduction: The Context of Race." In *Color Conscious: The Political Morality of Race*, ed. K. Anthony Appiah and Amy Gutmann, 3-29. Princeton: Princeton University Press.
Williams, Bernard. 1985. *Ethics and the Limits of Philosophy*. Cambridge: Harvard University Press.
Williams, Joan. 1987. "Critical Legal Studies: The Death of Transcendence and the Rise of the New Langdells." *New York University Law Review* 62:429-496.
Williams, Patricia. 1995. "*Metro Broadcasting, Inc. v. FCC*: Regrouping in Singular Times." in *Critical Race Theory*, eds. Kimberlé Crenshaw, Neil Gotanda, Gary Peller, and Kendall Thomas, 191-200. New York: New Press.

Winter, Steven. 1992. "For What It's Worth." *Law and Society Review* 26:789-818.

———. 1994. "Human Values in a Postmodern World." *Yale Journal of Law and the Humanities* 6:233-248.

Wittgenstein, Ludwig. 1973. *Philosophical Investigations*. Oxford: Basil Blackwell.

Wolin, Sheldon. 1960. *Politics and Vision: Continuity and Innovation in Western Political Thought*. Boston: Little, Brown.

Young, Iris Marion. 1990. *Justice and the Politics of Difference*. Princeton: Princeton University Press.

Zuckerman, Harriet. 1988. "The Sociology of Science." in *Handbook of Sociology*, ed. Neil Smelser, 511-574. Newbury Park, Calif.: Sage.

Index

Ackerman, Bruce, 81, 185n 18
Action, 1, 8, 22, 33, 48, 51, 64, 66–68, 70, 75, 96, 101–103, 141, 150, 151, 161, 165, 166, 177–179
   unintended consequences of, 144, 182n 15
Adams, John, 58
Adjudication, 62, 64, 96, 97, 110, 118, 136
Aesthetic sense in politics, 165–167
   as defensive "politics," 165
   as heightened subjectivism, 165
   in postmodernism, 165, 166, 187n 3
   in pragmatism, 165–167, 187n 4
      in pragmatist jurisprudence, 166, 187n 2
   and truth, 165
Affirmative action, 32, 43, 70, 74, 87, 88, 131, 139, 147
   set aside programs, 156
Agency,
   as free will, 20, 80
   individual, 16, 19, 144, 149
   postmodern account of, 81, 83
   of private legal subjects, 152, 153
   and structure, 140, 141, 143
   See also Structure; Structure and agency
Agreement,
   consensual, 6, 67, 102, 105, 109, 110, 115, 131
   foundations for, 6, 63
   normative, 6, 11, 184n 14
Allen v. State Board of Election, 57
Americans,
   African, 4, 23, 25, 40, 49, 53, 55, 56, 57, 70, 113, 114, 115, 139, 145–148, 150, 156–159, 180n 34, 181n 7. *See also* Identity; Race

Alaskan native, 145
Arab, 148
Asian, 49, 114, 115, 145–148
Creole, 146
Cuban, 49
European, 4, 23, 25, 26, 88, 145–147, 156
German, 114
Hispanic, 49, 115, 146
Italian, 114
Japanese, 25, 114
Korean, 146
Mexican, 49, 149
Native, 145, 148
Pacific Islander, 145
Anderson, Benedict, 163, 168, 171n 8, 174n 12, 188n 5
Anderson, Charles, 89
Antifoundationalism, 14, 78, 80, 178n 26, 180n 33. *See also* Foundationalism
Appiah, K. Anthony, 146–149
Argument, 72, 93, 102, 106, 180n 1
Aristotle, 13, 14, 187n 1
Authority, 93, 108, 124, 132, 136. *See also* Justice
Autonomy, 15, 34, 47, 51, 64, 81–83, 103, 117, 122, 125, 126, 130, 131, 134, 143, 145, 148, 150, 152, 156, 157, 162, 166, 167, 185n 17

Balkin, J. M., 80, 180n 33
Bauböck, Rainer, 128, 132, 135
Behavior, 1
   belief-guided, not truth-guided, 66
   norm governed, 19, 20, 64, 157
   other-regarding, 43
   self-regarding, 43
Belief, 71, 75–76, 102, 119

Belief, (cont.)
  analysis of, 162
  consequences of, 176n 5
  justification of, 66, 182n 19
  pragmatist account of, 177nn 17–19
  See also Truth
Bell, Derrick, 4, 5, 28, 29, 33, 35, 52, 172nn 14, 19
Benhabib, Seyla, 105, 106
Benjamin, Martin, 70
Bobbio, Norberto, 186n 6
Boundaries, 15, 180n 33
  indeterminate dimension of, 123–133
  normative boundaries that are closed, 125–130
  normative boundaries that are open, 130–133
  regulation of, 128
Bourdieu, Pierre, 173n 2, 183n 1, 185n 21
Braybrooke, David, 178n 22
Brown v. Allen, 177n 16
Brown v. Board of Education, 4, 30, 157
Bureaucracy, 138, 154, 163
Burtt, Shelley, 119, 120, 127, 134, 183n 9, 184n 16, 185n 17

Calder, Alexander, 164
Cardozo, Benjamin, 68, 183n 3
Carmichael, Stokely, 5, 6
Citizens, 1, 40, 93, 120, 128, 141, 144, 155, 159, 162
Citizenship, 15, 21, 23, 122–125, 128, 130, 131, 133–139, 164, 183n 9
  dual, 129
  indeterminate dimension of, 133–136
  poly-citizenship, 129
  in supra-national organizations, 129
Civil rights discourse, 43–44
Civil Rights movement, 4, 5, 30, 56
Coercion, 76, 101, 108, 117, 124, 136, 137, 157
Cohen, Felix, 62
Collins, Harry, 182n 14
Color blindness,
  in constitutional interpretation that turns out to be color conscious, 31
  demands impartiality, 43
  as entailed by proceduralism, 41
  historical absence in social norms, 114
  normative indeterminacy of, 32
  as racist, 42, 45
  in terms of law and morality, 16
  See also Color consciousness; Color consciousness and color blindness; Race
Color consciousness,
  as affirmative self-determination, 150
  as enabling, 150
  as facilitative of racial equality, 22–24, 71, 144
  irrational biases of, 44
  in legal structure, 158
  as a matter of racial identity, 142
  as not racist, 33, 74
  normative indeterminacy of, 32, 142
  as oppressive, 150
  in politics, 159
  in public policy, 70, 94, 149, 151, 154. See also Public policy
  as racist, 30, 74, 142, 144, 150
  urged by pragmatist law and public policy, 61
  See also Color blindness; Color consciousness and color blindness; Race
Color consciousness and color blindness, 139, 140, 157–159. See also Color blindness; Color consciousness; Complementarity; Race
Communication, 9, 18, 43, 46, 64, 84, 101, 108, 119, 126, 132, 151, 156, 167, 168, 186n 7
Communitarianism, 115, 117
Community,
  based on affinity, 49–50, 52
  diversity of, 105
  economic, 143
  ethical, 143
  as ideal, 117, 125
  imagined, 49, 163, 174 n 12
  interpretive, 46, 118, 164
  legal and political, 9, 16, 66, 78, 85–87, 95, 98, 99, 109, 115, 117, 128, 138, 154, 179n 29, 183n 1

INDEX

of states or nations, 132, 138
  normative, 15
  relationship to state, 119. *See also* State
  of world citizens, 153
  See also Group consciousness; Solidarity
Complementarity,
  of color consciousness and color blindness, 31, 141, 143, 144, 159. *See also* Color consciousness and color blindness
  of law and morality, 16, 20, 143, 144, 152, 153, 159. *See also* Law and morality
  of structure and agency, 143, 144, 157, 159. *See also* Structure and agency
Compromise, 69–71
Compulsion. *See* Coercion
Congress. *See* U. S. Congress
Connolly, William, 105, 106
Consequentialism, 66, 89, 110
Constitution, 19, 21, 32, 34, 46, 59, 73, 104, 121, 131, 135, 136, 141, 147, 153, 156, 172n 9, 184nn 13, 16. *See also* U. S. Constitution
Cooperation, 39–41, 101, 106, 118, 122, 136, 161, 164, 182n 16
Courts of law, 105, 127, 154. *See also* U.S. Supreme Court
Crenshaw, Kimberlé, 25, 29, 30, 43
Critical Legal Studies, 61, 62
Critique. *See* Social critique
Culture, 1, 9, 19, 23, 42, 79, 98, 104, 113, 121, 147, 163, 185n 2
  cultural capital, 88, 115
  culturally generalized modes of understanding, 46
  political culture, 46, 133, 135
  shared cultural categories, 46, 111, 125
  strength of against political marginalization, 39, 142

Dayton Board of Education v. Brinkman, 34
Declaration of Independence, 163
Deconstruction, 80, 180n 33
Deleuze, Gilles, 165, 179n 27
Deliberation, 41, 42, 51, 86, 128, 134, 137, 140, 157, 180n 2

Democracy, 64, 66, 81, 89, 104, 121, 138
  democratic theory, 144
  procedural concept of, 152, 153
Derrida, Jacques, 85, 87, 178n 23, 180n 33
Determinacy,
  epistemic, 1, 2, 40, 48, 85, 94
  normative, 1, 2, 11, 13, 40, 48, 77, 85, 94
Dewey, John, 66, 68, 69, 165, 166, 177n 15, 178n 19
Dialogue, 64, 82, 99, 118
Difference, 24, 49, 107, 135, 182n 16
  in distinction to homogeneity, 45, 46, 54, 99. *See also* Diversity; Heterogeneity
  recognition of, 54, 175n 15
  reduction to identity, 164
  relationship to universality, 54
Discourse. *See* Dialogue
Discrimination,
  race-based, 44, 50, 55, 88, 140, 175n 24, 185n 2
  sex-based, 49
Districting,
  multi-member or at large, 57
  race conscious, 57, 59
  single member, 57, 58
Diversity, 3, 8, 15, 40, 81, 84, 87, 88, 93, 97, 105, 133, 134, 147, 181n 8. *See also* Difference; Heterogeneity
Doctrine, 53, 62, 71–73, 136, 172n 9
Dogmatism, 67, 113, 173n 9
Douzinas, Costas, 81, 187n 3
Du Bois, W. E. B., 4, 5, 43, 47, 171n 2 (ch. 1), 172n 13
  double-consciousness, 43, 47
Durkheim, Émile, 47–49, 51, 56, 105, 155, 174n 10
Dworkin, Ronald, 69, 86, 176n 7

Egalitarianism, 127
Ehrenreich, Nancy, 81
Electoral districts, 141, 159
  color blind design for, 141. *See also* Color blindness
  color conscious design for, 141, 142. *See also* Color consciousness

Electoral districts (cont.)
  majority black, 157, 158
  as proxy for political interests, 57
  race-conscious electoral districting, 14, 41, 52, 53, 57-59, ch. 2
  redistricting, 158, 159
  See also Minority; Race; Representation; Voting
Ely, John Hart, 104
Emancipation Proclamation, 163
Emotional affect, 13, 44, 162, 173n 6
Enlightened localism, 2, 6-10, 13-16, 23, 24, 35, 40, 48, 50, 51, 56, 58, 59, 61, 64, 79, 80, 86, 87, 93, 95, 100, 103, 105-107, 112-115, 117, 123-126, 129-137, 139, 141-144, 152, 154, 158, 159, 161, 162, 164, 165, 167-169, 178n 25, 182n 16, 184n 13, 187n 1
  critical capacity of localism, 165-167
  harmony not unity as goal, 164, 165
  as horizontality not verticality, 167-169
  within tradition of social and political theory, 10-14
  See also Localism; Parochial localism; Situatedness
Epistemology, 1, 22, 45, 112, 113
  pragmatist, 63, 100, 176nn 3, 4. See also Pragmatism
  See also Knowledge
Equality,
  among communities, 138, 139
  among participants, 181n 6
  equal protection of the law, 158
  formal and substantive, 137
  as horizontal relationship, 132
  legal and political, 19, 21, 22, 27, 31, 40, 51, 59, 76, 77, 87, 106, 107, 113, 114, 130, 131, 135, 136, 138, 143, 157, 158
  of morally equal citizens, 157-159
  of political access, 51
  of opportunity, 27, 139
  racial, 6, 22-24, 27, 28, 31-33, 39, 41, 44, 61, 70, 71, 99, 107, 111, 113, 143, 181n 7, ch. 1, ch. 2, ch. 6. See also Race
  "separate but equal," 157
  sexual, 44, 127, 175n 13
  social, 87
  voting power, 158
  See also Inequality; Race; Voting
Ethnicity. See Minority
Ethnocentrism, 96, 97, 101, 178n 25, 181n 8
Etzioni, Amitai, 183n 2
European Enlightenment, 9, 77, 82, 86, 87, 103, 118, 127, 163. See also Modernity
European Union, 75, 129, 135, 138

Fairness, 18, 40-42, 48, 70, 93, 104, 115, 139, 140, 150, 162, 173n 4, 181n 8
Family, 117, 119, 126, 127, 134, 149
  parents, 119, 126, 184n 15
  religious, 120, 126, 127, 183n 9, 184n 13, 185n 17
  children, 119, 126, 184n 15, 185n 17
  civil rights of, 124, 184n 13
  principle of child's best interest, 124
  See also Public education; Rights
Fallibilism, 40, 64-67, 66, 73, 106, 110
Feldman, Stephen, 82
Feminism, 29, 80, 175n 13, 178n 26
Fish, Stanley, 82, 83, 87
Fisher, William, 61, 62
Force. See Coercion
Formalism, 44, 59, 104, 105
  formal right to legislative representation, 50
  legal, 172n 10
Foucault, Michel, 79, 82, 83, 165, 179nn 27-29
Foundationalism, 78, 109, 111, 113. See also Antifoundationalism
Fragmentation, 161, 162, 166, 187n 1. See also Unity under totalitarian order
  in attempts to understand society, 161
  democracy under conditions of, 161
  as lack of universally valid normative claims, 161

Index

possibility of non-authoritarian politics under, 162
social and political, 7, 16, 18, 163–168, 179n 29
Fraser, Nancy, 80, 178n 26
Freedom,
of conscience, 155
of movement, 135
of religious belief and practice, 155

Gadamer, Hans-Georg, 72, 173n 8
Galston, William, 72
Garfinkel, Harold, 171n 7, 186n 5
Gates, Henry Louis, 29
Gauthier, David, 182n 16
Gay Rights movement, 149
Geertz, Clifford, 46, 113, 173n 9
Gellner, Ernest, 83
Gender. *See* Sex
George III, 163
Giddens, Anthony, 74, 103, 144, 145, 150, 151, 182n 15
Gilbert, Nigel, 182n 12
Goldberg, Arthur, 72
Goldberg, John, 183n 3
Goodman, Nelson, 73
Goodrich, Peter, 81, 187n 3
Gotanda, Neil, 31
Gramsci, Antonio, 180n 1
Gregg, Benjamin, 171n 1 (ch. 1), 175n 13, 180n 34, 185n 18
Griswold v. Connecticut, 72
Group consciousness,
affiliation through proceduralism, 51, 58
does not subsume entire identity of individual members, 52
of a voluntary constituency based on interests, 49, 50, 53, 59
See also Community; Solidarity
Guattari, Félix, 165
Guinier, Lani, 52, 54, 56, 58, 175n 24
Gutmann, Amy, 142, 148, 150, 156, 185n 2

Habermas, Jürgen, 156, 180n 2, 187n 8
Hachamovitch, Yifat, 81, 187n 3

Hamilton, Charles 6
Hampshire, Stuart, 42, 103, 104, 110, 181nn 5, 8
Harpham, Geoffrey Galt, 181n 5, 183n 23
Hart, H. L. A., 22
Hegel, G. W. F., 175n 16
Hesse, Mary, 102, 108
Heterogeneity, 7, 39, 78, 81, 83, 93, 95, 98, 123, 161, 164, 168. *See also* Diversity
Hirschman, Albert, 122
Hobbes, Thomas, 104, 182n 16
Holmes, Oliver Wendell, 108
Homogeneity, 49, 50, 54, 81, 96, 98, 109, 128, 147, 168
normative, 75, 95, 99, 186n 6
Horwitz, Morton, 61, 62

Identity, 1, 105, 113, 130, 135, 182n 16
ascriptive, 89
as a citizen in terms of one set of collective identities, 144
class-bound, 1
cultural, 114
ethnic, 119
group-based, 45, 49, 54, 143, 145–148, 174n 11
individual, 147
interest-based, 56, 126
intersection of multiple identities, 29, 50, 52, 53, 114
national, 147
political, 28, 29, 117
politically and culturally "transvestite," 164
race-based, 1, 16, 52, 113, 142, 145, 147, 148, 150. *See also* Race
religious, 164
self-identification in racial terms, 24, 50, 89, 142, 143
self-identification in terms beyond race, 145, 146
sex-based, 1, 49
as structure, 149, 185n 3
Immigrants, 85, 119, 121, 129, 136, 138, 148, 149, 180n 34

Immigration, 15, 115, 117, 128-135, 137, ch. 5
  and rights of citizenship, 121-123
  and rights of residence, 121
  See also Rights
Impartiality. *See* Neutrality
Indeterminacy, 1, 3, 6, 11-13, 73, 74, 81, 178n 23
  coping with, 2, 40, 161
    by means of patterned behavior, 73-76, 83, 177n 17
  epistemic, 15, 16, 103, 108, 111
  law better than morality in resolving, 153
  of legal rules, 59, 61, 62, 85, 156, 171n 1 (ch. 1), 184n 16
  marks moral norms more deeply than legal norms, 153
  normative, 1-6, 9, 10, 12-13, 16, 19, 39, 40, 61, 77, 87, 93, 94, 110, 111, 118, 153-156, 159, 161, 164, 166, 169
  thesis of, 1, 2, 19, 78, 95, 112
Individualism,
  politics of, 145, 146
Inequality,
  as vertical or as hierarchical relationship, 132
  racial, 14, 32, 50, 98, 157, ch. 2
  See also Equality; Race; Voting
Interpretation, 1, 102, 118, 173n 8
  ad hoc, 28, 83
  affected persons should be among authoritative interpreters, 53
  of facts, 34, 93, 102, 154
  of indeterminate legal rules, 156
  of norms, 19, 22, 93, 112, 154
  of texts, 1, 15, 34, 72, 112, 154

Jackson, Robert, 73
James, William, 62, 68, 69, 176nn 4, 8
Jameson, Fredric, 187n 3
Jay, Martin, 167
Joas, Hans, 64, 68, 177n 17
Judges, 1, 2, 83, 84, 105, 110, 155, 172nn 9, 10, 179n 31

Judgments,
  aesthetic, 187nn 3, 4
  correct, 9, 93, 101
  judicial, 75, 87, 89, 177n 16
  legal in distinction to moral, 154
  normative, 8-10, 93, 103
  of standards, 100, 101
  See also Standards
Jurisprudence, 8, 14, 15, 77, 154, ch. 3
  pragmatist in distinction to postmodern, 78-89, 179n 31
Justice, 1, 2, 8, 15, 16, 70, 85-88, 93, 112, 113, 128, 140, 162, 166, 178n 24, 180n 33
  more than simply authority, 86-89. *See also* Authority
  politics of, 142
  racial, 33, 139, 142, 144, 152, 157
  singular not plural, 84-86, 179n 32
  standards of, 62
  transcendental, 85
  through proceduralism, 41

Kant, Immanuel, 63, 167, 187n 4
Karlan, Pamela, 56, 58, 175n 20
Karst, Kenneth, 138
Kelsen, Hans, 171n 6, 186n 6
Knowledge, 1, 63, 82, 103, 107, 182nn 19, 21
  contingent, 100
  moral, 9, 76, 161
  normative, 65-69
  as power, 101, 179n 28
  socially constructed, 98, 107
  transcendental, 77, 98
  See also Epistemology
Kuhn, Thomas, 109
Ku Klux Klan, 149

Landers, Scott, 61, 62
Language, 64-67, 72, 73, 81, 82, 84, 85, 98, 107, 109, 125, 131, 145, 151, 163, 168, 169, 182n 19, 188n 5
Law, 2, 7, 9, 15, 61, 66, 68, 71, 81, 110
  as amoral liberalism, 143
  as discursive exercise of morality, 152

interpretation and application of, 81, 87, 104, 171n 6, 172n 9
international, 153
as moral republicanism, 143
positive, 152, 156, 157
relation to morality, 152
requires non-legal norms, 153, 156
rule of, 72, 152, 156. *See* Proceduralism
as structure, 152, 157
supplements morality, 157
See also Law and morality; Morality; Norms; Rule
Law and morality, 16, 140, 141, 150-157, 161, ch. 6.
difference between legal and moral norms, 153
difference between legal and moral propositions, 153
functional difference of, 186n 6
and structure and agency, 152
as transformers of structure as confining, into structure as enabling, 143, 144
See also Complementarity; Law; Morality; Norms
Legal Positivism, 171n 6
Legal Pragmatism, 176n 7. *See also* Pragmatism
Legal Realism, 61, 62
Legal rights, 46, 48
Legal system, 1
as self-regulating, 186n 7
Legislation, 142, 154, 158
through proceduralism, 152
See also Law; Statutes
Legislators, 1, 51, 55, 56, 104, 128, 141, 144, 155
Legislature, 55, 58, 72, 154, 157, 159, 172n 10
Legitimacy, 41, 51, 76, 77, 79, 84, 97, 110, 118, 120, 128, 150
legal, 155, 156
See also Validity
Liberalism, 32, 89, 130, 143, 156, 157, 171n 6, 177n 15
economic, 151

political, 30, 104, 128, 145
Lincoln, Abraham, 163
Llewellyn, Karl, 61, 62, 172n 12, 187n 2
Localism, 3, 6, 8, 10, 35, 78-80, 85, 115, 162, 164, 180n 35
as antipolitical, 187n 1
as democratic theory, 93
in education, 124
in knowledge, 173n 9. *See also* Epistemology; Knowledge
as political proxy, 59
postmodern, 78-89
pragmatist, 78-89
standpoint of, 98, 181n 5
See also Enlightened localism; Parochial localism; Representation; Validity
Locke, John, 21
Logical positivism, 171n 6
L'Ouverture, Toussaint, 163
Lovibond, Sabina, 97
Luhmann, Niklas, 74, 141, 186n 7
Lyotard, Jean-François, 77-81, 84-87, 165, 178n 24, 180n 35, 187n 3

Machiavelli, Niccolò, 10-13
MacIntyre, Alisdair, 181n 5
Malcolm X, 6, 33
Margolis, Joseph, 65
Mead, George Herbert, 174n 11, 185n 3
Megill, Alan, 165
Memberships, 129
overlapping, 128, 129
See also Identity
Metro Broadcasting Company v. F. C. C., 30
Michelman, Frank, 179n 29
Milliken v. Bradley, 34
Minority, 88, 95, 156
electoral, 50, 52, 175nn 19, 20, 24
ethnic, 26, 70, 76, 107
racial, 56, 76, 88, 107, 141
religious, 76, 88, 107, 118
See also Electoral districts; Public education; Race; Voting
Modernity, 9, 75, 79, 81, 84, 85, 141, 165. *See also* European Enlightenment
Moore, Underhill, 179n 30

Moral Realism, 69, 71
Morality, 20, 104, 111, 143, 151
  moral dilemmas, 127
  moral reasoning, 44, 110
  moral relativism, 179n 32, 183n 23
  moral particularism, 14, 118
  moral understandings, 140
  moral universalism, 179n 32
  private, 166, 167
  internal relation to law, 152
  supplements law, 156, 157
Mulkay, Michael, 182n 12

Nagel, Thomas, 44, 45, 96, 173n 3
Natural law, 71, 77, 155, 171n 6
Naturalization, 114, 131, 135
Needs, 76, 105, 124, 125, 128, 130
Neighborhood, 5, 6, 33, 39, 58, 115, 117, 124, 183n 2
Neutrality, 93
  in application of norms, 19, 94, 106
  approaching race in terms of, 41–45
  ethnic, 146
  as impartiality, 41–45, 104, 173nn 6, 7
  normative, 3, 19, 26, 40, 41, 105, 110
  procedural, 20, 41, 42
  religious, 127
  standards of, 43
  as view from nowhere, 96, 110
  See also Proceduralism
Nicholson, Linda, 80, 178n 26
Nietzsche, Friedrich, 149, 173n 2, 186n 4
Normativity, 3, 7
Norms, 1, 2, 19, 20, 27, 28, 32, 34, 48, 63, 70, 78, 80, 93–95, 164, 181n 3
  consensual, 109, 119
  constitutional, 19, 153
  contain inconsistent premises, 22, 32, 33
  contingent meaning and application of, 22, 25–28, 30–32
  as cultural practice, 96
  deviant, 43, 75
  of equality, 41, 114
  of fairness, 41, 48
  of inquiry, 99
  interpretation of, 22–25, 28–30, 34, 97
  legal and moral, 20, 34, 63, 68, 78, 153–156
  meritocratic, 26, 27
  moral, of civil disobedience, critique, or revolution, 153
  objective, 19
  political, 1, 15, 20
  pragmatist, 20
  of public policy, 20
  shaped by, but more than, prohibitions, 111
  social, 1, 2, 15, 20, 94, 150
  social constructedness of racial and sexual, 26
  stabilizing capacity of, 153
  thick or thin, 104, 105, 185n 18
Nussbaum, Martha, 80, 179n 32

Objectivism, 2, 99, 108
  cultural, 99, 109
  as impartiality, 44–45
  pragmatist notion of, 110
  strong, 2, 42
  weak, 2, 80, 87, 108
  See also Subjectivism

Parochial localism, 6–9, 23, 24, 79, 95, 96, 99, 104, 105, 117, 123, 136, 143, 161. *See also* Localism; Enlightened localism
Participation, 5, 18, 32, 41, 42, 48, 50, 53–57, 89, 93, 104, 106, 112, 125, 128, 131, 136, 137, 142, 152, 157, 162, 168, 180n 34, 183n 2
Peirce, Charles Sanders, 63, 67, 68, 69, 177n 17, 178nn 18, 19
Peller, Gary 6, 23, 27
Pitkin, Hanna, 51, 53
Plato, 10–13
Plessy, Homer Adolphe, 142, 143
Plessy v. Ferguson, 107, 143,
Political unity,
  as nationalism, 163
  pluralism as problem for, 164, 165, 180n 34

with universalistic features, 18, 161, 163, 164, 167, 168
without universalistic features, 162, 173n 6, 187n 1
Politics, 1, 7, 9, 11, 174n 11
of authenticity, 146
of interiority, 166
of normative indeterminacy, 4
of recognition, 146
Posner, Richard, 110, 172n 9, 179n 31
Postmodernism, 14, 15, 63, 77–87, 179nn 27, 29, 180n 33, 187n 3, ch. 3. *See also* Validity
Pound, Roscoe, 61, 62
Power, 3, 82, 112, 119, 136, 179n 28
Prado, C. C., 65
Pragmatism, 6, 14, 39, 59, 63, 71, 93, 95, 97, 103, 110, 112, 113, 117, 161, ch. 2; ch. 3
behavior, pragmatist account of, 179n 30
as belief-oriented, 67
belief, pragmatist account of, 75, 76. *See also* Belief
as consequence-guided, 68
as a form of relativism, 63, 101
guides to behavior, 63
historical antecedents to this book's position, 61–63
legal, 176n 7. *See also* Legal pragmatism
social order, pragmatist account of, 71–75
this book's position on, 63–65
treatment of normative conflicts, 177n 15
truth, pragmatist account of, 63
See also Validity
Predictability, 9, 62, 72–74, 77, 100
Principles, 1, 68–70, 72–74, 94, 177n 10
normative, 69–77
Proceduralism, 6, 14, 31, 39, 40, 41, 48–51, 54, 59, 63, 93, 95, 96, 102, 103, 117, 141, 161, 172n 1, 180n 34, ch. 2
color-blind, 54
of deliberative democracy, 152, 155, 159

fair outcomes of, 42
geographic, 58
group-specific, 54
inclusive form of, 55–59
as means to legal equality, 54, 182n 16
modified toward greater civic inclusion, 55–59
as non-neutral method of progressive politics, 158
as normatively neutral, 104
as normatively thin, 105
political representation through popular voting, 40, 45–47, 56, 57
race-conscious, 51–55
in social critique, 96
universalist, 180n 2
See also Neutrality
Progress. *See* Social change
Public discussion. *See* Deliberation
Public education, 34, 35, 109, 115, 117, 125, 127, 128, 130, 134, 149, 155, 157, 162, 163
compulsory, 15, 115, 120, 121, 124, 125, 130–133, 136, 137, 184 n 15, ch. 5. *See also* Family; Rights
curriculum, 120, 121
equal opportunity in, 172n 14
local control over, 34, 35, 39
See also Minority; Race
Public policy, 1, 8, 9, 15, 61, 66, 71, 74, 75, 94, 105, 115, 118, 119, 123–125, 127, 129, 130, 133, 135–137, 139, 147, 149, 157, 161, ch. 5
color-conscious, 70, 113, 114, 130, 141, 146, 152
color-neutral, 142
and indeterminate rule of legal equality, 139, 140

Quine, Willard V. O., 103, 107, 108, 182n 19

Race, 4, 26, 31, 41, 42, 45, 46, 52, 53, 77, 80, 107, 113–115, 119, 141, 146, 149, 151, 156, 163

Race (cont.)
  as mode of resistance, 24, 25
  racial neutrality, 23, 27, 30, 33. See also Neutrality
  normative indeterminacy of, 142, 145
  as political coalition, 29, 54
  as proxy for representation of political interests, 14, 41, 52, 53, 57–59
racial injustice, 94, 141, 142, 155, 157, 158
racial integration,
  of public schools, 4–6, 22, 23, 39, 87, 137, 157, 172n 19
racial segregation, 32, 107, 158
  of public schools, 21, 137, 171n 2 (intro.), 172n 13
  as self-segregation, 39
  as residential segregation, 57, 58
  See also Color blindness; Color consciousness; Color consciousness and color blindness; Electoral districts; Equality; Identity; Inequality; Public education; Representation
Racism, 4, 24, 26, 27, 29, 30, 32, 33, 42, 51, 58, 74, 84, 98, 99, 124, 137, 139, 142, 146, 149, 171n 8
Radin, Margaret Jane, 179n 29
Radin, Max, 172n 9
Rationality, 1, 64, 86, 87, 103, 110, 127, 134, 173n 6
Rawls, John, 121, 182n 16
Reciprocity, 82, 100, 114, 115, 122, 140
Reductionism, 8, 101
Reed, Thomas, 61, 62
Refugee, 121, 129, 133, 165
Relativism, 2, 6, 7, 8, 40, 59, 61, 63–65, 93, 95, 100, 101, 108, 109, 112, 113, 178n 25, 181n 8
  pragmatist in distinction to postmodern, 77–87
  See also Enlightened localism; Fragmentation; Localism; Pragmatism; Universalism; Validity

Religion, 7, 70, 76, 85, 86, 102, 119, 129, 130, 136, 146, 149, 155, 163
  freedom of, 120
  fundamentalism in, 105, 126, 128, 183n 9, 185n 17
Representation, 41
  group, 48, 52, 55, 56
  as linked to voting, 51, 55, 130, 158
  by proxy, 14, 41, 52, 53, 57–59
  should include affected persons, 53
  by voters who form their own electoral districts, 56
  See also Electoral districts; Localism; Race; Voting
Republicanism, 143, 151
Reynolds v. Sims, 57
Rhoads, John, 28
Rights, 15
  among equals or unequals, 136–138
  of citizenship, 121–123, 128, 130, 138. See also Immigration
  civil, 123–126, 135–137
  of emigration and of immigration, 122, 132. See also Immigration
  of entrance or exit, 133, 136
  of federal government to regulate interstate commerce, 73
  human, 155. See also Natural law
  as legal not moral, 155
  indeterminate dimension of, 136–139
  individual, 137, 143, 151, 157
  of parents over children's curriculum, 119–121, 124, 184n 15. See also Family; Public education
  political, 104, 120, 130, 157, 166
  to privacy, 73
Rorty, Richard, 101, 107–110, 165–167, 178n 25, 181n 8
Rule,
  interpretation of, 62, 136
  legal, 20, 21, 34, 62, 87, 166
  normative, 1, 19, 108
  pragmatist, 78
  rule-governed creativity, 151
  rule-governed politics, 152

rule-governed social behavior, 7
scientific, 109
social, 1, 2, 20, 94
See also Law; Legislation; Statutes

Scanlan, John, 139
Schlag, Pierre, 78
Scholars, 1, 103
Schusterman, Richard, 167
Science, 77, 108, 110, 182n 22
   natural, 102, 107, 109, 182nn 11–14
   social, 62, 101, 107, 108, 127
Secularism,
   in education, 120, 121, 185n 17
   rationalist secularism, 134, 163
   secular normativity of law, 140, 152, 156
   secular normativity of politics, 18, 152, 158
   secular political culture, 76, 107, 127, 128, 130
Self-delusion, 83, 84
Self-determination, 81, 121, 125, 143, 144, 150, 153, 155
   individual, 82, 107, 149, 162
   of legal community, 18, 128, 138, 152, 171n 6
Self-interest, 8, 98, 99, 101, 104, 108, 181n 7
Self-reflection, 8, 103, 113, 181n 8
Sellars, Wilfred, 107, 108, 182nn 19, 22
Selznick, Philip, 183n 2
Sex, 102, 107, 114, 119, 147
   women, 26, 29, 44, 49, 53, 148
   homosexual, 26, 146, 148
   men, 26, 29
   as predicate of inequality, 27, 184n 16
Sexism, 29, 52, 84
Shared understandings, 145, 181n 8
   as achieved by participants, 168
   generation of through normative structures, 125, 152, 163, 174n 10
   individual need interpretations, 46
   as means for coping with indeterminacy, 39, 40, 109
   norms, as form of, 40, 118
   particular or local understandings, 46, 97, 98, 111, 125
   See also Standpoint
Shklar, Judith, 81
Situatedness,
   in enlightened localism, 7, 8, 130
   in history and culture, 72
   and impartiality, 41
   in racial localism, 24
   of social critique, 79, 94, 110–113
   of truth, 165
   See also Enlightened localism; Localism; Neutrality; Social critique
Skepticism, 81, 179n 27
   rule, 166
Slavery, 96, 113, 153, 163
Smiley, Marion, 178n 26
Smith, Adam, 10, 13, 14
Smith, Barbara Herrnstein, 181n 3
Smith, Steven, 176n 7
Social change, 76, 77, 93, 131
Social class, 107, 114, 115, 147
   consciousness of, 94
   as identity, 29
   middle class, 114, 115
   as predicate of inequality, 27
Social constructivism as distinguished from essentialism, 51–54
Social critique, 1, 7, 8, 15, 16, 71, 81, 89, 93, 102, 110–112, 114, 117, 161, 167, ch. 4,
   centered, 94, 95
   critique among competing belief systems, 15, 84, ch. 4
   from a decentered standpoint, 79, 80, 94, 95, 97–100, 112, 113
   as a form of pragmatism, 108–110
   as a form of proceduralism, 103–107
   more than localism less than universalism, 95–97
   normative, 79–81, 153, 182n 12
   norms of, 20
   not empiricist, 107, 108
   parochial in distinction to enlightened form of, 80, 95

Social critique (*cont.*)
  as post-empiricist persuasion, 101–103, 108
  in postmodern aesthetics, 187n 3
  rational 166, 167
  relativism of, 100, 101
  situatedness of, 110, 111
  standards of, 110
  See also Situatedness
Social integration, 1, 13, 39, 46, 105, 117, 136, 143
  through conscious or unexamined communal belief, 155
  through internalization of norms, 49, 151
Solidarity,
  as achieved not given, 155
  ascriptive identity as means of, 89
  in the context of the intersection of multiple identities, 50
  as cultural embeddedness, 3
  as *Gemeinschaft* or *Gesellschaft*, 168, 188n 6
  within marginalized or oppressed groups, 48, 49
  model of, 47, 48
  as participatory political life, 16, 152
  as "particular" or "universal," 47
  with persons previously discriminated against, 131
  by similarities and differences, 47, 48, 49
  through colonial racism, 171n 8
  through race-based identity, 142, 143
  under conditions of social fragmentation, 167, 168
  See also Community; Group consciousness
Solipsism, 109
Stability, 71, 72, 74, 94, 99, 103, 106, 110, 120, 177n 17
Standards,
  cognitive or epistemic, 7, 9, 100, 101, 108, 161
  local, 8, 14, 78, 79, 97, 106, ch. 3
  of meaning and value, 109
  normative, 7, 9, 93, 97, 161, 181n 6

  universally valid, 180n 2
  See also Judgments
Standpoint,
  decentered, 15, 80, 83, 88, 94, 96, 97–99, 100, 114, 140, ch. 4
  extra-personal, 99
  internal, 99
  local, 161, 181n 7
  non-local, 99, 161
  parochial, 111
  of relativism, 100
  reflexive, 2, 8, 151
  universal, 111
State, 119, 149, 173n 6
  as enforcer of legal norms, 154
  interdependence of states, 122
  legal authority over curriculum, 120
  as nation-state, 128, 138
  in relation to parent and child, 119-121, 126
  regulation through boundaries, 128
Statutes, 1, 73, 79, 155, 156, 172nn 9, 12.
  See also Law; Legislation
Structure,
  and agency, 140, 141, 143
  as color consciousnessness, 150
  as constraining, 145
  duality of, 144
  as enabling, 145, 148, 150
  as individual rights and liberties, 152
  as oppressive, 148, 150
  as rules and resources, 144
  social, 16, 19
  See also Agency; Structure and agency
Structure and agency, 144–150
  and color consciousness, 149
  and law and morality, 152
  mutual dependence of, 144, 145, 148, 149, 151, 152
  normative order, as product of, 151
  See also Agency; Complementarity; Structure
Subjectivism, 2, 80, 99. *See also* Objectivism
Sunstein, Cass, 104

Supreme Court. *See* U.S. Supreme
Court

Thebaud, Jean-Loup, 84, 86
Tolerance, 7, 75, 97, 120, 127, 130, 161
Tönnies, Ferdinand, 168, 169, 188n 6
Tribe, Laurence, 31, 35
Truman, Harry, 157
Truth, 65, 69, 102, 107, 173n 7, 180n 2
 absolute, 66, 67, 101, 127
 as belief, 65, 66
 all claims to are fallible, 67, 68
 coherence theory of, 66
 correspondence theory of, 65, 68, 176n 4
 criteria of evaluation, 101, 102
 as generated by experience, consequences, and action, 68, 69
 as opinion, 69
 a Peirceian theory of, 67
 as plural, 97, 181n 6
 pragmatist notion of, 110, 176n 8. *See also* Pragmatism
 as property of language, 65–67
 See also Belief
Turner, Bryan, 129
Twain, Mark, 163

United Nations, 155
United States v. Lopez, 73
Unity under totalitarian order, 161, 162. *See also* Fragmentation
Universalism, 7, 8, 14, 16, 23, 24, 30, 51, 63, 84, 98, 114, 115, 117, 125, 176n 3
 false, 85
 as imagined unity, 163
 "in drag," 163
 in normative claims, 95, 100, 105, 162, 168
 See also Relativism; Validity
U. S. Congress, 14, 50, 57, 73, 141, 150, 156, 158, 177n 12
U. S. Constitution, 30, 31, 32, 44, 56, 57, 72, 73, 104, 114, 177n 12, 184n 16
 constitutionalism, 19, 30, 32, 136, 144, 152
 Ninth Amendment, 72
 Fourteenth Amendment, 21, 30, 77, 158, 187n 10
 Fifteenth Amendment, 56
 Nineteenth Amendment, 44
 See also Constitution
U. S. Supreme Court, 11, 21, 22, 24, 47, 56, 57, 73, 107, 120, 137, 143, 157, 177n 16

Validity, 21, 22, 27, 112
 claims to, 8, 93, 181n 5
 cognitive, 7
 of conviction, 8
 discursive, 1
 internal, 102
 in interpretation or application of norms, 2, 19, 164
 local, 2, 161. *See also* Localism
 postmodern, 79. *See also* Postmodernism
 pragmatist notion of, 110, 178n 19, 179n 31. *See also* Pragmatism
 universal, 2, 7, 63, 67, 86, 106, 111, 161, 163, 167, 180n 2, 187n 4. *See also* Universalism
 See also Legitimacy
Values,
 communal, 183n 2
 cultural, 6, 9, 19–21, 26, 43, 80, 95, 96, 100, 109, 110, 115, 117–119, 129, 133, 134, 148, 150, 185n 2
 democratic, 120
 normative, 7, 10, 11, 14–16, 31, 41, 51, 62, 69, 70, 80, 83, 84, 86, 95, 103, 104, 107, 108, 120, 125, 134, 135, 152, 154, 172n 18, 178n 26, 179nn 27, 32, 183n 9
Voting, 141, 150
 equally weighted vote, 141
 equal voting power, 50, 59, 141, 180n 34
 local control in majority-black electoral districts, 39
 procedural framework for, 107

Voting (*cont.*)
  racial-bloc, 157
  racially polarized, 56
  right to vote, 44, 52, 173n 5, 175n 17
  vote dilution of racial minorities, 14, 57–59, ch. 2, 175n 20
  See also Electoral districts; Equality; Inequality; Race
Voting Rights Act of 1965, 56, 57

Wallace, Anthony, 105
Walzer, Michael, 112, 113, 122
Weber, Samuel, 84
Wilkins, David, 150

Williams, Bernard, 181n 5
Williams, Joan, 73
Williams, Patricia, 24
Winter, Steven, 80, 83, 179nn 27, 29
Wisconsin v. Yoder, 120
Wittgenstein, Ludwig, 73, 81
Wolin, Sheldon, 161, 162, 164, 165, 167, 168, 187n 1

Young, Iris, 45, 52, 54, 158, 173n 6, 178n 26

Zuckerman, Harriet, 182nn 11, 13